Nobility and Annihilation

in Marguerite Porete's

Mirror of Simple Souls

SUNY series in Western Esoteric Traditions

David Appelbaum, editor

Nobility and Annihilation

in Marguerite Porete's

Mirror of Simple Souls

JOANNE MAGUIRE ROBINSON

STATE UNIVERSITY OF NEW YORK PRESS

Published by
STATE UNIVERSITY OF NEW YORK PRESS
ALBANY

© 2001 State University of New York

Printed in the United States of America

For information, address
State University of New York Press,
90 State Street, Suite 700, Albany, NY 12207

Production and book design, Laurie Searl
Marketing, Anne M. Valentine

Library of Congress Cataloging-in-Publication Data

Robinson, Joanne Maguire, 1966–
    Nobility and annihilation in Marguerite Porete's Mirror of simple souls / Joanne Maguire Robinson.
        p.   cm.
    Includes bibliographical references and index.
    ISBN 0-7914-4967-X—ISBN 0-7914-4968-8 (pbk.: alk. paper)
    1. Contemplation—History of doctrines—Middle Ages, 600–1500. 2. Porete, Marguerite, ca. 1250–1310. Miroir des simples ãmes. 3. Mysticism—France—History—Middle Ages, 600–1500. 4. Women mystics—France—History. I. Title.
BV5091.C7 R62 2001
248.2'2—dc21

                                                00-045679

10   9   8   7   6   5   4   3   2   1

For

Mom and Dad,

with love and thanks

CONTENTS

ACKNOWLEDGMENTS

This work, which is concerned in part with the lineage of ideas and of people, would not have been possible without the support of mentors, friends, and family. A special thanks to Gene Gallagher at Connecticut College, an outstanding teacher who enticed me into a life of teaching and scholarship, and to George McCormack and the late Larry Robinson, both of whom fostered a love of learning when it made all the difference. I hope to live up to their legacy of exceptional teaching. My dissertation readers at the University of Chicago, David Tracy and Peter Dembowski, shared their expertise freely and graciously in the early stages of this project. I remain most indebted to Bernard McGinn, advisor, friend, and tireless and brilliant scholar. For him, an Irish blessing: *Sláinte!*

Thanks also to my friends at the University of Chicago and in Charlotte, some of whom have never read a word of this manuscript but all of whom helped to get me through and beyond my doctoral work: the Anderson family, Emily Baird and Darren Dowell, Trish Beckman, Paul and Sylvie and the girls, Eddie Howells, Sarita Tamayo, and, always, Jill Mancina, who came to mind many a time when the pages weren't simply producing themselves. Thanks also to my colleagues in Bernard McGinn's Christian Mysticism seminar in 1993, as well as to the Fellows of the 1994–1995 Institute for the Advanced Study of Religion, all of whom gave constructive advice when this project was in its formative stages.

This work was supported, in part, by funds provided by the University of North Carolina at Charlotte. I graciously acknowledge this Junior Faculty stipend support during the summers of 1997, 1998, and 1999. I will always be grateful for the outstanding work of the interlibrary loan staff of Atkins Library. This project would have been impossible without their particular magic. Thanks also to all faculty, staff, and students of the Department of Religious Studies for supporting my work.

I am especially grateful to my editorial team at the State University of New York Press, for taking on this project and for patiently answering my many questions. I am also grateful to the three anonymous reviewers, who saw what I couldn't see and provided crucial suggestions for improving this work. I am fully responsible for all remaining errors in wording or content.

Above all, I am indebted to my family. My animal muses—Lotta, Sturgeon, and Sophie—have kept faithful watch, warming my lap as I worked. My husband James has never failed to bring me back down to earth and remind me that life cannot be lived entirely through books. I thank him for his love and for providing treats and laughter when they were most needed.

This book is, in its way, about ancestors and family, and it is dedicated most broadly to my grandparents, my parents, and my sister, Kathleen. But it is especially for my mother and father, who inspired in me a life of reading, writing, and thinking. There are no adequate words of thanks for all they have done for me. I hope this book serves in some small way as a tribute to them.

INTRODUCTION

Marguerite Porete's complex and at times discordant *Mirror of Simple Souls* was received into a world hungry for new spiritual ideas and experiences yet wary of innovation. The enduring popularity of her text, the ways in which she has been classified by medieval and modern observers, and her execution as a relapsed heretic in 1310 attest to this pervasive tension. Porete became the target for condemnation in large part for her doctrine of annihilation and its associated ideas, which appeared uniquely innovative to some of her contemporaries. Put simply, Porete challenges the traditional Christian conception of the radically debased nature of fallen humanity by asserting the nobility and freedom of certain individual souls. She expresses her radical ideas about the virtual existence of the Trinity in the soul and the ramifications of that indwelling for mystical union through a distinctly late medieval understanding of spiritual nobility, cleverly employing motifs that suit her doctrine of the preexistence of all things in God. In doing so, Porete shifts the focus of Christian life away from systematic discipline based on the institutional church as mediator of all knowledge of, and access to, God. She thus explicitly rejects the tradition of affective spirituality by attacking the "works-based" ethic of the official church and by carving out a new path for what she considers the soul's eternal vocation: union with God.

Much is unclear about the author and the message of *Le Mirouer des simples ames anienties et qui seulement demourent en vouloir et desir d'amour (Mirror of Simple Annihilated Souls and Those Who Only Remain in Will and Desire of Love)*. Yet it is abundantly clear that the *Mirror* makes a striking departure from traditional church doctrine in its radical doctrine of annihilation, which, despite solid theological foundations, had never been explicitly promulgated by any Christian thinker. Porete claims as no author before her—male or female—that a soul can divest itself of the created state of willing, knowing, and having in order to realize the pre-creational state of non-willing, non-knowing, and non-having. The soul is not by nature divine, but it is, through the transformation of love, divinizable, enabling even the embodied, earthly soul to achieve a lasting and essential union with God. The doctrine of annihilation of the soul was never a mainstream theological doctrine before or after Marguerite Porete, yet it reveals profound insights into the possible relationship between God and the soul.

The central contention of this book is that Marguerite Porete bases her theological speculations on an explicitly nongendered classification of souls into noble and non-noble, a hierarchy based on a God-given inborn spiritual status. Such a division, which reflects developing definitions and practices in the secular sphere, serves Porete well in defining her audience and in expressing her radical theology. The amount of recent scholarship on Porete reflects a wide range of interpretations available to modern readers. This is one such interpretation, which takes as its foundation the idea that Porete considered herself one of the "simple souls" of her title—and thus one of the few noble souls—despite numerous medieval and modern claims to the contrary. This book examines the ways in which Marguerite Porete conforms to and departs from medieval literary and theological ideas to assert the possibility of utter annihilation of the soul in earthly life. It advances on previous scholarship in looking directly at Porete's ontological presuppositions, her understanding of the relationship of the Creator to creatures, and the way these issues affect her conception of union with—or transformation into—the divine. In particular, it focuses on her speculative insight into the nature of the "noble soul" and her innate capacity for attaining annihilation in relation to other uses of this motif.

Porete's condemnation was doubtless tied to the vernacular form in which she set her message coupled with a thoroughgoing elitism. The paradoxes of this situation are many. Theoretically, the medieval church aimed to uphold an ecumenical, archaic Christian ideal of spiritual equality alongside a deeply merit-based hierarchical system. This system might appear eminently equitable, allowing all who were willing to strive toward spiritual perfection to do so. Yet such earthly "perfection" could be achieved only through the aid and mediation of the institutional church. That church relied on an explicitly hierarchical chain of command and sanctity for its authority. In the world of the *Mirror*, by contrast, each soul possesses a core identity that determines its place in the spiritual hierarchy and its potential for annihilation. It does not need the mediation of the church nor does it need works. In promoting a theology of exclusion and elitism based on inborn nobility, Porete threatened a system that aimed, in theory, to be both inclusive and universal even while maintaining a tight control over its adherents. This work will show that Porete's treatise reflects a history of esoteric speculation on the nature of humanity and the possibility for union with God during earthly life, which she expresses in distinctly medieval and courtly language.

Porete's *Mirror* certainly appealed to many people. This text was read widely during Porete's lifetime, as attests the range of extant manuscripts in

Old French, Latin, Italian, and Middle English; it is also clear that the book enjoyed renown after Porete's execution, particularly in the fifteenth century (due in no small part to the fact that many manuscripts circulated under the name of John van Ruusbroec). Other versions of the *Mirouer* continued to circulate anonymously or under other male pseudonyms for 650 years. Scholarship on the work has increased steadily since Romana Guarnieri identified its author in 1946, and many translations have been completed to date. It is worth noting that Guarnieri's positive identification did not stop the editors of a recent English translation of the work to preface the text with the notation that it was written by an anonymous male mystic. This oversight, made thirty-five years after Guarnieri's discovery, perhaps indicates a reluctance on the part of scholars and readers to grant philosophical ingenuity—if not genius—to women authors.

Scholarship on the *Mirror* and its author has evolved in definable stages over fifty years. The audacity of the ideas in the *Mirror*, along with the fact of its author's condemnation and execution, justifiably provoked many earlier scholars to occupy themselves with the question of her heterodoxy. Some of these scholars "tried" Porete and condemned her, as did her medieval accusers. More recently, historians have tended to view Porete's condemnation as the result of being in the wrong place at the wrong time: she was, for these scholars, a political pawn for whom an active life, arrogant pertinacity, and political circumstances proved a deadly combination. More recent work has moved away from heresy hunting and toward attempts at classification, much of which is anachronistic or inaccurate in Porete's case. Most notably, much scholarship on "women's spirituality," in particular, fails to account for the work and fate of the beguine burned at the stake in 1310.

The fault here lies in part with the assumption that gender was the pivotal matrix for all medieval women's understanding and expression of their own experience, theology, and spirituality. Porete's text explicitly classifies the world into noble and non-noble, and to overlook this scheme in favor of solely gender-based explorations can sidetrack the issue in a way Porete might never have intended. The question of gender in relation to this and other late medieval texts has been covered extensively by other scholars, many of whom have significantly informed this work. As a complement to those studies, this book examines the interplay of social structure, creative imagination, and theological constructs. It does not aim to dismiss the obviously gender-based images and themes in the *Mirror* or to cast aside the themes of courtly love; it endeavors, rather, to look at the *Mirror* from another perspective to explore another set of reflections, and to show that this perspective is validated within the text itself.

Porete's work stands out in high relief against a background of medieval women's writings, not least because most of her fellow authors in vernacular languages adhered to traditional theological doctrines and refrained from making the kind of bold claims found in the *Mirror*. Porete places little emphasis on Christological, penitentially ascetic, paramystical, or even contemplative modes of movement toward God, and she neglects many of the fundamental hallmarks of medieval mystical treatises, such as authorizing visions, biblicism, Christocentrism, an obsession with sinfulness, and devotion to the church, its liturgical cycles, and the Eucharist. The sum of these elements, as identified by scholars such as Caroline Walker Bynum in her groundbreaking *Holy Feast, Holy Fast: The Religious Significance of Food to Medieval Women*, and expanded upon by many scholars in subsequent years, add up to what Porete proves are overly simplified characterizations of late medieval "women's spirituality." Bynum herself, fully aware of the disjunction that Marguerite Porete's speculative writing introduces into her thesis, readily describes Porete as an anomaly. Indeed, Porete was an anomaly in her time and remains an anomaly today.

This investigation is thus concerned with trying to understand this anomaly by looking at Porete's adoption of social ideas as part of her theological speculations. It combines the much-studied topic of medieval nobility (and medieval social structure more generally) with the relatively understudied *Mirror of Simple Souls*. The first chapter provides historical and literary background to the related terms *nobility* and *lineage*, accompanied by brief interpretive essays. The texts and authors examined here (including Hrotsvit of Gandersheim, Hildegard of Bingen, Bernard of Clairvaux, the authors of the *Roman de la Rose*, and Hadewijch of Brabant) represent some of the more influential understandings of nobility as social class and as theological metaphor. More importantly, however, this chapter underscores the lack of tidy, unambiguous definitions in the Middle Ages. This chapter illustrates several commonly held meanings, echoes of which can be found in Porete's work, such as Hrotsvit's insistence on noble beauty and bearing; Hildegard's certainty about the divine ordination of social hierarchy; Bernard's call for egalitarianism among those who have chosen the nobility of service to the church; the emphasis on earned nobility in the *Roman de la Rose*; and Hadewijch's elitism and insistence on the noble *imago* of the soul. Porete adopts and rejects these motifs, weaving together what she chooses to describe as annihilation and the souls who are capable of achieving that lofty state.

Chapter 2 provides an overview of Porete's contemporary situation as well as an outline of the basic elements of her text. It argues that Porete fits only loosely in several established contemporary categories, and that this lack of certain status in the social world contributed to her negative reception at the hands of skeptics. Another contributor was her elitist stance, which affects her understandings of her audience and her own authorship, issues that will reemerge in chapter 4. The chapter then focuses on the theological vocabulary and essential constructs that form the foundation of her speculative ideas. These include her doctrines of two churches, two types of souls, three soul-deaths, and seven levels/stages of annihilation, as well as her pivotal doctrine of "Taking Leave of the Virtues." Porete speculates about a church and society conducive to simple souls, predicated on the notion of the return of the soul to its precreated existence while still embodied. Simple souls, the noble souls who attain annihilation, can have an unmediated relationship with God because of their noble lineage. Her insistence that such souls achieve such a status while still embodied and not through works or church mediation predictably alarmed her contemporaries.

Chapter 3 delves more deeply into Porete's cosmological and anthropological speculations, all of which feed into her doctrine of annihilation. This chapter illustrates how Porete upholds traditional Christian doctrine in believing that wretched humanity possesses absolutely no power to correct its inherited defects; nevertheless, she shifts the discussion in revolutionary ways based on her theological ideas. This chapter focuses on Porete's ways of describing God the Trinity as well as the creation and fall of humanity following a brief consideration of some of the foundational philosophical and theological issues that bear on Porete's doctrine of the utter abnegation of the soul. Her understanding of this pivotal event shapes what is perhaps best understood as her "two paths" of creation and return. The "higher" path leads to annihilation. Porete departs from traditional soteriology in placing the onus on the individual and the focus on the human will, not on Christ, who is the worthiest exemplar but who cannot coerce human beings to sacrifice their wills. To be sure, Christ's redemption enabled good Christians to merit their own salvation by following the commandments and relying on the mediation of the institutional church as the means to the grace of God. Yet Porete takes this idea further. For Porete, recognition of humanity's utterly debased state prompts a saving recognition of God's goodness, a salvation that coexists alongside and complements the salvation wrought by Jesus Christ. Indeed, she goes so far as to assert that certain souls become "redeemers" because they recognize that they are completely debased and thereby witness to God's absolute goodness. This union is an ontological union of indistinction (not simply a participation) of the soul with its Creator. This claim has significant cosmological (as well as political) implications.

These theological ideas find fruition in Porete's doctrine of annihilation, which is the explicit subject of chapter 4. Porete's foundational cosmological scheme, which is tied to a theological anthropology placing humanity as a key cosmological pivot, leads her to guide a select few not to Adam's Paradise but to the land of annihilation. This chapter presents the ways in which Porete describes the soul in annihilation, in part by using traditional metaphorical mystical imagery. Yet the key becomes Porete's unique conjunction of ideas related to spiritual nobility and annihilation. Who can achieve this state? For whom is her *Mirror* written? Porete's message is explicitly elitist and esoteric: her ideas, although expressed in a vernacular language, are designed for an inner circle of disciples, and her *Mirror* is directed solely to them. Her message is unknown—and will remain unknown—to all but a privileged few noble and noble annihilated souls. Simply put, those who read and cannot understand never will understand. Although Porete has been accused of being "elitist" in a negative way, this chapter shows that her elitism is justified within the world view she constructs. Without the motif of lineage and nobility, Porete's doctrine of annihilation would be shorn of much of its content and expressive force.

Marguerite Porete relies upon yet goes beyond any of her predecessors in her doctrine of annihilation, especially as she claims that the soul "becomes what God is." Although it is evident from passages in the *Mirror* that Porete considered herself a noble conduit for a saving message, it is also clear that she was aware that her message was obscure and esoteric and radical. It was indeed presumptuous for any medieval theologian, particularly a woman, to claim that a certain "class" of souls can advance beyond merely worldly Christian perfection—as exemplified in bodily *imitatio Christi*—to achieve annihilation of the will and transformation into God. To do so, Porete privileges instead a notion of the essential freedom and inborn ability of individual souls. This quest for annihilation relies only minimally on the ministrations of the institutional church. In fact, after a pivotal point in the process of annihilation, the soul can surpass *all* embodied creation to realize the true goal of Christian life: annihilation of the will and transformation into God. Such a soul is at once noble and common, mirroring God's ineffable transcendence and immanence. This nobility is not truly part of an earthly, human lineage, although that is the basis for the overarching metaphor. Such nobility is traced to the soul's virtual existence in the Trinity. For both Porete's metaphor and for the soul's essential status, inborn nobility is the one crucial component.

✦   CHAPTER ONE   ✦

NOBILITY AS HISTORICAL REALITY AND
THEOLOGICAL MOTIF

Most students of western European history are familiar with a trifunctional model of medieval social organization. Commonly associated
with modern scholar Georges Duby and found in medieval documents in
various forms, this model compartmentalizes medieval society into those
who pray (*oratores*), those who fight (*bellatores*), and those who work (*lab-
oratores*).[1] The appeal of this popular classification is, in part, its neatness,
yet that is also its greatest fault. As Giles Constable explains in an extended essay, such a classification relies too fully on occupational status
and thus obscures more fruitful and at times overlapping ways of classifying
individuals and groups.[2] Constable explores other social classifications,
such as those based on gender or marital status; founded on age or generation, geographical location, or ethnic origin; rooted in earned merit,
function, rank, or on level of responsibility; and based in inborn or inherited status. Some social systems express a necessary symbiosis of roles
within society (such as clergy, warriors, and laborers), while others assert
a hierarchy of power and prestige (such as royal, aristocratic, and common,
or lord and serf). Certain divisions, such as those based on ancestry, can
be considered immutable in individuals although their valuation in a given
society can fluctuate. Others, such as status in the eyes of the church,
might admit of change in individuals (through, for instance, repentance)

1

while the standards (such as church doctrine regarding sin and repentance)
might remain essentially static over time.

Constable's call for alternative ways of conceiving medieval social structure aids the reader of Porete's *Mirror*, in which a trifunctional model is of little relevance. As explained more fully in the following chapters, Porete
adopts as her central image an immutable, inborn nobility of certain chosen
souls. This crux of her exclusive and revolutionary theology derives, at least in
part, from a pivotal social distinction in the secular world. It is the task of this
chapter to show that despite—or perhaps because of—its labile nature, the
term *noble* became a powerful part of the late medieval theological imagination. In particular, a debate swirled around the distinction between nobility of
blood or nobility of virtue in the later Middle Ages, and the clamor of this debate echoed in literature and theological writing. In Porete's time, nobility in
the secular world was associated more often with foundation in an ancient
race than with earned social status, and the consequences of this emphasis can
be seen in Porete's writing as well as in her unfortunate fate.

The shifting and ambiguous nature of the terms *nobility* and *noble* makes
certainty in definition difficult—if not impossible—for the historian. Maurice
Keen, for instance, readily admits that his conclusions—and those of other
scholars—are necessarily inconsistent.

> Late medieval ideas about nobility, it seems to me, did not owe their
> shape to any single, unitary influence. Rather, in an effort to make sense
> of contemporary conditions, and to explain what was of value in current
> conventions, what valueless and unacceptable, writers on the subject
> blended a series of approaches, Christian, chivalrous, Aristotelian,
> Romanist and humanist.[3]

Porete and the authors with whom she is compared in this work mixed a variety of sources in their works and thus none of them can be said to express one
"correct" definition of nobility. They each use the term to express a spiritual
or social ideal in a complex and changing world. A true synthesis of such dis-
parate usages would be impossible and, worse, unfair to the sources it aims to
reconstruct. One can certainly provide interpretive answers to certain questions, such as: Who comprised the medieval nobility? Was that nobility
granted based on merit, or was it inherited through a long family line? If one
were noble in blood, must one then be noble in deed as well in order to maintain that status? If one was noble in deed alone but born to a low station,
might one be considered truly noble? What qualities of character would one
expect to find in noble individuals or families? One can venture answers to
these questions, but the answers are not neat.

Many authors and texts could be chosen to illustrate the range of uses
for the term *nobility* in literary and theological works. The authors chosen
here are an exclusive few, chosen to represent a certain range of possibilities

for "nobility" and "noble" in theological and mystical contexts.[4] These include Hrotsvit of Gandersheim (935–1000), who follows traditional martyrology language in associating nobility with beauty and fine bearing, and Bernard of Clairvaux (1090–1153), who called for eliminating worldly distinctions within the folds of monastic institutions. This examination will look especially closely at three perspectives: *Le Roman de la Rose*, Hildegard of Bingen (1098–1179), and Hadewijch of Brabant (thirteenth century). Explicit similarities and divergences with Porete will be explored more fully in the book's conclusion. Unfortunately, the scope of this work excludes many other relevant writers and texts.[5] All of these sources do illustrate in important ways the power of social classification (and nobility in particular), yet only a few can be chosen here as representatives of key "types" of theological speculation.[6] This survey will highlight some of the essential theological constructions Porete imposes on the term *nobility* (and the closely related term *lineage*) in her *Mirror of Simple Souls*, which will be explored more fully in the following chapters.[7]

RECONSTRUCTING THE MEDIEVAL NOBILITY

This investigation assumes that Porete did not set out to describe the social world in which she found herself, although it assumes a degree of correlation between the literary and theological use of these motifs and its basis in social fact.[8] This study does not aim at a single, clear picture or at a simplified definition of what proves to be a tremendously abstruse term. As noted above, the modern lack of consensus on the issue seems simply to replicate the lack of consensus in medieval sources. Maurice Keen explains this conundrum as follows:

> If one asks how [late medieval people] could hope to have it so many ways, to maintain for instance that virtue was the foundation of true nobility but that princely recognition was essential to make it valid while at the same time proclaiming the acceptability of the hereditary principle, the answer is, simply, that they are reflecting the tensions and ambiguities of contemporary aspirations and of contemporary conditions.[9]

In short, lack of clarity on this issue is a reflection of the rapidly changing society from which these sources come, one that was assimilating a money economy, a growing merchant class, and an influx of new spiritual movements, as described in more detail in the following chapter.[10] Porete found herself in the maelstrom of these changes, and her response to them certainly contributed to the shape of her theology.

Lucid and contemporary theorizing about any given social order is rare, yet awareness of social order is ubiquitous. All individuals in all societies are enmeshed in social orders that affect and even direct their movements and potential. This is apparent in a range of written sources. Literature, legal charters, chronicles, wills, and theological works often attest to a concern for and awareness of "the powers that be" and the horizon for advancement or change in any given time or place. Consider, for instance, the figure of the Bel Inconnu of Arthurian legend, who is ignorant of his ancestry only to realize he is of a lineage of brave knights; the increased use of *sermones ad status* in the later Middle Ages; or the *debats d'honneur* and *specula* for those in many walks of life, both of which were popular in the later Middle Ages into the Renaissance.[11]

Or consider the ways in which early Christians found ways to both reflect or reject the prevailing social order in which they found themselves.[12] As Wayne Meeks points out in *The First Urban Christians*, early Christians used kinship terms to describe relationships within the group. Those terms were symbolic of a hierarchy that had been theoretically expunged, because members of the group were understood to be united by common possession of the Spirit and thus equal.[13] This unity set the growing Christian community against (or above) its pagan neighbors while aiming for equality within the group. The rhetoric of Paul's letters aims at an ideal of eliminating markers of hierarchy or differentiation within the group. For instance, in Galatians 3:28, Paul tells his readers that among those who accept Christian doctrine, "There is neither Jew nor Greek, there is neither slave nor free, there is neither male nor female; for you are all one in Christ Jesus."[14] This rhetoric underscores the ideal that Jesus conferred saving grace to all who follow him.

This aspect of Pauline rhetoric never found a foothold in the world (if it was ever meant to). Internal differentiation set in quickly as certain individuals came to be thought to possess "more Spirit" than others, evidenced in, for instance, the rising "cult of the saints" described so vividly by Peter Brown or the growing hierarchy of church offices. As Christianity became institutionalized, it followed the timeworn rule that true egalitarianism exists only temporarily in any society. Indeed, the medieval church that derived from this seed of equality became defined by an intense focus on merit and hierarchy. From Charlemagne's plea to "Let everyone serve God faithfully in that order in which he is placed" to Pope Gregory VII's statement that "The dispensation of divine providence ordered that there should be distinct grades and orders," the Western Christian world has tended to value a merit-based, hierarchical system of works while accepting that individuals are born to certain stations in life.[15]

The huge historical corpus of interpretations of the medieval nobility attests to two enduring truths: a notable lack of consensus on some of the most basic lines of inquiry coupled with a great silence on the issue from the perspective of historical theology.[16] Both the interest and lack of consensus stem in part from the many contradictory or ambiguous references to nobility and lineage found in medieval chronicles, legal documents, and literary works. "Lineage" is relatively easy to define: a lineage (Old French *lignage, lygnage,* or Latin *genus*) denotes an unbroken line of consanguinity, usually through the male line. The emergence of genealogies in the eleventh and twelfth centuries signals a growing consciousness of lineages in medieval culture, leading one scholar to assert that "the rise of the *lignage* family was the fundamental social fact of thirteenth century France."[17] The power of noble lineages led, in some cases, to seeking out or appropriating ancestors, because recalling eminent founding figures or epic origins legitimated claims to high social and moral status. In consequence, these lineages were, at times, completely mythic. Even so, they remain an important witness to the tremendous power of a single idea from which others spring. That idea, put simply, is that blood matters in establishing worldly power.[18]

"Nobility," however, remains a protean puzzle. The Latin *nobilis* (Old French *gentil, franche*) and *nobilitas* (Old French *noblesse, noblece, or gentilece, franchise*) were commonly associated with terms such as *clarissimus, praeclarus, illustris,* and *venerabilis* and were often—although not always—divided into *genere nobilis* (noble by birth) or *divitiis nobilis* (noble by wealth/merit), as described below.[19] Modern scholars have encountered difficulty in establishing unambiguous definitions; as a case in point, one standard dictionary lists seven definitions of *nobilis* in use during the Middle Ages.[20] An overarching generalization can be made that, prior to the twelfth century, "noble" was a term used primarily in learned, largely ecclesiastical circles; after the twelfth century, it gained more widespread usage in secular society.[21] Yet within that range, scholars are faced with a dizzying array of viewpoints, as one finds reference to an abstract "nobility" of character or bearing, to nobility as a social class, to noble acts and noble things and noble institutions, to ennobling oneself through works, to inheriting nobility through the mother's line or the father's line, to the relative "level" of nobility of certain professions.[22]

The complexity and quantity of the sources continues to feed the scholarly debate, which began in earnest in the 1960s.[23] Marc Bloch could perhaps be credited with initiating the ongoing discussions and disagreements regarding the origins and nature of the European nobility.[24] Bloch insists that nobility as a distinct social class arose in the eleventh and twelfth centuries, when the basis of social status shifted from merit to inheritance. According to Bloch, those who held aristocratic power from late antiquity until the eleventh century did not do so based on inherited power; rather, they earned their status through personal ambition and ability. Hence, there was no officially recognized nobility of blood prior to the eleventh century. Yet this view, which was considered a breakthrough in its time, has been seriously challenged in various ways by Georges Duby, Gerd Tellenbach, Léopold Genicot,

and others.[25] These changes have been due, in part, to the changing interests
and methodologies of scholars.[26] Some scholars have argued for more complex
reconstructions of the ideas of nobility and lineage or have aimed to reconstruct the daily life of nobles as closely as possible.[27] Constance Bouchard, for
instance, has shown that scholarly debates over the purported "newness" or
"oldness" of medieval nobility have been overly simplistic by arguing for the
Carolingian roots of the purported "new" nobility.[28] Others have turned to regional studies.[29] None have focused exclusively on themes of nobility and lineage in spiritual texts.

Throughout these studies, however, one anthropological and theological theme continually arises, as it did in the Middle Ages. The problem is
summed up (and purportedly solved) by a well-known contemporary of
Porete. Dante Alighieri (1265–1321) writes in *Il Convivio* that "if Adam himself was noble, we are all noble, and if he was base, we are all base, which eradicates any distinction between these conditions and so eradicates the conditions themselves."[30] He goes on to argue that "nobility" is earned through
virtuous conduct and that nobility must be "engendered anew" in succeeding
generations. Dante argues that nobility is, in short, "the perfection of the nature proper to each thing," including plants and animals and inanimate ob-
jects.[31] He refutes those who claim that nobility is based on inherited wealth
and fine manners, passed on through time. No, he insists, riches are intrinsi-
cally ignoble and lineage alone neither ensures nor confers nobility, as a lineage itself has no soul and thus cannot be correctly called noble.[32]

> So let none of the Uberti of Florence or the Visconti family of Milan say
> "Because I am of such a race I am noble," for the divine seed does not fall
> upon a race (that is, family stock) but on individuals; and as will be
> proved below, family stock does not make individuals noble, although in-
> dividuals make family stock noble.[33]

Nobility is thus a quality earned through virtue and good character.

Here Dante rehearses a well-worn argument: human beings, all descended from one forbear, have no other way to distinguish themselves other
than through virtue or vice.[34] For Dante, lineage confers nothing nor does it
rescue the bad man from his ways; in fact, more is required of those who are
high-born. "Thus he who is descended of noble stock through his father or
some ancestor, and is also evil, is not only base but basest and deserving of
contempt and scorn more than any other ill-bred person."[35] It is not surprising
that this view is found in so many other texts, since it provides an answer to a
key social and theological dilemma that is based on quantifiable works and
behaviors.[36] Nor is it surprising that it was a mainstay of much Christian anthropology. Adam, as the sinful progenitor of humanity, was thought to have
bequeathed sinfulness to his descendants. The only hope to distinguish

oneself from the mass of sinful humanity was through works and virtues, aided by divine grace. Those on this side of the argument held that humanity was descended from one root and that, therefore, only individual moral excellence (*probitas morum*) distinguishes one individual from another.[37] Such a system rewards those who strive. Yet this was not the only possible solution, as Porete assures her readers, because it overlooks the power of an "ontological" nobility.

The discussion in Dante's *Convivio* gets at a central issue in both medieval and modern debates over the medieval nobility: is blood or merit the primary arbiter in determining noble status? Scholars have uncovered a tendency by the twelfth century to privilege nobility of blood over nobility of virtue.[38] According to Maurice Keen, around the twelfth century lineage began to take "pride of place over vocation" in establishing nobility, thus narrowing but not completely eliminating the chances that knights and others could earn a noble title.[39] Nobility came to rest on the notion of foundation in an ancient race and inborn authority and power, while knighthood was achieved largely through prowess and public military service.[40] Nobility and knighthood, once considered identical by scholars, were not necessarily linked. Nobility was at times declared by royal certificate in the form of patents of nobility; at other times, that certificate merely underscored a recognized family lineage.[41]

In an important sense, of course, these two categories were not mutually exclusive, yet one was always given higher status in determining nobility, as we will see in Porete's *Mirror*. In general, those who were noble by blood were expected to be virtuous in deed, and those who were virtuous in deed could thereby uncover a "hidden" nobility.[42] Yet before delving further into the debate about blood or virtue, it is possible to present a description of characteristics shared by those called "noble," apart from how the status was attained. For instance, nobles commonly were expected to own property and a common patronym that was possessed by all members of the lineage.[43] In secular custom, the title of "noble" came to be granted only to those who possessed fixed, inalienable property, transferred through the generations of one family in unbroken succession. This property belonged to the lineage itself rather than to individuals. Linked to this fixed residence was a family name, often related closely to the name of the family castle, giving the lineage an identity based on geographical rootedness.[44] Family identity was also promoted in several public ways; for instance, through family gifts to monasteries and through other charitable works done in the family name. This fixed residence of noble families contrasts markedly with the mobility of the growing merchant class, which can be said to have experienced more change in location and status than the landed nobles. This theme of rootedness is found in many theological texts. Another common attribute was freedom from mundane affairs and a direct link to the monarch. Nobles enjoyed unparalleled political liberty and immunity from certain laws. As Léopold Genicot asserts in the following passage, the late medieval noble was defined primarily by his freedom in many spheres:

> At the end of the middle ages the image of the noble was fully delineated: he was a person directly linked to the sovereign, free from all banal exactions, authorized to judge, exempt from the parochial system, a man who neither worked nor traded.[45]

It is no surprise to note that nobles often comprised much of the ruling class.[46] And it is not surprising that this element became prominent in theological works: the noble soul is the soul closest to God.

Yet a noble was defined not only by what he owned or by his extraordinary rights; in fact, noble behavior and bearing were tremendously important. This code was based in large part on courtly models. Nobles were expected to embody such virtues as prowess, courage, loyalty, and largesse, and thus to distinguish themselves physically and morally from commoners. Closely connected to this idea was an overwhelming moral denotation, in which nobility was associated with good character, moral worth, magnanimity, and ethical goodness.[47] Nobles were thus united to one another and easily recognized by others, as described below in the writings of Hrotsvit of Gandersheim. These common attributes were the raw material on which theological and literary writers built: a common name, property, certain privileges, freedom, a distinguished code of conduct, and a high level of education relative to others. As we shall see, rather free reinterpretations abound.

These interrelated themes are found often in mystical texts, particularly those that adopt themes from the so-called "courtly love tradition," which itself has been the subject of much scholarly wrangling.[48] This investigation is not centrally concerned with this tradition and its influence on mystical writing; nevertheless, many themes predominate in the courtly love tradition that will arise here. To put it very briefly, in the courtly love model starting with the writings of troubadours, the focus of drama is on the relation of reverence and proper behavior between a lover (the poet) and the beloved, who is both socially and morally superior to the lover and thus unattainable. She describes in courtly language the anguishing distance and nearness of God to the soul who longs for Him.[49] The beloved appears to embody all virtue, and the poet reveres her and obeys her will, enduring all trials and distance for the sake of this lofty love. The love of a relatively low-status individual for a superior was thought to be particularly ennobling. In these tales, only the noblest of lovers can endure all trials for the sake of such a seemingly hopeless and endless love; only the noblest of lovers can be entirely *simplece*, without duplicity, fully loyal to the beloved. This yearning and thwarted desire for a faroff beloved can be found as a commonplace in twelfth- and thirteenth-century literature and will be represented below primarily by Hadewijch of Brabant.

HROTSVIT OF GANDERSHEIM: THE BEAUTY OF HIGH BIRTH

Porete certainly adopts many of these themes, as will be seen more fully in the following chapters. Yet she twists themes of nobility and lineage and "courtly love" in revolutionary ways; the authors examined here also adopt and transform themes and expressions from these loosely connected "traditions." Perhaps the simplest example is provided by Hrotsvit of Gandersheim (c. 935–1000), a writer of hagiographic plays who spent much of her life as a Benedictine nun at the convent in Gandersheim. She is commonly regarded as the first German woman poet.[50] Social status—and particularly noble status—plays a central role in her creative image making.[51] She thus joins a long tradition of associating the outer physical status of the human being with inner worth: the evil, the bad, the corrupt are described as ugly, while the noble, the good, the valiant are described as beautiful.[52] Examples of this abound in her writing as they do in early church martyrologies.[53]

For instance, she praises the benevolence of a noble wife in the following way:

> Of noble descent she was, endowed with special gifts,
> And counted mighty kings among her fine ancestors.
> Her noble countenance shone forth in stellar beauty,
> Wondrously reflecting her worthy family line.[54]

Here Hrotsvit follows the model of praising illustrious ancestors, which have endowed their descendants with a physical mark of greatness that reflects their inner goodness. One encounters this emphasis on noble bearing throughout Hrotsvit's works. In her tale of "The Martyrdom of the Holy Virgins Agape, Chionia, and Hirena," Diocletian remarks to one of the women he has imprisoned that "The renown of your free and noble descent / and the brightness of your beauty demand / that you be married to one of the foremost men of my court."[55] Here the ideal is that such extraordinary beauty must be preserved through careful breeding. Likewise, in the "Martyrdom of the Holy Virgins Fides, Spes, and Karitas," the Emperor Hadrian remarks of the young girls before him that

> The beauty of every one of them stuns my senses;
> I cannot stop admiring the nobility of their bearing,
> their many excellences . . .
> You appear to be of noble descent.
> I would like to know from where you came,
> who are your ancestors, and what is your name?[56]

The girls' mother, Sapientia, responds that she knows that pride in ancestry is not becoming to a Christian, she is not afraid to describe her family's eminence. Hadrian responds that "The splendor of your noble ancestry illumines your face;/and wisdom, inherent in your name, flows in your speech's grace."[57] Again, Hrotsvit follows the traditional portrait of the martyr: physically beautiful and noble in bearing, able to withstand persecution and easily recognized as especial holiness. Hrotsvit here represents a much wider usage, in which external acts and physical beauty are significant signs of an inner nobility, of interior peace and fortitude, and of enduring virtue. Porete does not adopt this particular usage, except insofar as the annihilated soul appears beautiful to God. Hildegard of Bingen uses this theme as shown below, yet her practical understandings of social status within the convent are perhaps more relevant to Porete's writing.

HILDEGARD OF BINGEN: ELITISM UPHELD

Hildegard of Bingen was born in 1098 of noble parents and died in 1179 in Rupertsberg, where she had served as abbess. Hildegard was a precocious visionary and reformer who wrote lyric poems, musical compositions, treatises on medicine, many letters, hagiographical biographies, and the monumental *Scivias* (1141–1152).[58] This work, meant to be a comprehensive account of the Creator's care and plans for his creatures, presents twenty-six prophetic, apocalyptic visions focusing on the church, the divine-human relationship, and redemption. It depicts humanity as the exalted image of God, the supreme reflection of the divinity; nevertheless, that image is fallen and in need of grace. In her view, human beings are microcosms of the whole, granted free will and a powerful intellect. In her cosmology, all of creation yearns to return to its Creator, yet this return will never be complete during human life on earth. The human soul wanders in a harsh and unforgiving land of exile, a prodigal daughter "driven from [her] inheritance" who seeks to return from her path of error.[59] The *Scivias* and selections from her letters form the core of this investigation.[60]

Like Hrotsvit, Hildegard employs "noble" most often as a modifier for the highest virtues to show that they endow their possessor with impregnability and ensured success.[61] "Noble" becomes a staple descriptor throughout her works as she connects nobility and outward appearance and bearing. For instance, she describes Christ as a youthful man who is pale, manly, and noble in appearance. He is both beautiful and pale, poor yet noble.

> His face is manly and noble, for He is the strong Lion who has destroyed death and the noble Sinless One Who was visibly born of the virgin. But he is pale; for He did not seek earthly honor by earthly means, but was gentle, poor and humble with a holy humility.[62]

Here strength and beauty and nobility come together in one supreme exemplar.[63] Yet other things, such as cities, church buildings, and certain individuals (chaste priests and virgins, for example), can share in such nobility; that is, they can be impenetrable, victorious, beyond corruption.[64] They cannot be breached. Church buildings, for instance, those built with "the most noble of stones," will stand indefinitely.[65] Her personification of Judaism in the form of a huge woman named Synagogue, for instance, "foreshadowed the bulwarks and defenses of the noble and chosen City," the triumphant Christianity.[66] Hildegard exults that Christians can proudly state, "I take off the Old Testament, and I put on the noble Son of God with His justice in holiness and truth."[67] She extends this physical strength to the very physical body of Jesus Christ and of those who embody His example of patience and constancy.[68]

Yet Hildegard's adoption of this motif also has practical implications. Hildegard insists, for instance, on the value of what she sees as eternal distinctions "between peole of inner and outer life, spirtual and secular people, and greater and lesser people."[69] God has established ranks for all creatures, including the angels. Hildegard is careful to point out that "they are all loved by God, although they are not equal in rank."[70] The goal of the human life on earth is to do well in one's given rank, safe in the knowledge that God loves all for their merit, humility, and works.[71] This and other passages give us important insight into Hildegard's social vision, in which individuals can move between levels, both spiritually and in the secular realm, yet in which one's rank is always considered of paramount importance.[72]

Hildegard is quite open in asserting a necessary hierarchy in the world if not on a spiritual plane, as well as in insisting on inborn characteristics proper to given ranks. Certain traits and types of knowledge are natural to the noble. For instance, Hildegard proposes an analogy of a king who, lacking a body of matured noble warriors, gathers an army of common folk who seem suitable for leadership. Later, however, "as justice required," the matured offspring of the nobles are promoted beyond the commoners as commanders of the army.[73] This parable makes it clear that certain characteristics are inherent in the noble that can only be approximated in the commoner: given a choice, commanders will chose those born with certain abilities over those who might learn them. The attributes of the warrior, including courage and steadfastness, can be found "inborn" in those of noble lineage.

This notion of inborn attributes extends to Hildegard's ideas about the redemption of fallen humanity. The noblest soul of all is Jesus Christ, the noble son of God who opened heaven. God explains to Hildegard in a vision that "because Adam transgressed My precept, he and his race were without a law until the time that prefigured the nobility of My Son."[74] Her depictions of this ransoming depends on seed and fertility metaphors, both of which imply lineage and inborn characteristics. For instance, "God gave the earth a new vigor when Noah brought forth in his vineyard that noble seed of obedience which Adam, like a wanton boy, rejected in his foolishment."[75] Those who reject heaven are "cut off from the noble work of God's hands, from all honor and from the beatitude of the celestial vision, and exiled from the Living Fruit and the root of the Just Tree."[76]

It is clear that this salvation could not be accomplished by any other than Jesus Christ. He was of "the root of Jesse, who was the foundation of the royal race from which the stainless mother had her origin."[77] Jesus came from a human mother of the proper lineage at the necessary juncture in history, to ransom a human race initially created for the high calling of spiritual nobility. She writes, "But when the human race was created, oh!oh!oh! the noble Seed, and oh!oh!oh! the sweetest Offshoot, the Son of God, was born human at the end of times for the sake of humanity."[78] In short, Adam cut humanity off from its rightful lineage, and Jesus Christ restored it.[79] For fallen humans, then, the only way to recover the lost nobility is to imitate Christ's high nobility and resolute endurance. God helps those who resist despair, she says, patiently enduring despite the difficulties such a soul must encounter.[80] Virtues lead to "the members of Christ" becoming "nobly perfected in splendor and united to their Head."[82]

It seems, from the above description, that all of humanity was leveled by Adam's sin. Yet, for Hildegard, both earthly and heavenly life are hierarchically ordered, with God as the noblest of all.[83] This hierarchy is designed by God for the good of all. "For in secular affairs there are lesser and greater nobles, servants and followers; and in spiritual matters there are the excellent and the superior, the obeyers and the enforcers."[84] These distinctions are determined by divine institution in direct response to human selfishness.

> There was excess and vaunting because no people honored any other people, and everyone was doing as he pleased; and this would have continued if God, in His infinite wisdom, had not done away with it. Therefore, He made distinctions between one people and another. He made the lesser subject to the greater in the service of obedience, and made the greater help and serve the lesser with intelligence and devotion, just as it was granted to Jacob by his father, inspired by the Holy Spirit, to be lord of his brothers.[85]

It is clear that, to Hildegard, God has made each of his creatures to fulfill a particular role. She goes further in Letter 6, in which she reports to Pope Eugenius what the "Living Light" had said to her. She explains that those "sealed" with balsam on foreheads will remain sealed and will thereafter have no business with the unsealed.[86] Nevertheless, the unsealed can cross over and associate with the sealed, thereby aiming for the better part.

Perhaps the most telling example of Hildegard's world view comes in her correspondence with Mistress Tengswich, Prioress of Echternach. It is certainly the most discussed. Tengswich writes first to Hildegard to inquire about "strange and irregular" practices in the Rupertsburg convent. Some of those practices are related to the apparent immodesty of the virgins on feast days, which seems to deny the words of 1 Tim 2:9. Tengswich goes on:

> Moreover, that which seems no less strange to us is the fact that you admit into your community only those women from noble, well-established families and absolutely reject others who are of lower birth and of less wealth. Thus we are struck with wonder and are reeling in confusion when we ponder quietly in our heart that the Lord himself brought into the primitive Church humble fishermen and poor people, and that, later, at the conversion of the gentiles, the blessed Peter said: "In truth, I perceive that God is no respecter of persons" [Acts 10:34; cf. Rom 2:11]. Nor should you be unmindful of the words of the Apostle in Corinthians: "Not many mighty, not many noble, but God hath chosen the contemptible and ignoble things of this world" [1 Cor 1:26–28].[87]

Tengwich thus accuses Hildegard of breaking with church tradition and denying the authority of scripture in establishing an elitist standard for members of the Rupertsburg convent.

Hildegard responds that her view concurs with the divine plan. God Himself ensures that lower orders not overtake higher as is shown in the stories of Satan and Adam, who "wanted to fly higher than they had been placed" and were duly punished.[88] Earthly rank and difference must be respected, and one must practice humility when among equals. She illustrates this with a metaphor from the realm of animal husbandry. Who, she asks, "would gather all his livestock indiscriminately into one barn—the cattle, the asses, the sheep, the kids?" They must be kept separate, she insists,

> lest people of varying status, herded all together, be dispersed through the pride of their elevation, on the one hand, or the disgrace of their decline, on the other, and especially lest the nobility of their character be torn asunder when they slaughter one another out of hatred. Such destruction naturally results when the higher order falls upon the lower, and the lower rises above the higher.[89]

Hildegard here appeals to divine inspiration, rather to the text of the New Testament as does Tengswich.[90] Hildegard has been criticized by modern scholars for this elitism; Peter Dronke, for instance, even goes so far as to criticize Hildegard on this point, imagining she was capable of rising higher than this level.[91] Emilie Zum Brunn and Georgette Epiney-Burgard seem to concur with Dronke when they note that "in spite of the universal character of her visions, Hildegard did not go beyond the feudal conceptions of her age. For she defined a hierarchical theory of convent life, as oppposed to a more evangelical experience."[92] These authors seem to see Hildegard from Tengswich's perspective: as a renegade against a divine decree of egalitarianism in church. Yet in this regard, Porete and Hildegard are soulmates. For both, what might be perceived as "snobbishness" is firmly based in an understanding of personal divine illumination. Bernard of Clairvaux had another interpretation of the divine decree.

BERNARD OF CLAIRVAUX: EGALITARIANISM UPHELD

Bernard of Clairvaux (1090–1153), founder and abbot of the Cistercian abbey of Clairvaux and a leading churchman of his day, was a noted mystic who wrote extensively on political, theological, spiritual, and ecclesiastical issues.[93] This investigation will look most closely at his letters, in large part because they span the gap between his theological agenda and his pastoral efforts. Bernard is perhaps the foremost representative of the tradition of using images and metaphors from feudal life and chivalry in didactic, spiritual writing.[94] For Bernard, human life—and monastic life in particular—is an ongoing military-style combat: one becomes a *miles Christi* not only by crusading against the infidels but by embodying *imitatio Christi*. His interests and his language favor images of military battles and Christian knighthood and he uses the term *nobility* explicitly within those contexts.[95] Yet Bernard is a worthy counterpart for this examination because he eschewed ideas of ordained hierarchy in the hopes of establishing "classless" institutions, whether monastic or military. Like Hildegard and Hrotsvit, Bernard was himself of a noble family, yet he insisted that "in nature, none is inferior, none is superior; none is placed ahead or behind; and none is noble or nonnoble, for nature creates us all equal."[96] Accordingly, distinctions among individuals must be made according to merit, not on the basis of status at birth.[97] Bernard's theological anthropology is stated in a brief below:

> To use terms familiar to you: man is a rational and mortal animal. The one we are by the grace of the Creator, the other as a consequence of sin. By our reason we share in the nobility of the angels, by our mortality in the weakness of animals.[98]

What one does with one's mortal and weak state is at stake in Bernard's writings, which are imbued with ideas about mystical union with God. Part of the preparation for such a high goal is the shedding of earthly honor. In his extensive correspondence, Bernard urges his fellow nobles to jettison their noble status and secular power in exchange for the greater nobility of service to the church.[99] For instance, Bernard writes to a noble youth who he believes is wasting his intellect and "noble bearing" in futile secular study "when they would be so much better used in the service of Christ." If the youth would but give up his riches and give himself to God,

> [God] will take away all those gifts which have earned you such spec-
> tacular, but such treacherous, applause in your own country. Noble
> birth, a lithe body, a comely appearance, a distinguished bearing, are
> great acquisitions, but the credit of them belongs to him who gave
> them.[100]

Here one sees Bernard referring to the traditional assocation of nobility and
appearance. Yet he does not value these worldly attributes, including notori-
ety, as they are meaningless in comparison to the higher calling of the
Christian. Bernard also wrote to one of a group of noble youths, all of whom
turned their lives to church service. He begins by quoting 1 Cor. 1:26, which
Mistress Tengswich had also chosen in making her point to Hildegard.

> I read that God did not choose "many noble, many wise, or many mighty"
> but now contrary to the usual rule he has converted by his wonderful
> power a whole band of such. They have deemed the glory of this world
> worthless; they have trampled on the flower of their youth; they have
> held their noble lineage of no account; they have considered worldly wis-
> dom foolishness . . . all the privileges, honours, and dignities of their po-
> sition they have treated as things no better than dung that they might
> gain Christ.[101]

His companion letter to the youth's parents explains that "[i]f God is making
your son his own, as well as yours, so that he may become even richer, even
more noble, even more distinguished and, what is better than all this, so that
from being a sinner he may become a saint, what do either you or he lose?"[102]
In Bernard's view, abandoning worldly social status has infinite rewards. And
the sacrifice is more meaningful if it is greater: to give up noble worldly status
is harder than abandoning worldly penury.

Bernard does sanction the nobility of virtue, most particularly when it is
found in those least likely to display it: those of the worldly nobility. He despise worldly riches and praises those who embrace poverty.

> The title of poverty is a noble one, which God himself is pleased to com-
> mend through the mouth of his Prophet when he says: "I am the man
> that sees my poverty." Poverty is a surer title to nobility than all the pur-
> ple and pearls of a king.[103]

Here "nobility" is clearly not worldly nobility but spiritual nobility: high status before God if not before other people. Yet status in the world cannot be
completely overlooked. Bernard writes that "it is not easy to know whether
the baser sort lack the glory of the world by their own choice or by force of circumstances. I certainly praise anyone who is virtuous through necessity, but I
praise far more her who is virtuous by the free choice of her will."[104] Likewise,
in a letter to the virgin Sophia, he takes the opportunity to note that few nobles take this path, and he implies that the difficulty in giving up worldly

riches makes the sacrifice all the more praiseworthy and virtuous than it is for those to whom poverty is a "necessity."

Again, he begins by quoting the passage from 1 Corinthians:

> "Not many noble, but the base things the world hath God chosen." Hence you are indeed blessed amongst others of your rank, because while they are contending for worldly glory you, by your very contempt for it, are exalted much more gloriously and by a far truer glory. You are far more distinguished and honorable for being one of so few than for being one of a great family. For what you have been able to do by the grace of God is yours, but what you have by your birth is the gift of your ancestors. And what is yours is all the more precious for being so rare.[105]

Bernard thus notes that moral vigor accompanied by inherited nobility is rare. He remarks that "God is not at all a respecter of persons and yet, I don't know why it is, virtue is far more pleasing in the nobility. Perhaps because it is more evident."[106] Bernard welcomed former worldly nobles into the folds of his monastic institutions, stressing the new identity as monk that excluded any advantage based on birth and emphasized the acquisition of humble merit. His ideas are perhaps best expressed in his "In Praise of New Knighthood." In that short work, Bernard praises the knights by remarking that "[t]here is no distinction of persons among them, and deference is shown to merit rather than to noble blood. They rival one another in mutual consideration, and they carry one another's burdens, thus fulfilling the law of Christ."[107] This idea of earning merit for oneself is continually reiterated in *Le Roman de la Rose*.

LE ROMAN DE LA ROSE: THE NOBILITY OF VIRTUE

Le Roman de la Rose was perhaps the most influential vernacular allegorical poem of the Middle Ages. It was written by Guillaume de Lorris, who wrote the first 4,000 lines of the tale between 1225 and 1230, and Jean de Meun, who continued the work (albeit in a distinctive vein) and finished it in the 1270s.[108] Little is known of these authors, and the evidence for their dual authorship, generally accepted by scholars, is provided only within the text itself. The *Roman* is an account of a young man's dream, in which he falls in love, is separated from his beloved, endures torments during the separation, and overcomes several obstacles before finally possessing his beloved. This is a conventional plot for a courtly romance. This tale has survived in hundreds of manuscripts, all of which testify to the text's tremendous popularity from the time of its writing through the sixteenth century. The vast corpus of critical work on this text attests to its enduring fascination for modern scholars.[109] The *Roman de la Rose* provides an engaging secular counterpart to the *Mirror of Simple Souls* in several important ways. Perhaps most importantly, the allegorical structure of the *Roman* was widely influential in teaching those of Porete's generation how to express abstractions, such as Love and, most particularly, love at a distance. This is evident in the allegorical dialogue form of the *Mirror*. Even more similarities can be found in the apparent world views of each text, best seen by looking at the more theological aspects of the *Roman*.

The speculations presented by the God of Nature in the *Roman de la Rose* are founded on two fundamental assertions that are central to the plot: that human free will and divine omniscience are completely compatible, and that true nobility derives primarily from individual virtue, not from inborn class status. The cosmological system of the *Roman* rests on the notion that all created things will return to their beginning.[110] The allegorical figure of Nature presents the example of the heavens, which revolve slowly back toward their origin so that in thirty-six thousand years they will return to the point at which God first created them.[111] God created the visible world from a blueprint that existed in his mind from eternity:

> [B]efore [the world] had external existence [God] held the loveliness of
> its form preordained eternally in his thought. There he found the model
> and all that he needed. . . . Nothing had existence outside his thought,
> for he who has need of nothing caused all to spring from nothing.
> Nothing prompted him to do this except his gracious, generous, courte-
> ous will, free from envy, which is the font of all life.[112]

Here, as in Porete, the ideas on which the world was formed are the very thoughts of God. This notion is here blended with courtly virtues attributed to God: courtesy, largesse, and the absence of envy. All of these ideas are found also in the *Mirror*, as will be seen in the following chapters.

The *Roman* posits Nature as the former of corruptible things and God as the creator of eternal things. Nature explains that God—as a traditional triad of power, goodness, and wisdom—creates human beings eternally by his will and then entrusts Nature to form humanity in God's own image.[113] Nature goes on to describe how all men, created as "new miniature worlds" (microcosms), are born through her "alike in their nakedness, strong and weak, high and low. I make them all equal in their human estate; Fortune does the rest."[114] Humanity, like all of created nature, will return to her origin in God; however, she will not follow the predictable pattern set by heavens or by other natural phenomenon. Humanity will return to God to face judgment for her waywardness in using her free will to remove herself from God and from the laws of nature.[115] God foreknew this recalcitrance, yet this divine foreknowledge does not detract from human free will:

> God sees [any action] now as if it had already happened. He has seen it
> from eternity, by true demonstration in his eternal mirror, which none

but he can polish, without taking away from free will. This mirror is God himself, from whom we took our being.[116]

Divine foreknowledge does not keep virtue, vice, and Fortune from shaping an individual's destiny.[117] Free will, the master of both body and soul, is more powerful than destiny alone.[118]

Theoretically, no individual is excused from following reason and using free will to act in praise of God.[119] Nevertheless, it is apparent that the lover in the tale seeks his beloved with impunity while ignoring the advice of Reason. This is a crucial parallel to Porete's understanding of the ultimate fate of reason in the realm of love, as described in the following chapter. Those who wish to live in love must move beyond reason. In the *Roman de la Rose*, then, the lover places his heart and body entirely in the service of the God of Love. The lover does not, however, place himself in Love's service without the express invitation of Love; indeed, the lover must be "courteous and noble" at the outset in order to be permitted to serve the God of Love. The rewards for this service are unsurpassed.

> Serving [the God of Love] is without fail painful and burdensome, but I make you a great gift, and you ought to be grateful to have such a good master and a Lord of such renown, for Love holds the standard and banner of courtesy and is of such good manners, so kind, free, and gentle, that whoever is able to serve and honor him becomes free from baseness and misconduct and from bad practice.[120]

A good and gentle Lord imparts those qualities to the servant who serves him well. The servant, by serving, becomes free from baseness, from vile habits, and from impropriety. Yet he must be high-born to be allowed into the Lord's service at all, meriting the highest master and thereby attaining the highest likeness to that master. After the God of Love accepts the courteous and noble lover into vassalage, he will raise that lover to "high rank, as long as [the lover] does not relinquish it by wickedness."[121] The lover, however noble, must continue to merit even his servitude.

In proper service to the God of Love, moreover, the lover loses all ability to act on his own account. "My heart is yours and not my own, for it must—for good or ill—do your will. No one can take it from you."[122] This notion is repeated later in the narrative, when the lover reports that any pains endured in the service of Love cannot hurt him. An examination of the quest of the lovers in each of the tales (the young man in the *Roman* and the soul in the *Mirror*) reveals a shared necessity for the lover to place himself fully in the service of Love, forsaking all individual willing and all attention to the dictates of Reason. All is in the hands of God: "I," says the lover, "can no longer take an active part."[123] This notion is reiterated by Marguerite Porete in expressing the utter passivity of the soul in both creation and in annihilation. The lover in the service of love is beyond harm from any created thing.[124]

Yet in the *Roman*, nobility is not necessarily inborn. Clerks and others who have learned the appropriate virtues are constrained to strive toward achieving nobility and are faulted more than the simple, foolish folk (and even princes) who do not have that understanding.[125] Those who wish to attain nobility, the "most honorable thing on earth," must proceed from goodness of heart. Low birth is not itself an impediment to attaining noble rank; indeed, Nature cites many cases in which a high-born heart was proven to be base and a low-born heart was nobler than a king's.[126] There is considerable flexibility in this notion of nobility, which revolves primarily around the virtuous disposition of an individual's heart and the learning that individual has had regarding proper noble behavior. Thus, Nature states clearly that "nobody is noble who is not intent on virtue, nor is anyone base except for his vices."[127]

It is apparent in the *Roman* that lineage alone is not strong enough to establish or to enable an individual to sustain virtuous conduct. Indeed, those who look to a lineage and claim nobility thereby must bear in mind that any nobility to which they lay claim as an "inheritance" was originally earned by their forebears. Noble ancestors are constrained to live up to the example set by those who came before. Nature explains that

> nobility comes from good courage, for nobility of the lineage fails if it is not from goodness of heart. Thus must [the noble person] imitate the prowess of his forebears, who gained nobility though great effort. [Those forebears] took all of their virtues with them and gave only their possessions to their heirs, who received nothing else from them, neither nobility nor worth, unless they can earn nobility by works, by their sense, or by virtue.[128]

To claim nobility based on lineage alone is thus to steal nobility from another: one must earn the nobility gained by one's forebears yet again in order to lay claim to nobility.[129] The value of imitation of those forebears is reiterated several times in the text. For instance, the figure of Genius explains the value of maintaining the purity and fecundity of one's lineage by exhorting his hearers to "Remember your excellent fathers and venerable mothers! Model your actions upon theirs, and beware of betraying your ancestry."[130] Although nobility can be achieved by a low-born individual, it will not enter into a base heart: the noble heart is generous, courteous, gracious, compassionate, and inclined to largesse, one of the most essential virtues of the lover.[131] Those who love are those who give, according to the *Roman de la Rose*: "Nobody ever knew how to love who disliked giving."[132] Avarice is despised by God, who loves generosity and charity.[133]

As in the *Mirror*, those who love in anticipation of gain are merchants, who foolishly seek treasure they will never fully possess. The largesse of the noble is contrasted to the avarice and pettiness of merchants, who never have enough and are at constant war with themselves and others. Merchants possess "wretched hearts" and are concerned only with amassing and augmenting stores of wealth, wealth that will never suffice, no matter how much it amounts to.[134] Even worse is poverty, which seems to be considered totally negative throughout this tale.[135] Noble folks possess hearts that do not love for wealth or with anticipation of profit.[136] In contrast, the merchant has set himself a nearly impossible task: to acquire property that belongs by right to others. He thus

> aspires to drink the whole of the Seine but is never able to do it, because always some remains. This is the burning anguish, the everlasting torment, the agonizing conflict that tears at his vitals and tortures him with his lack; it is that the more he gains, the more he lacks.[137]

The merchant is thus in servitude to a quest he cannot end. Yet those who listen to the counsel of Reason might be led to understand that those things that the merchant seeks are never properly his own. Reason insists that all people possess

> something much better and more precious. Those gifts are rightly yours that you feel within you and understand so well in yourself, which remain with you always and may not leave you so as to serve others likewise. The other, external, gifts are not worth [anything] . . . for you should know that everything you own is enclosed within yourself.[138]

This notion—that all that one ever needs is enclosed within—belies the efforts of merchants and others who seek worldly gain. It is the means by which nobility, once earned, is maintained. With Hadewijch of Brabant, we enter a world in which nobility is both granted eternally to the soul and must be earned in earthly life.

HADEWIJCH OF BRABANT: THE SOUL'S NOBLE IMAGE AND LIKENESS

With Hadewijch we come closest to the theological world of Marguerite Porete. Hadewijch, like Porete, was a Beguine who lived in the thirteenth century, and details of her biography are extremely scarce. It is likely that she was born into a noble family.[139] Like Porete, Hadewijch saw herself as the conduit for a truth that was hidden to all but a particular few, her fellow "brave knights."[140] Like Porete, too, Hadewijch describes the fully matured noble person as untouched by commands or counsels of those "aliens" who do not understand the secret message and thus aim to destroy God. For both, the world is divided into noble and non-noble, or nobles and "alien rustics." Both of these authors use nobility as a central theme, as a concept that significantly informs and shapes their theologies. Yet the differences between the two are equally striking and essential to this investigation. This investigation will rely on a mix of Hadewijch's poetry, prose, and letters, all of which employ a complex of imagery from courtly life, law, and war.[141]

Like many others before her, Hadewijch employs the image of human life as a pilgrimage or exile in an inhospitable land. On this pilgrimage, those who follow the virtues "must in noble-mindedness fear no difficulty . . ."[142] The soul is exiled on rough roads in a foreign land and seeks only to return "home" to God.[143]

> Now understand the deepest essence of your soul, what "soul" is. Soul is a being that can be beheld by God and by which, again, God can be beheld. Soul is also a being that wishes to content God; it maintains a worthy state of being as long as it has not fallen beneath anything that is alien to it and less than the soul's own dignity. If it maintains this worthy state, the soul is a bottomless abyss in which God suffices to himself; and his own self-sufficiency ever finds fruition to the full in this soul, as the soul, for its part, ever does in him.[144]

The soul, then, is a "mirror" for God when it becomes worthy of that status through earthly works. When that status is achieved (or, more appropriately, recovered), the soul and God become one. In short, "the sign that anyone possesses grace is a holy life."[145]

Like Hildegard and Hrotsvit, Hadewijch often refers to patience and "noble bearing" under tremendous suffering, failure, abandonment, affliction, and works, noting that nobility of soul alone enables endurance.[146] She assures her readers that "God consoles all noble souls" despite affliction, which is a salutary grace in the almost unbearable condition of waiting for God; indeed, "Love is so noble and liberal, she withholds no man's reward (Tob. 4:15)."[147] Hadewijch assumes that no soul will receive God without wrenching suffering while awaiting the beloved. She asks

> How can the noble soul keep on—
> Yes, it is the noblest of all creatures,
> Which of its nature must love in the highest degree—
> When it does not have its Beloved?[148]

It keeps on, Hadewijch responds, by periodic, unexpected consolations from God, or Love. This time of waiting unfailingly "depresses the noble soul; but when it reaches this state, hope in God's goodness consoles it once more. But one must err and suffer before being thus freed."[149] The result of living an exemplary life and enduring Love's absence will be that Love will give herself fully to the soul.

> But before Love thus bursts her dikes, and before she ravishes man out of himself and so touches him with herself that he is one spirit and one being with her and in her, he must offer her noble

service and the life of exile—noble service in all works of virtue, and a life of exile in all obedience.[150]

This is the ultimate goal:

> For when the soul has nothing else but God, and when it retains no will but lives exclusively according to his will alone; and when the soul is brought to nought and with God's will wills all that he wills, and is en-gulfed in him, and is brought to nought—then he is exalted above the earth, and then he draws all things to him; and so the soul becomes with him all that he himself is.[151]

Similar ideas are prominent in Porete's writings: the bringing of the soul to "nought" and living God's will and simultaneous exaltation and abnegation.

Hadewijch clearly bases her ideas in the creation of humanity as the image and likeness of God and insists that the soul thereby has an inner grace. She calls to the "free, noble, and highborn souls,/Not only called but chosen . . ." to whom god gives insight to enlighten their exile.[152] She thus exhorts her readers to "earnestly maintain the noble perfection of your in-valuable and perfect soul."[153] Hadewijch closely identifies "noble souls" as di-rectly descended from Love; moreover, she makes it clear that status must be continually maintained both by Love and by the soul itself.

> O Love, those who are of your lineage
> You nourish with your nature according to your lineage;
> Whoever spared his nature, keeping back something from
>   you,
> Was left remote from your nature;
> But he whom your nature ever enlightened
> Remained enlightened in your nature,
> So that he lived according to perfection.[154]

Only certain souls can live with God; put simply, "No stranger lives in God."[155] For Hadewijch, as for Hildegard, the hierarchy of humanity is di-vinely decreed. God is provident toward every human in any station of life.

> And each of his perfections gives according to the condition of its birth and function. Mercy gives God's gifts to all the indigent people who are utterly poor and ensnared in all sorts of vices, because of which they re-main infamous and ragged. Charity guards the common people of the kingdom and gives each of them what he needs. Wisdom arrays all the noble knights who, in burning desire, labor with great combat and fierce assault for noble Love. Perfection gives the peers of the kingdom the lordship over their land, like the sovereign dominion of the sover-eign soul I am speaking of who, with a sovereign and perfect will and perfect works, has obtained her noble mode of living by all the will of Love.[156]

This emphasis on lineage and inborn wisdom is also a prominent theme for Porete.

Finally, Hadewijch, unlike the other authors surveyed here yet much like Porete, maintained the essential esotericism of her message. Hadewijch displays characteristic scorn for those of the merchant class and other "rustics." The following passage captures how seamlessly Hadewijch melds earthly and spiritual nobility and contains many of the themes she relies on throughout her works: the outward marks of nobility, the grace of God that enables the noble soul to withstand difficult challenges, and the incorrigible ignorance of ignoble souls:

> A free man's nobility we can recognize
> In jousts and in noble deeds;
> With the pride of noble minds, he wades through
> Where the storm of Love withstands him.
> For in jousts a knight receives praise
> Of which he appears worthy because of love.
> Love is so strong a buttress:
> It is right that men suffer for his sake . . .
> From slothful hearts and ignoble minds
> Remains hidden the great good
> Which those well understand
> Who live in the madness of love . . .[157]

Hadewijch often refers to "aliens" or "rustics," by which she means those who have certain saving knowledge hidden from them and live in fear; in contrast, noble souls, like good warriors, have no fear.[158] "Aliens" never know the inebriation that accompanies unity with Love: "This remains wholly hidden from aliens,/But well known to the wise."[159] In the following passage, Hadewijch combines many of her central ideas: the affinity of Love for the virtuous soul; the ever-present reality of difficult testing; and the secret nature of this doctrine.

> Oh, what I mean and have long meant,
> God has indeed shown to noble souls
> To whom he has allotted the torments of love
> To give them fruition of Love's nature;
> Before the All unites itself to the all,
> Sour bitterness must be tasted.
> Love comes and consoles us; she goes away and knocks us
>   down.
> This initiates our adventure.
> But how one grasps the All with the all,
> Alien rustics will never know.[160]

Those who can never know are intimidated and alarmed by their ignorance. They are unwilling to accept the doctrine out of fear of the unknown.

> But from the truth and justice of the judgments it has received in the divine countenance, it appears to ignoble men awesome and unheard of (Exod. 34:29–30). And when these ignoble men see that the soul is then wholly arrayed according to truth and well-regulated in all ways, how fearful and alarming it is to them![161]

These "ignoble" people are "of small perception" and thus move away from love, fearing they will lose rather than gain and thus become content with "alien consolations" and worldly spoils.[162] Such a soul never sheds her beggar's garments and thus "has not the form or badge of honor/By which Love recognizes what is hers."[163] Love knows the heraldic images that certify the wearer's status: the garments are good acts, the heraldic symbolism of high birth and appropriate conduct. "This is the colored apparel, best adorned/With blazons of nobility, to the honor of high Love."[164] Here Hadewijch employs the motif of the outward appearance of worldly nobility as a key to the inner spiritual identity of the truly noble soul.

Noble souls are such in their image and likeness to God; however, in their fallenness they must rely on worldly works to maintain that spiritual status. For Hadewijch, *imitatio Christi* is absolutely essential to "being one" with God. In Letter 18, Hadewijch invokes a favorite metaphor of maturation, addressing the soul directly: the soul will come to full growth, "according to the measure of the dignity in which you are loved and destined by God! Conform wisely and valiantly, as one undaunted, to all that is meet for you, and act in all things according to your free nobility."[165] Action and conforming to standards of virtue become key elements here as Hadewijch speaks repeatedly of "noble service" to Love, or God. This emphasis on noble service is reminiscent of Bernard's insistence on the higher nobility of service to the church. Both authors stressed the importance of works and suffering, and both argued that the path to this freedom from suffering is *imitatio Christi*. Hadewijch notes that "We must be continually aware that noble service and suffering in exile are proper to man's condition; such was the share of Jesus Christ when he lived on earth as Man."[166] This emphasis on works distinguishes Hadewijch from Porete. In one letter, Hadewijch notes that "He who loves God loves his works. His works are noble virtues; therefore he who loves God loves virtues."[167] *Imitatio Christi* is, for Hadewijch, living in Love, herself described as noble. "The greatest radiance anyone can have on earth is truth in works of justice performed in imitation of the Son, and to practice that truth with regard to all that exists, for the glory of the noble *love that God is* (1 John 4:16)."[168] As we will see in the following chapters, Porete's doctrine of annihilation required removal from all earthly affections, even love of works done in imitation of Christ. All souls owe courtly service to the Beloved.

These authors have illustrated the ways in which nobility and lineage have been adopted in theological and literary thought. It is clear in all of them that "nobility" sets an individual (or an institution, such as the church) apart from the "common herd." Yet how do these social distinctions exist? To what extent is one what one inherits, or to what extent is status earned? The answers to those questions are not easy. Examples from the Hebrew Bible, for instance, are inconclusive: Cain and Abel came from the same father but were of opposed temperaments, while David was raised from being the son of a shepherd to being a king. The tension between nobility of blood and nobility of virtue resonates in Christian theological texts. The medieval authors examined above tended to privilege virtue over inheritance in determining "true" (herein referred to as "theological") nobility. This is true even of those who insisted that humanity was created in the image and likeness of God and that likeness must be continually sought in earthly life. The reason for this might quite simply derive from the Genesis narrative of Adam's primeval fall and the later doctrine of original sin. The Christian lineage was seen to be derived from the root of Adam and and all his ancestors were considered willful and sinful. This wrong was righted by Jesus Christ's redemption; however, the need for works and virtues remained. Those who resisted these "natural" sinful inclinations were considered especially virtuous.

In the words of R. Howard Bloch in *Etymologies and Genealogies: A Literary Anthropology of the French Middle Ages*, choosing blood over virtue in establishing a noble lineage ensures that "sameness engenders sameness; and [that] the magical tie to an origin is preserved."[169] Bloch asserts that recourse to an ancient (if mythic) origin is a "deep, though historically determined, mental structure" to legitimate power and assert moral superiority.[170] Assuming this dynamic applies equally to theological ideas, much of Christian theological anthropology capitalized on the negative association of the "magical tie" to sinful Adam, thus defining humanity in a particular way and explaining an apparent need for redemption and mediation. Certainly, the implications of privileging either blood (lineage) or merit (deeds) in the establishment of spiritual nobility and status in the eyes of the church can be profound. Porete, as we shall see, used the tie to an ancient origin in a different, more positive way. Porete maintains the key single ancestor of humanity but shifts the terms of the debate in distinctive ways. In Porete's *Mirror*, the affinity of the lover for the beloved and the innate ability of the lover to attain the beloved, despite impediments, make annihilation possible.

✚   CHAPTER TWO   ✚

THE "BEGUINE CLERGERESSE"
AND HER MIRROR

The execution of Marguerite Porete on June 1, 1310, is the earliest recorded death sentence for mystical heresy in Western Christianity. For Porete, that day was the culmination of years of struggle against authority. Ecclesiastical officials had learned of the suspect doctrines espoused in the *Mirror* by 1306, when the Bishop of Cambrai ordered the book burned publicly in Porete's presence and issued a stern warning to her to cease circulating her ideas or writings.[1] She ignored his reprimand. Two years later, Philip of Marigny, the new Bishop of Cambrai, accused her of giving her book to another bishop as well as of teaching her views to uneducated folk. Local inquisitorial judges sent Porete to appear before the Dominican Inquisitor in Paris, where Porete and a loyal supporter were jailed for eighteen months. During this time she refused to respond to her inquisitors' questions.[2] The Inquisitor, William Humbert, then presented fifteen articles excerpted out of the context of her book to a panel of twenty-one regents from the University of Paris. They summarily declared Porete a relapsed heretic, and they turned her over to secular authorities on May 31, 1310. She was burned at the stake a day later in the Place de Grève in Paris.[3]

Who was this woman? We know very little about the author of the *Mirror of Simple Souls* beyond evidence within the text and the documents relating to her trial and condemnation.[4] And this scant evidence is largely

27

skewed and biased. Many of the sources that have survived were hostile to Porete, and she is predictably hostile to her detractors within her text. Although we know far more about what Porete taught than about who she was, a brief historical synopsis can help to reconstruct her likely circumstances as well as outline key issues within the text itself.[5] A brief review of the categorizations into which Porete has been placed—and into which she fits only loosely—seems to justify Bernard McGinn's inventive designation: Porete, along with Angela of Foligno, Hadewijch of Antwerp, and Mechtild of Magdeburg, is one of the "four female Evangelists" whose work deserves careful and respectful consideration in the history of mysticism.[6]

As explained in the Introduction, this investigation generally avoids questions of heresy, which have been covered fully and continue to be explored by other scholars.[7] Others have also looked more closely at her apophatic mystical language and other aspects of her theological ideas.[8] It is also not centrally concerned with questions commonly associated with what has become known as feminist discourse.[9] This is not "women's history" in any other way than it focuses on a writer who was a woman who lived a religious life outside the structure of monastic life; who was well educated and inclined toward mystical speculation; and who stirred up controversy with a stubbornness found only rarely among her contemporaries. It is more properly categorized as an interpretive exploration of a distinctive mode of spirituality. It casts Porete as a representative of what Bernard McGinn has termed the "new mysticism" that arose in the thirteenth century, particularly in the realm of "new forms of language and modes of representation of mystical consciousness."[10]

That Porete lived a life outside the established orders is clear both in her *Mirror* and in trial documents, which refer to Porete as a beguine, a "beguine clergeresse," or a "pseudo-mulier."[11] These appellations may or may not be accurate: certainly the charge that Porete was a "pseudo-mulier" comes from a hostile source. It must be remembered, too, that many of the sources that do survive are hostile toward the women whose condemnations they record.[12] Inquisitor's condemnations, papal directives, and the pejorative writings of churchmen cannot be relied upon to tell us much about the "real" life of heretical beguines in this period. This is reflected in unsupported accusations by modern scholars. Ernest McDonnell, for instance, proposes a category of "petty heresiarchs of the Marguerite Porete type" in *The Beguines and the Beghards*. He writes that

> Margaret no longer belonged to the church-schooled, orthodox beguines of Belgium and northern France from whom she could very well have come as a native of Hainaut. She must have been an unattached beguine, with no fixed residence, regarding mendicancy as a means of livelihood, pursuing a life of moral laxity, and refusing to submit to authority. For the fourteenth century she was a sectarian, far removed from the beginae clausae who dominated the extraregular scene in Belgium.[13]

There is no evidence for most of these claims. Much of what McDonnell asserts simply reiterates the accusations of hostile authorities. Indeed, when not openly denouncing these marginal women, medieval and modern sources often display bewilderment as to the beguines' status in general and to Porete's status in particular, as described in more detail below.[14] The text of *The Mirror of Simple Souls* attests that Porete held some of the views allegedly espoused by beguines and "Free Spirits," as far as those doctrines can be reconstructed based on condemnation documents. Yet it is equally clear that she stands alone in the unique expression and content of her thought.

One cannot definitively classify Porete as a beguine, in part because the label itself refers to a shifting set of doctrines and lifestyles. "Beguine" was a general title that was used primarily to describe women pursuing what Herbert Grundmann describes broadly as an "extra-cloistral form of feminine religiosity." This general definition masks the tremendous complexities in the spiritual paths of growing numbers of *mulieres religiosae* from the beginning of the thirteenth through the middle of the fourteenth century.[15] Fortunately, a few reliable generalizations emerge from the sources. It seems fairly certain that beguine groups first flourished around 1200 in the diocese of Liège, moving from there through the Rhineland and south to the Alps, and into northern France and Bohemia. Cologne and Paris were vital centers. Attempts to ascertain the institutional origins of these extraregular movements have met with varied success. The first evidence for a beguine "movement" (if it can be classified as such) comes from the early thirteenth century, at a time when both ecclesiastical and secular authorities were becoming increasingly wary of deviant influences in society.[16] The monastic ideal of a life lived in stability and contemplation gave way in the wake of the Gregorian reforms to religious lives more often marked by itinerant preaching, teaching, and radical poverty. Boundaries between clerical and lay piety thus gradually blurred, at once providing new opportunities for lay religious life while—at times—alarming ecclesiastical authorities.

Pinpointing the origins of this "movement" is made particularly difficult by the apparent absence of a founding moment or figure or any agreement as to the origin of the name.[17] Some scholars have characterized the emergence of the women's movement as "spontaneous," despite evidence to the contrary. Carol Neel and others have shown convincing connections of beguines to earlier movements, yet determining the extent of beguine connections to other informal and formally established groups has been contentious as well.[18] For instance, institutions such as Prémontré and Cîteaux, as well as certain lay sisterhoods that proliferated in the twelfth century, may also have provided models of extraregular life upon which the beguines built.[19] It is certainly true that opportunities to join existing orders fluctuated in the twelfth and thirteenth centuries, and many women were forced to seek innovative alternate routes, such as forming communities outside of the established orders.[20]

Some scholars have posited stages of development for the movement, despite a scarcity of evidence to support anything resembling linear development across western Europe.[21] Others have turned away from attempting to classify this movement and have turned instead to regional studies focusing on other issues.[22]

On the face of it, beguines seemed to hold many of the ideals of more established religious orders. They can be characterized by commitment to two virtues—poverty and chastity—and to manual labor. Most beguines lived in cities and worked in the world to support themselves. They usually resided either within an established beguine community or with their families, and they did not submit to the perpetual vows of the regular orders; in fact, they could abandon the beguine life at will, either to marry or to enter a regular order. It appears that some beguines lived under a rule; others, however, lived apart from any formal obedience or community.[23] As this short description attests, beguine life admitted of tremendous variety and structural diversity. This problem of definition certainly plagued Porete's contemporaries. For instance, Gilbert of Tournai, a Franciscan, lamented that "[t]here are among us women whom we have no idea what to call, ordinary women or nuns, because they live neither in the world nor out of it."[24] This perplexity is reflected in modern times by Richard Kieckhefer, who remarks that "beguine" was a vernacular and nontechnical term for "various forms of community, for itinerant, beggars, and in general for religious enthusiasm of all kinds."[25] In short, "beguine" could be used to describe a saintly women working among the needy, a pious woman living with her family in the city, a woman living in a loose form of religious community, or a contumacious heretic. This range of definitions and the lack of easy categorization and control likely prompted ecclesiastical and secular authorities to investigate and punish certain "extraregular" women.

Porete has also been called the founder of another "anomalous" group, the heretical sect of the Free Spirits.[26] This claim is based on similarities between the doctrines allegedly espoused by this "Brethren" and those found in the *Mirror of Simple Souls*. As evidenced in the bull *Ad nostrum*, Free Spirits were believed to hold that embodied humans could become one with God in this life; that certain individuals could dispense with the ministrations of the Church; and that moral strictures were fundamentally irrelevant to living the divine life on earth.[27] This bull, which was promulgated in 1311 at the Council of Vienne, focused on eight "doctrines" of the "Brethren" of the Free Spirit, several of which were thought to reflect some of Porete's teachings. Robert Lerner has called this bull the "birth certificate" of the Free Spirit "movement," a document that attests the existence of a subversive brotherhood where, he asserts, none truly existed.[28] At this stage of scholarship, there is no irrefutable evidence to support the claim that Porete was a Free Spirit, although such claims can still be found in fairly recent work.[29]

What is certain about Porete, as attest the extant inquisitorial documents and the Vienne decrees (particularly *Ad nostrum*), is that authorities were alarmed by her espousal of a doctrine that included surpassing the traditional earthly path toward Christian perfection (as mediated through the Church and Jesus Christ). There are notable parallels between the doctrines of the so-called Free Spirit "brethren" and those found in Porete's *Mirror*. The earlier Paris condemnation of Porete in 1309, for instance, includes the following two articles (the first and fifteenth), excerpted from the *Mirror*:

> That the annihilated soul is freed from the Virtues and nor is she any longer in the service, because she does not have them as far as their practice is concerned, but the virtues obey according to her good pleasure.
>
> That such a soul has no concern for the consolations of God nor for his gifts, and she neither ought nor is able to care, because her total intent is toward God, and otherwise her efforts toward God would be impeded.[30]

One can see how these assertions might alarm those loyal to an institution founded on a merit-based system of works-righteousness and wary of individual freedom within its ranks. Yet these excerpted passages belie Porete's more complex doctrine. The soul in the *Mirror* does yearn to attain a "pre-Adamic" state within earthly life, yet the motive for this is far more complex and profound than mere freedom from works. Porete wanted to surpass *all* embodied creation *while remaining within it* in order to realize the true goal of human life: annihilation of the will and transformation into God.

It must be noted that Porete's condemnation was not the first or the last aimed at regulating new religious movements. Restrictions began as early as 1215, when the Fourth Lateran Council declared that all new religious orders had to conform to existing rules and forms. This decree was reiterated in 1274 at the Second Council of Lyons and at the Council of Vienne in 1311. Vienne struck hard at the beguines in two bulls: *Cum de quibusdam mulieribus* (Clem. 3.11.1) and *Ad nostrum* (Clem. 5.3.3). The first decree castigated women for discussing the Holy Trinity and for offering opinions to others regarding the sacraments, yet it contained an "escape clause" to allow those women living an upright life in the community to continue to do so. The second focused on doctrinal issues and was much harsher in its rhetoric of condemnation.[31]

What also seems certain is that this surge of women's piety was fostered by interrelated social and spiritual factors brought to bear on a society in a period of transition. Scholars tend to agree that the *Frauenbewegung* was part of the *vita apostolica* movements of the twelfth and thirteenth centuries, which found their deepest roots in the papal reform of the eleventh and twelfth centuries.[32] One inadvertent offshoot of these reforms was a backlash among the laity, primarily manifested in an increase in lay piety, anticlericalism, and vernacular preaching.[33] Fortunately, the implications of this move to the vernacular are finally being recognized by scholars, as it becomes clear that the terms *scholastic* and *monastic* do not do justice in categorizing the huge corpus of vernacular texts from the thirteenth and fourteenth centuries.[34] Accompanying this "democratization" of spirituality comes a body of innovative mystical literature, much of it written by women. These texts, although in many ways quite different from one another, show that these women of the "new mysticism" shared several key elements. Here we will focus in on Porete's adoption of nobility and lineage motifs to describe the utter abnegation of the human soul in annihilation.[35] Porete held that only certain noble souls could ever understand her message; fewer still could surpass the earliest stages of the seven-stage journey to achieve the goal of annihilation. This nearly anonymous woman, who could be said to have belonged only loosely to defined groups, outlines that teaching in her *Mirror of Simple Souls*.[36]

NEITHER LOWLY WRITER NOR LOWLY READER

Like much in her treatise, Porete's claims to authorship depart from contemporary paradigms. Women writers traditionally relied on claims to divine inspiration, whether through visions or spoken messages, to legitimate their questionable authority. Not only does Porete downplay this traditional claim to authority: she even goes so far as to castigate learned theologians, actives, and contemplatives as unworthy recipients of her lofty message. She writes for fellow noble souls and leaves the rest open to the dangers of her message. She seems to be referring to herself when she writes:

> And so this mendicant creature wrote what you hear. And she desired that her neighbors might find God in her, through writings and words; that is to say and mean, that she wished that her neighbors become the perfect ones she described (at least all those to whom she desired to say this).[37]

According to the author of this text, God transformed this particular "begging" soul because she was "nobly born" and thus privy to the secrets of the divine court. The allegorical figure of Love discloses the author's royal lineage with a play on words by remarking: "O very high-born one, says Love to this precious pearl, it is well that you have entered the only noble manor, where no one enters if he is not of your lineage, without bastardy."[38] Love thus authorizes Porete as a conduit for divine truth, without relying on authorizing visions or apologies for her lowly status. Her nobility is recognized and she thus gains admittance to the lofty secrets of the divine court.

Trying to pin down the intended readers or "hearers" of this text is as complex as trying to ascertain the author's true identity.[39] Porete quite plainly identifies her audience in many places in her book; however, she provides so many contradictory declarations in this regard that it is difficult to be sure of her intentions. For whom did Marguerite Porete write the *Mirror of Simple Souls and Those Who Remain in Desire and Will?* The title alone indicates two possible audiences: she wrote it for both the simple (or annihilated) souls and for those who have not yet achieved annihilation. This title seems to welcome all human readers and listeners, but, following the logic of the text as a whole, the second description probably refers not to *all* human beings, however fallen and in servitude to works, but to those who *can* become annihilated but have not yet arrived at that state. The text includes an invitation to all by proclaiming its own accessibility. For instance, Reason opens Chapter 1 by insisting on explanations of the message for actives, contemplatives, and "perhaps those annihilated by true love."[40] A similar invitation is extended to "common folk" in Chapter 13. Yet this apparent opening to those who will not be able to grasp its message does not indicate that the book was written for all.

Indeed, most of the evidence within the text indicates that Porete intended for her work to be read and heard only by those who can understand its message and achieve its goal. Porete contrasts these noble ones with the donkeys who are so rude and misled by Reason that Soul hides from them: "Because of their rudeness I must be silent and hide my language, which I learned in the secrets at the secret court . . ."[41] These donkeys are steered away from the path to annihilation and blindly follow the dictates of Reason and of the earthly church.[42] Porete explains her characterization of these folk with a reference to scripture:

> These folk that I call donkeys seek God in creatures, in monasteries for prayer, in a created paradise, in human words and in scripture. Alas, without doubt, in these folk Benjamin has not been born, because Rachel lives, and Rachel must die in the birthing of Benjamin. Until Rachel dies, Benjamin cannot be born.[43]

Porete's use of the derogatory term *donkey* serves her purpose in highlighting the supreme nobility and purity and freedom of annihilated souls. The donkey's rudeness and commonness is in direct contrast to the gentility and courtesy of the far-away King who is the object of the soul's love. This dialectic of nobility and commonality is the core of Porete's thought, and it is not surprising that it is reflected in her descriptions of her audience and of humanity as a whole. In fact, commonality and baseness are key to her doctrine of annihilation.

Porete and those learned men whom she asked to read and defend the *Mirror* certainly recognized the danger in distributing her book to those who knew no better than to "take the shell and leave the kernel."[44] One of the monks who certified the orthodoxy of the *Mirror* remarked that "not many should see it, because . . . they could set aside the life to which they were called in aspiring to the one at which they will never arrive."[45] At the very least, any reader must be humble and proceed by faith and love in order to understand the wisdom of the *Mirror*.[46] This qualification alone leaves out a sizable portion of Porete's possible audience. Within the text lie further clues that the book was written only for those who can be allowed into the court of the king, that is, for those who can attain annihilation and no others. Porete identifies those who will understand her message by exclusion. She does not write to those who are led by Reason, the "masters of the natural senses, nor any of the masters of Scripture, nor those who remain in the love of the obedience to the Virtues, none perceive this, nor will they perceive what is intended."[47] Only those "whom Fine Love calls" can understand this message.[48] Porete implies here that some of her "hearers" will possess an inborn affinity for her message and that all of her efforts at teaching the others will be, at best, in vain and, at worst, damaging. Her message is esoteric; in short, "Scripture does not teach it, nor the human mind comprehend it, nor does creaturely work deserve to grasp or comprehend it."[49] Knowledge of the way cannot be learned or deserved. Those who read the *Mirror* and are not "of this kind" will never understand. Yet, for the reader of this book, understanding can come through a close reading of the text.

THE TEXT OF THE *MIRROR OF SIMPLE SOULS*

The *Mirror of Simple Souls* is a dialogue in the Boethian tradition in which three principal allegorical figures—*Dame Amour* (Love), *L'Ame Adneantie* (the Annihilated Soul), and *Raison* (Reason)—discuss seven stages of the soul toward annihilation and glorification. The result can appear to be, at times, a jumble of unrelated ideas and disconnected notions, which has prompted Nicholas Watson to remark on "the book's lack of comprehensibility."[50] The same author calls the book a "highly-charged theological fantasia" that is, in essence, a performative "meditation on translation."[51] As Watson notes,

> To view the *Mirouer* as a heretical "Bible," or a systematic treatise whose aim is to teach a set of preformulated positions, is to fail to notice its performative aspect as a book whose prime intention is not public but personal: a book which exists to convert even its own author to the life it imagines.[52]

This interpretation of Porete's *Mirror* opposes Watson on this point. Porete is explicitly not interested in converting others, and she was certain of her own "conversion," if that word is even appropriate for what she means with her doctrine of annihilation. This and the following chapters will show that Porete had a clear agenda throughout her text, although the thread of her thought might prove difficult to follow at times.

Porete chooses a personification narrative to present her theological speculations. True to this genre, her allegorical characters maintain their identities and particular temperaments throughout the text.[53] Love is the personification of God in the narrative, as Porete clearly states: "I am God, says Love, since Love is God and God is Love."[55] Love is also the primary identification of the Holy Spirit, the person of the Trinity who both maintains the bonds within the Trinity and links humanity to divinity. The implications of this identification are profound. The Holy Spirit works within the Annihilated Soul so that the Soul "is God by the condition of Love. . . . by the righteousness of Love."[55] The Soul and Love work together in the dialogue as the Soul comes to increasing understanding of her calling. Most importantly, over the course of the narrative the Soul develops spiritually and intellectually as she comes to greater understanding of Love's lessons.[56]

Reason—as the representative of the institutional church, the clergy, and the common understanding of scripture—spends the first eighty-seven chapters of the *Mirror* questioning Love and the Soul regarding the progress of the soul to annihilation. She is continually astounded and repelled by most of the things Love and the Soul say about the soul's annihilation in God. Thus, Reason is the ideal spokesperson for what Porete sees as the huge number of misled and one-eyed souls who are so ardent in practicing the Virtues that they value nothing else. These folks will achieve salvation through the grace of Christ's sacrifice, but they will never enjoy the glorified life of annihilation. They are common, not noble, a distinction that underlies Porete's entire program.

Love grants that Reason's path is taken by many and is fitting for some; nevertheless, worldly works and membership in the earthly hierarchy are only a passing stage on the path to annihilation. No created thing is a proper guide, not even the church that mediates sacraments to the needy laity. Annihilated souls are guided not by Reason but by "that one alone who is so strong that he can never die, whose teaching is not written, neither by the works of exemplars or by human teachings, for one cannot give form to his gift."[57] Porete here introduces the essential apophaticism that guides her thought. More importantly, perhaps, she implies that the role of Jesus Christ, whose example is recorded so fully in scripture, must be reevaluated. She seeks above all identity with God as the eternal, hidden, one ground of all, as described more fully in the following chapter. According to the *Mirror*, any soul that seeks anything other than willing nothing, knowing nothing, and having nothing is hopelessly lost or has been deceived. Reason personifies those who honor and follow the church and the Virtues and are thereby misled. She thus serves as a foil for the lessons about annihilation presented by Love and the Soul. As the inquisitor in the dialogue, Reason plagues Love and the Soul with questions that bring them to the point of exasperation. Finally, their counterarguments cause Reason to faint away and die. She is thus dismissed in the midst of the drama.

Early in the narrative Porete lays out the contrast between those who follow Reason and those who follow Love. Here Reason tries to explain what a soul must desire and do on the path to perfection:

> For my intellect and my judgment and all my counsel is the best that I know how to counsel: that one desire contempt, poverty, and all manner of tribulations, and masses and sermons, and fasts and prayers, that one have fear of all kinds of love, whatever they might be, for the perils which can be there, and that one desire above all paradise, and that one have fear of hell; that one refuse all manner of honors and temporal things, and all comforts, in obstructing Nature [in] what she asks, except those things without which the Soul could not live, as in the exemplar of the suffering and passion of our Lord Jesus Christ.[58]

Reason thus outlines traditional doctrine in advocating works of charity, self-abnegation, and *imitatio Christi* as the steps toward a proper Christian life. The soul following this path is advised to despise the world, to avoid any earthly affection or attachment, and to avoid hell and desire paradise. Reason directs the soul to imitate Jesus Christ in his suffering, so that imitation of Christ becomes the goal of Christian life. Whatever Jesus Christ thought to be a "necessity" is permitted these souls, yet all other needs of nature are scorned. Importantly, this type of soul is expected to fear "all kinds of love" as dangerous deceptions.

Reason's viewpoint as expressed in this passage is countered by the voice of Love. Love assures Reason that annihilated souls are *not* slaves to works; in fact, they become completely indifferent to any outside influence as God works His will in them. Love asserts that

> Such souls, those whom Fine Love calls, have equally shame as honor, honor as shame; poverty as wealth, and wealth as poverty; torment from God and His creatures as comfort from God and from His creatures; being loved as hated, and hated as loved; being in hell as in paradise, and in paradise as in hell; and being in small estate as in great, and great estate as small. . . . For such Souls no longer possess any will, except what God wills in them . . .[59]

This type of soul is free of the traditional model of piety sketched above by Reason. She has no desire or fear or work. She takes both good and bad in equal measure, neither despising nor welcoming either. This soul possesses no will and thus becomes no-thing.

This key dichotomy is reflected in Porete's doctrine of annihilation, a spiritual state that can be reached only by certain noble souls. It is central to Porete's entire program that she sees humanity and its institutions as fundamentally dualistic: she divides the world into two types of souls (lost and sad) and two churches (Holy Church the Little and Holy Church the Great). The seven stages of annihilation (outlined below) are attainable in different measure for these two kinds of souls within the folds of two churches. Lost souls remain obedient to Reason and the Virtues and are content with their lot. They will be saved because they live in the grace ushered in by Christ's sacrifice, but they will never live the divine life. They will not be glorified. They are eternally encumbered with themselves and thus are perpetual slaves to themselves, to the Virtues, to the dictates of the church. Lost souls

> completely mortify the body in doing works of charity; and they have such great pleasure in their works that they have no awareness that there might be any better being than the being of the works of the Virtues and death by martyrdom, in desiring to persevere in this with the aid of an orison filled with prayers, in the multiplication of good will, always for the purpose of retaining what these folk possess, as if this might be the best of all the beings that could be.[60]

These souls never realize that their will and their continuous work impede their progress. They are beggars who seek outside themselves—in masses and sermons and temporal things—what they have within.[61] They follow Reason and are ultimately misled.

Sad souls, on the other hand, see that lost souls are deceived, and they recognize there is an assured way for them to reach a more lofty goal. Both lost and unannihilated sad souls are "servants and merchants, but [sad souls] act more wisely than do [lost souls]."[62] The gospel figures of Mary and Martha embody these types. Martha, the type of the lost soul, "is too impeded and she does not know it" in caring for the earthly needs of Jesus Christ.[63] Mary, on the other hand, is a sad soul who endures no earthly impediments in loving Christ and possesses just "one sole intent, which makes her have peace."[64] Martha can never achieve peace, because she continually attempts to achieve the impossible by immersing herself in works. She is never sure she can complete them or do them correctly. Porete insists that this anxiety is unremitting until the soul abandons works entirely. Only noble sad souls see that this abandonment is possible, and thus only sad souls advance on the road to annihilation. Sad souls are not yet annihilated souls, but they are able to become so by means of an indwelling nobility and the transformation of love. The sad souls are the noble souls to whom the *Mirror* is addressed.

Not surprisingly, Porete insists that these two types of souls belong to two churches: Holy Church the Little (or Holy-Church-Below-This-Church) and Holy Church the Great. Those lost souls who belong to Holy Church the Little, which is governed by Reason, cling to Scriptures and the teachings of earthly exemplars. Membership in this lower Holy Church is an early stage in the process of annihilation, although eventually the "soul who is [annihilated] no longer seeks God through penitence, nor through any sacrament of the

Holy Church."[65] When the soul is "in the greatest perfection of being . . . she no longer takes Holy Church as exemplar in her life" and joins Holy Church the Great, which is governed by Love.[66] The higher church sustains, teaches, and feeds the lower church through love of the Trinity itself.[67] In fact, it supersedes and judges the earthly church for the greater benefit of all. For Porete, this Greater Church is the true church, invisible and not dependent on earthly sacraments and scriptures. Only sad souls who are the anonymous members of Holy Church the Great will become annihilated and thus live without fear, without anxiety, without shame, without reproach, and without the Virtues. Only such sad, noble souls are capable of enduring on the long road toward annihilation.

THE SEVEN-STAGE PATH TO ANNIHILATION

Porete describes the way to annihilation through stages of increasing perfection, an arduous journey at the end of which the soul lives the divine life. Sad souls must travel a long road to come to the place of clarification and annihilation, where they attain their pre-created state of nothingness. At the beginning of her book, Porete describes how the soul at the first of the seven stages of annihilation is "touched by God" in grace and thereafter lives without sin. The soul is then "carried by divine graces" through the seven stages. At the fifth and sixth stages she becomes established and comes to possess "the fullness of her perfection through divine fruition in the land of life."[68] The stages of perfection are purificatory and developmental, aimed at divesting the human being of worldly loves and willing. Impediments on the path, which are ultimately the result of misused will, are overcome and dispelled only in giving the will entirely to God, its proper owner.

Porete spells out the seven stages to annihilation most fully in Chapter 118 of the *Mirror of Simple Souls*. As described earlier and explored more fully in the following chapters, only select "noble" sad souls can achieve all six of the stages possible in this life (the seventh is reserved for the soul after death).[69] Souls on this path must endure three deaths: to sin, to nature, and to the spirit. The first "death to sin" gives birth to the life of grace and the ability to do what God commands.[70] This is the status of ordinary believers, who live in obedience to the commandments. The second death is death to nature, which enables the soul to move into the second stage and greater purification. This is the life of evangelical perfection, in obedience to the Virtues and under submission to Reason.[71] Yet this *vita apostolica* is not Porete's ultimate goal, because human works are limited. The final death is death of the spirit, by which souls "live the divine life" and are thus unencumbered and free.[72] For the life of the spirit to cede to the divine life, the soul must abandon Reason, willing, and the Virtues.

The handwritten note at top: The seven stages end with the annihilation of the will.

In sum, these seven stages, steps, or, perhaps most accurately "states," begin in a state of grace under the rule of the commandments, with purity rather than depravity: they end with the annihilation of the will. These stages are quite distinct and incomparable. Love tells Reason that

> There are seven steps, each one of higher intellect than the former, without comparison. As one might speak of a drop of water in the whole ocean, which is very great, so one might speak of the difference between the first stage of grace and the second, and so on with the rest, without comparison.[73]

Nevertheless, these stages conform to simple categorization: souls in any of the first four stages continue to labor in some degree of servitude because they continue to possess will, but souls in the fifth and sixth stages are "unencumbered" of will and, consequently, of all created things, including masses, sermons, prayers, and other worldly works. These souls become "neither lost nor sad . . . in the depths of the fifth stage with the Lover."[74] The freed soul is no longer tormented by the necessity of practicing good works; moreover, once the soul has reached the fifth stage she becomes firmly "established" and can never slide back to a lower stage. This is worth noting, as it is a departure from the notion of a merely momentary and fleeting "union" with God, after which the soul and body return to normal. The annihilated soul is, thereafter, always "without a why."

The first stage begins on a high level with souls who have already pledged to follow the commandments for the rest of their lives. These commandments are absolutely necessary to salvation in the earthly, ecclesiastical realm.[75] These souls have died to sin and have committed to a life following the two supreme commandments to love God and neighbor. Placing this death to sin so early in the journey underscores how advanced Porete expects souls to be even in this earliest stage of the return. Souls who embark on this path struggle not with sin but with willfulness. The soul that is dead to sin follows the commandments in a state of grace, while no "color or taste or odor of anything prohibited by God" remains in her.[76] Nevertheless, the soul in this stage still fears God's lofty and difficult commandments. This anxiety, which is borne of the recognition of the arduous and futile nature of earthly work, is a tremendous impediment to advancement. Yet courageous and diligent souls are able to climb higher to the second stage by surpassing the commandments "in the work of mortification of nature, in despising riches, delights and honors, in order to accomplish the perfection of the evangelical counsel of which Jesus Christ is the exemplar."[77]

This second stage can begin only when the soul has died to nature; that is, when the soul has ceased to obey the body's incessant demands in choosing to follow the counsel of evangelical perfection. This stage demands strenuous

Freedom is gained only by
abandoning the will

discipline and ongoing sacrifice in imitation of Christ. Jesus Christ is the exemplar of evangelical perfection for those who are in the second stage. He valorizes works and sacrifice through his own example:

> Jesus Christ exalted [works] by His own body, who saw the bestiality of those in this labor who would be saved, and for them He certainly came. And Jesus Christ, who would not ever will to lose them, has bound them to Himself through His death, and through His Gospels, and through His Scriptures where laboring folk are guided.[78]

By placing imitation of Christ so low in the stages of perfection, Porete implies that those souls who imitate Christ in his suffering and sacrifice as the means to annihilation are *ultimately* misled. Their works will never suffice for the debt that is owed either to Christ Himself or to God, to whom each individual soul remains accountable, even after Christ's considerable ransom. This repayment is accomplished only in the fifth stage in abandoning the will.[79] Jesus Christ and his apostles are useful exemplars in their earthly conduct; however, Jesus Christ is most important as an exemplar in willing the divine will. Even if lost souls "strive each day with themselves to enlarge upon the perfection of the apostles by the effort of the will, they will not be unencumbered from themselves . . . that is, neither from the body nor from the soul."[80] Freedom is gained only by abandoning the will. Each noble soul must do this herself in order to achieve annihilation, because the sacrifice of Jesus Christ was not sufficient to accomplish this task. This issue will be covered more fully in the following chapter.

It is essential at this stage to reiterate Porete's understanding of the practical necessity and ultimate futility of human work. She provides an analogy for the necessity of God's aid in human production by noting the role of work in the growth of grain. When "the wise laborer has plowed and hoed the earth and placed the wheat in it, all his power cannot do any more . . . and this you can see through the sense of nature."[81] God must do the rest of the work. "How the grain decays, how it revives and yields fruit one hundredfold through great multiplying, no one knows but God, the only one who does this work; but this happens only after the laborer has done his work and not before."[82]

The sower could spend days and nights working the soil, but in the end his anxiety will be for nought. The sower's work is nothing without God's aid. In keeping with this idea, Porete extolls passivity after strenuous work in explaining how Mary Magdalen came to love Jesus Christ. Mary accomplished her own work and then "rested without doing any work of herself, and God accomplished His work gently in Mary, for Mary, without Mary."[83] Mary first tills and sows; that is, she achieves the works of perfection and maintains pure intention. Yet Mary's labor is limited. Mary and the sower are like the soul in the abyss of the fifth stage: they can do nothing more without divine intervention. At this stage alone God lifts souls up.[84]

This paradigm—doing the work and then allowing God to work within—illluminates Porete's teaching regarding the Virtues, which will be examined in more detail at the end of this chapter. Porete describes such servitude to works as an impoverishing and perhaps fatal exercise in futility. Those who accept the Virtues as their master serve a "poor lord," and "those who serve a poor Lord a long time becomes poor in waiting for a small wage."[85] Moreover, those who live by the Virtues "perish," for the Virtues do not teach the essential lesson of annihilation. The Virtues were made by Love to serve—not to encumber—the soul. The annihilated soul "takes leave of the Virtues" and thus becomes free.

In the third stage, the soul sacrifices these works, which she loves dearly. **3rd stage** The love of works is disordered but exceedingly strong; most importantly, it distorts the soul's perception of spiritual priorities. "For no death would be martyrdom to [the soul in the third stage] except abstaining from the work she loves, which is the delight of her pleasure and the life of her will which is nourished by this."[86] The soul must now move away from material things to focus on abandoning her will. Before forsaking the Virtues absolutely, however, the Soul must pass through the treacherous fourth stage, which is a turning point and a testing ground. By the fourth stage, the soul is completely absorbed in contemplation of God and has abandoned all labor and obedience. **4th stage** Unfortunately, in this stage the soul still believes "that there is no higher life than to have this over which she has lordship. For love has so grandly satisfied her with delights that she does not believe that God has a greater gift to give to this Soul here below . . ."[87]

Life in this stage seems as sweet and perfect as the soul could imagine. Yet the soul does not know that she is "inebriated" and thus deluded: she does not see how "dazzled" she has become in the brightness of love. The soul does no more works, but she still remains in will. As explained above, the soul advances from the first to the fourth stage by stripping away the things of the world, first by ascesis and then through abandoning works and, with those works, the anxiety that attends them. For the soul finally free of anxiety, the fourth stage seems to represent human perfection. Yet even in this stage the soul is to some degree burdened and in servitude, because she has yet to abandon her will. She has throughout these four stages labored in a life according to the self or to the spirit. She must die to the spirit, as she has already died to self (to sin and to nature), in order to move beyond this deceptive fourth stage to the true life of the fifth and sixth stages.

The origin of the human soul and the freedom of the will are of utmost importance in the final stages, as described in more detail in the following chapters. The annihilated soul realizes, without the work of her will, her pre-created state, the glory of her eternal existence within the Trinity and the Trinity within her. Porete's understanding of creation, Fall, redemption, and annihilation places the ultimate focus of annihilation on individual souls, not on Adam or Christ. Adam used his will, so the soul must cease using hers and follow Christ in doing God's will. By this the soul returns to her source. Consequently, the soul in the fifth and sixth stages is "established" there, although she continues to move according to God's will. Porete describes the movement of the soul into the fifth stage as catalyzed by "one rapturous overflow of the movement of Divine Light," which shows the soul what is and what is not and thereby moves the soul from where she ought not to be to where she ought to be.[88] There she stays, without threat of regression. Periodically such souls are raptured by the Trinity to a "vision" of absolute peace and glory, a glimpse of the glory that the disembodied soul will enjoy eternally in the seventh stage, which is granted only after bodily death. Thus the soul realizes its true identity as divine. Before examining the cosmological and anthropological underpinnings of these doctrines, we must delve into Porete's central and controversial doctrine of "Taking Leave of the Virtues."

"TAKING LEAVE OF THE VIRTUES" AND POSSESSING ALL

This notion of annihilation as a state in which the soul is "established" and thus continues to live in the world without need of the world is expressed most clearly in Porete's doctrine of "Taking Leave of the Virtues." As noted above, the first recorded condemnation of Porete includes the following excerpted article: "That the annihilated soul is freed from the Virtues and nor is she any longer in the service, because she does not have them as far as their practice is concerned, but the virtues obey according to her good pleasure."[89] This article describes a key doctrine in Porete's arsenal. As she describes it, an annihilated soul remains in the world in bodily form yet becomes impassive to anything outside of herself. The soul must, therefore, become indifferent to church teachings as well, including the scriptures, sacraments, works, and Virtues. An examination of this doctrine, which vexed and angered inquisitorial authorities, will illustrate the radical nature of Porete's teachings.

As just described, Porete does not completely dismiss the traditional path to salvation through obedience to the commandments in her seven-stage path to annihilation. She insists that grace and *imitatio Christi* are early and necessary steps in the process of regaining the soul's prior existence. The created world and its virtues and vices are a necessary part of the path to annihilation. Porete states emphatically that none can achieve the highest restful repose without working first.[90] One must obey the Virtues, as a sower must sow each seed, in order to progress on the path. She describes this as passing through a rough ocean, a baptism by works, after which the soul attains the country of peace.

> This Soul has perceived by divine light the being of the land of which she must be. And [she] has crossed the sea in order to suck the marrow of the high cedar. For no one receives nor attains this marrow if he does not cross this high sea, if he does not plunge his will into its waves.[91]

The sea represents the soul's passage through the created world, a way to leave one's enemies behind, as Moses did in crossing the Red Sea.[92] The created world is one stage of being. The sad soul sees that another, higher level of peaceful being exists in a land beyond a tumultuous sea. These are the two paths of the soul, which will be explored in more detail in the following chapters.

This freedom, then, is attained only through prior obedience to the Virtues. She outlines the requisite commandments that lead to salvation: to love God "with all our heart, all our soul, and all our strength; and ourselves as we ought, and our neighbors as ourselves."[93] She expands on these commandments, noting specifically that each of them, including the command to love oneself as one ought, resolve to doing God's will. She concludes that "these commands are necessary for the salvation of all. Nobody can have grace with a lesser way."[94]

In annihilation, however, the Virtues serve the soul. This is, to Porete, the correct and natural order of things. Porete explains that a man who serves a master can become "richer and wiser" than the master. He is then free to choose a better master or free himself from servitude. This move can prompt the first master to enslave himself entirely to his former servant. This is precisely what ought to happen with the soul and the Virtues. The soul serves the Virtues until she surpasses them and has no need of them, and then the Virtues serve the soul. The soul then belongs to God rather than to the Virtues. She serves the highest master and thus attains the highest state of being.[95] Souls who were once slaves to works become free after serving an apprenticeship of sorts "when they lived in the love and obedience of you, Lady Reason, and also of the other Virtues. And having lived there, they have become free."[96] She describes such a soul as follows:

> A Soul
> who is saved by faith without works
> who is only in love
> who does nothing for God
> who leaves nothing to do for God
> to whom nothing can be taught
> from whom nothing can be taken
> nor given
> and who possesses no will.[97]

How does the soul achieve such a state? Porete at first counsels absolute adherence to the rules of evangelical perfection as expressed in the words of Jesus in Matthew 19:20–21. The young man who has followed the commandments throughout his life is told by Christ: "One thing you must do, if you want to be perfect. Go and sell all of your possessions and give them to the poor, and then follow me, and you will have treasure in the heavens."[98] In this passage, perfection consists in abandoning all "possessions" and following Christ absolutely in supreme love or charity. Porete then goes on to explicate the hallmarks of a life lived in Charity.

> Charity obeys no created thing except Love. Charity possesses nothing of her own, and should she possess something she does not say that it belongs to her. Charity abandons her own need and attends to the need of others. Charity asks no payment from anyone for some good or pleasure that she has accomplished. Charity has no shame, nor fear, nor anxiety. She is so upright that she cannot bow on account of anything that might happen to her. Charity neither makes nor takes account of anything under the sun, for the whole world is only refuse and leftovers. Charity gives to all what she possesses of worth, without retaining anything for herself, and with this she often promises what she does not possess through her great largesse, in the hope that the more she gives the more remains with her. Charity is such a wise merchant that she earns profits everywhere where others lose, and she escapes the bonds that bind others and thus she has great multiplicity of what pleases Love.[99]

Here, under the familiar guise of the teachings of evangelical perfection, Porete anticipates essential elements of her doctrine of annihilation. Ideally, Charity obeys Love alone; abandons and ignores all created things while attending to those in need; has no fear or anxiety or shame; gives her "possessions" freely without regard to their limit; and escapes the "bonds" that tie most other souls to earth. Those who live a life of Charity are considered truly holy, truly set apart from the mass of humanity. Nevertheless, Charity still "pleases" Love; still "obeys" Love; still has "hope" that her largesse with be rewarded; still suffers under the weight of what Porete will later term "burdens from multiplicities of love"; and still continues to ignore her own needs.[100] In Porete's terms, those who live lives governed by Charity continue to possess will; although they may appear saintly and poor, they are in the most essential sense neither.[101] Charity is the perfection of the Virtues, but Porete's goal is to dismiss the Virtues entirely in order to live in "freeness of Charity."

Porete appeals instead to the souls who can live "*beyond* the work of Poverty and *above* the work of Charity."[102] The embodied, unannihilated soul lives in a state of constant anxiety, unsure about the efficacy of her works and uncertain about her standing before God. Yet, as described above, the freed annihilated soul has no "anxiety about any sin which she might ever have committed, nor about suffering which God might have suffered for her, nor about the sins or anxiety in which her neighbors remain."[103] This impassivity is not meant to imply that the soul no longer actually does any works; rather, it is meant to show that the compulsion felt by fallen souls is obliterated in annihilation. The soul is capable of helping her neighbors, yet she does not feel compelled to do so.

Porete insists that the key to this "above and beyond" status is Humility, the supreme virtue for souls attaining annihilation. The soul only comes to realize her true nature when she recognizes her extreme wretchedness in the light of God's goodness, as described in more detail in chapter 4. The annihilated soul understands that her wretchedness is so great that it has no "beginning, middle, or end, only a bottomless abyss."[104] This recognition gives birth to Humility, who "seats her on the throne, who reigns without pride."[105] The soul in annihilation becomes the "most sweet abyssed one . . . at the bottom without bottom of total humility . . ."[106] This fifth stage is the lowest place, an abyss of poverty, an abyss of humility, or quite simply a "valley." In essence, the soul must hit bottom before she can ascend: she must become completely passive as well. The soul in the fifth stage "seats herself in the bottom of the valley, from which she sees the height of the mountain . . ."[107] Those who embrace the humility of their true station live "another life, which we call the peace of charity in the annihilated life."[108] Souls in such abject humility seem to be quite like those who follow the supreme virtue of charity, yet they are purely impassive, purely will-less. The distinction between those who live by the rules of charity and those who are annihilated is subtle but crucial to understanding annihilation.

Porete expresses this distinction best when she describes the relationship between such souls and the Virtues. Those who struggle constantly to fulfill the commands of evangelical perfection continue to struggle within the world of created things. Porete depicts this life as a "great and perilous war! . . . one must certainly call such a strenuous life sickness and a life of war."[109] The soul who follows the rules of charity blindly is a slave, in distress, in pain. Yet when that soul takes leave of the Virtues, she is suddenly unencumbered of that burden and supremely free.

> Virtues, I take my leave of you forever,
> I will possess a heart most free and gay;
> Your service is too constant, you know well.
> Once I placed my heart in you, retaining nothing;
> You know that I was totally abandoned to you;
> Once a slave to you, I am delivered from it.
> I had placed my heart completely in you, you know well.
> Thus I lived a while in great distress,
> I suffered many grave torments, endured many pains.
> It is a miracle that I have somehow escaped alive.

The Virtues are meant to serve Love. (handwritten)

> This being so, I no longer care: I am parted from you,
> For which I thank God on high; this day is good to me.
> I am parted from your dominations, which so vexed me.
> I was never more free, except as departed from you.
> I am parted from your dominations, in peace I rest.[110]

The soul thus surpasses and abandons the Virtues. Porete here describes the world as a schoolroom in which the annihilated soul moves beyond the elementary, corporeal level. This seems to follow the standard formula of increasing spiritual maturity. Yet she also asserts that the soul can actually bypass *all* lessons after a certain stage and thus cease developing. The soul "took lessons in [Reason's] school through desire of the works of the Virtues. Now she has entered upon and is so surpassing in divine learning that she begins to read where you take your end."[111] The burdensome earning of virtue becomes unnecessary, and the soul who has become annihilated does not simply serve a better master. Indeed, the "nobility of the courtesy of [the Soul's] spouse would not deign to leave the soul in any sort of servitude," not least in servitude to Reason.[112] When the Master is Love, even the Virtues serve Love. The soul in annihilation has become Love, and the Virtues thus serve the soul.

Nevertheless, this freedom from the burdensome weight of the Virtues does not mean that the soul ceases to possess them. The Virtues remain within the soul always, although they are masterfully hidden. The personified allegorical Virtues in the narrative seem to anticipate Porete's difficulties with the authorities by remarking that anyone who asserts that those who live by the Virtues alone will perish ought to be considered "a heretic and a bad Christian."[113] Porete makes it clear, however, that the Virtues are meant to serve Love, to be messengers for God.[114] It is proper that the unencumbered soul becomes so far removed from the work of the Virtues that she "cannot understand their language."[115] The Virtues obey the soul, however, and are so perfectly enclosed within the soul that nobody, not even those in the spiritual Holy Church, is able to discern them within. The annihilated soul becomes the master of the Virtues, who serve her absolutely, and which she fulfills without desire and out of habit.[116] When she does the "work" of the Virtues it is not out of compulsion or with the hopes of advancement toward divine life; rather, it is because God wills through her. The Virtues, as God's messengers, work through the soul, without the soul, serving the soul just as they serve God, who is Love. The three cardinal Virtues of Faith, Hope, and Charity are within all annihilated souls eternally. They further ennoble the soul and guard Love. Nevertheless, these Virtues do not know what these souls are, any more than do other created things or the Holy Church.[117]

For Porete, then, the Virtues serve the souls who once lived in absolute obedience to their demands. The most controversial implication of this doctrine is the implication that embodied souls can take advantage of whatever they might want or need in life, without regard. Those souls who achieve annihilation live in the world without reproach; therefore, they do not deprive themselves of what their bodies require of necessity nor do they serve the Virtues, whatever Reason might counsel. Indeed, to deprive the body of what it needs would be "to fault the innocence and to encumber the peace in which such a Soul rests from all things."[118] Porete goes on:

> For who would make his conscience guilty about taking the necessities from the four elements, as light from heaven, warmth from fire, dew from the water and from the earth that sustains us? We receive the service of the four elements in all the ways that Nature has need of them without reproach to Reason. These elements were graciously made by God as other things. As such Souls make use of all things made and created of which Nature has need, in complete peace of heart, so they make of the earth upon which they walk.[119]

This necessity of the annihilated soul to "use" all things granted by nature is explained in part by God's absolute largesse. The Trinitarian God "promised" through goodness and largesse that all that God possessed would be possessed by the properly oriented soul. The soul possesses what earthly things she possesses by means of the will, and that will stands between the soul and God. The soul who renders all back to God—without wishing anything in return—forsakes not only those possessions but also the mediation of the human will. In this state, what is God's becomes properly the soul's through the transformation of Love. "Thus what we possess in us, says the Holy Spirit, is by divine nature, and this Soul possesses it from us in herself by right of Love."[120]

Consequently, the soul—once nothing—becomes "as rich as God is" in annihilation.[121] The full, perfect Love offered by God is what the soul wants and needs, so she takes what is His as if it were her own.[122] Thus, to follow the courtly metaphor, if God, the Lover, is totally rich, the soul as beloved cannot be poor.[123] When the soul gives everything to the Trinity "without wishing anything in return in heaven or on earth, but for the sake of the will [of the Trinity] alone," the Trinity renders all it possesses to the soul "by right of love."[124] When the annihilated soul returns her will to God, the whole Trinity works through her, "for the one who gives all, possesses all, and not otherwise."[125] This insistence on God's absolute *largesse* is fully in keeping with courtly mysticism.

In summary, the annihilated soul, once in servitude to the body and to the Virtues, becomes free, noble, and unencumbered. Such a soul thus

> leaves the dead to bury the dead, and the sad ones to work the Virtues, and so she rests from the least part of her in the greater part, but she uses all things. The greater part shows her her nothingness, naked without

covering; such nakedness shows her the All Powerful through the goodness of divine righteousness. These showings make her . . . always naked,
All and Nothing, as long as they hold her in their embrace.[126]

In this passage Porete refers to the "greater part" within the soul, which overtakes the "least part." This realization makes the soul both "All" and "nothing," the intersection of which is where God and human meet. This meeting,
ineffable yet entirely real to Porete, must be expressed in metaphorical language. We will explore this language more fully in the following chapter.

Irving Singer seems to capture the essence of Porete's theological
agenda in his monumental, multivolume *The Nature of Love*. Singer remarks
that it is a commonplace in the courtly and romantic traditions that the lover
"discovers the hidden reality that is herself" in her beloved.[127] This is surely an
undercurrent in Porete's work: by attaining annihilation through recognizing
the soul's wretchedness, the soul paradoxically discovers her true identity in
her virtual existence in the Trinity. Noble souls can advance on the path to
annihilation by virtue of an ability to recognize their own wretchedness, not
through begging for something outside of themselves.[128] The soul who abandons her will and loves God alone finds herself in God: the soul becomes a
mirror for God, and God becomes the "mirror" of the simple soul.[129] The soul
through annihilation realizes her fundamental identity with God in the ultimate ground of reality, a realization that is made possible only through shared
noble qualities.

This basic map of the textual territory of Porete's *Mirror* has outlined
her teachings about two types of souls and churches, three deaths, her seven-
stage path to annihilation, and her doctrine of "Taking Leave of the Virtues"
as well as her construction of her own authority and audience. All of these elements underscore the uncompromising and esoteric nature of her message. A
study of her cosmological and anthropological speculations will set the stage
for a detailed study of Porete's doctrine of annihilation and the implications of
the metaphors she adopts to explain it.

✟ CHAPTER THREE ✟

GOD, THE SOUL, AND NO-THINGNESS

The *Mirror of Simple Souls* begins with paired but distinct fables of love, one of earthly love and one of divine love. The first "little exemplum of love" is narrated by Love. The second is related by the Soul. These lengthy passages together contain the theological keys to—and the framework for this exploration of—the esoteric anthropology of the *Mirror*. Love tells the following tale:

> Once upon a time, there was a maiden, daughter of a king, of great heart and nobility and also of noble character; and she lived in a far off land. So it happened that this maiden heard tell of the great gentle courtesy and nobility of the king, Alexander, and very soon her will loved him because of the great renown of his gentility. But this maiden was so far from this great lord, in whom she had fixed her love from herself, that she was able neither to see him nor to have him. Thus she was inconsolable in herself, for no love except this one would be sufficient for her. When she saw that this faraway love, *who was so close within her, was so far outside of her, she thought to herself that she would comfort her melancholy by imagining some figure of her love,* by whom she was continually wounded in heart. And so she had an image painted which would represent the semblance of the king she loved, an image as close as possible to that which presented itself to her in her love for him and in the affection of the love which captured her. And by means of this image with her other works she dreamed of the king.

Then Soul interjects to tell her own tale.

In truly similar fashion, speaks the Soul who had this book written, I tell you of such a thing: I heard tell of a king of great power who was by gentle courtesy and by very great courtesy of nobility and largesse a noble Alexander. *But he was so far from me, and I from him, that I did not know how to take comfort for myself.*

And for the sake of my memory of him, he gave me this book, which makes present in some manner his love itself. But it is no hindrance that I have his image, for it is *not* that I am in a strange land and far from the palace where the very noble friends of this Lord dwell, who are completely pure, perfect, and free through the gifts of this king with whom they remain.[1]

These two passages are predicated on the twin notions of presence and absence as expressed in an extended courtly metaphor.[2] They echo themes seen in earlier thinkers: the dilemma of the soul, distant from yet ineffably near God; the notion of an image as the binding force between the two; and the particular powers both from within and without the soul that enable a re-union. Yet these two passages attest to very different experiences of love in the world.

The first of these twin passages is rich with motifs that express Porete's conception of the dilemma of the common fallen (in Porete's terms, "lost") human soul, at once far from yet ineffably near God, who is Love. It opens with an admission that the high-born maiden is informed of the "courtesy" and "nobility" of the great Alexander.[3] Her knowledge of him thus comes from hearing of his virtuous reputation, not from her own experience of him. This knowledge causes her *will* to love him alone, despite (or perhaps because of) the distance between them. In order to comfort herself, the maiden has an image created of the king, to resemble both her mind's vision of him and the love she has for him. It is essential to note that the maiden undertakes to comfort herself by having this image made. The king does not reciprocate, nor does he offer his services in any way. This image is described as an aid to "dreaming" of the king; however, as such it is only one of the maiden's many works. The maiden never knows more of the king than what her imagination and tales of his gentility tell her. This is certainly a high and exalted love; however, the love the maiden has for the king plays itself out only in her imagination and her works. The king remains in a realm apart. This sums up the dilemma of the lost soul.

Soul's tale is distinctly different, and the divergences between these accounts are keys to Porete's message. Both lovers recognize the paradox of the simultaneous nearness and distance of their beloved, and both resort to "images" of their love in that absence. The maiden has a painted image: the soul has "this book." Both of these images manifest love; however, the maiden's image manifests the love she has for the king, while the Soul's image makes present the king's love itself, directly from the king. The maiden's love, encumbered by works, is not reciprocated, except in her imagination. The Soul's love is answered in the form of a book, a gift from the king. The Soul thus *ap-*

pears to be contented from "without," although her proximity to the king within his court and among his friends makes the soul the direct recipient of the king's largesse.[4] The sad soul has an advantage over the lost soul: she has an affinity for the king, and the king takes notice of her. Consequently, Soul takes care to note that the image granted to her by the king is not a hindrance to her love (implying, it seems, that the maiden's fabricated image might be an encumbrance). The maiden's image—along with her other works—enables her to dream of the king but not to have him. The Soul's book, in contrast, is evidence of the Soul's proximity to the king. The soul is explicitly *not* exiled from the king but dwells among fellow noble souls in the king's court. In sum, the fallen soul, embodied in the maiden, might appear to be highborn, but she cannot escape the world of constant work and striving. In contrast, the noble annihilated soul dwells in the peace of repose with God.

The dialectic of presence and absence in these exempla, a dialectic that mirrors that of God's simultaneous immanence and transcendence, plays itself out over the course of the *Mirror*. These tales exemplify love mediated through works and love without mediator, love merely imagined and love realized, noble love that remains on the earthly level and noble love that realizes its lofty divine calling. Only certain noble souls discern that they are called to an unmediated, reciprocal union with God, the overflowing, good, magnanimous ground of all being. God's overflowing of himself in creating souls and the material world means that all things participate in some degree in the divine essence. Human souls are set apart from other creatures because of an eternal indwelling mark of the Trinity within, complemented by a reciprocal mark of the soul in the Trinity itself. By means of this image, certain noble souls can, during earthly life, attain a seemingly paradoxical state of embodied "nothingness."

This chapter will lay the theoretical groundwork for such a radical claim by examining Porete's conception of God, the courteous and noble allegorical king of the opening exempla, and by exploring the relationships that inhere within God and between God and the Soul. This examination will show that, for Porete, the human soul is created from nothing and bound, if it is noble and aided by Love, to return to that glorious pre-created state. Such a soul returns from being to Being, regaining the passivity and nothingness it possessed prior to creation. It experiences an appropriately unmediated, reciprocal union with the God who is All. Three questions will guide this inquiry. First, on what theological basis does Porete, who insists upon the absolute unlikeness of humanity to divinity in nature, assert a complete and reciprocal union of both? Second, how does she conceive of the roles of Adam and Jesus Christ in humanity's fall from and return to God? Finally, how does the embodiment of the soul figure in the soul's dilemma? Exploring the cosmological and theological speculations in her thought is the essential first step in answering these questions.

GOD AS TRINITARIAN GROUND AND CREATOR

Marguerite Porete provides her readers with little explicit theological and cosmological speculation, but this modest testimony provides solid ground for her doctrine of annihilation.[5] She relies on three key doctrines that guide her understanding of the relationship between Creator and creatures and of the process of annihilation. The first pivotal doctrine is that God the Father is the source without source of the Trinity and, by extension, of all of creation. God is Being and the ground of all being; therefore, all created things derive their existence from God. Nevertheless, God remains radically distinct from creation. The second doctrine is that God creates all from nothing and that all created things will return to that nothingness.[6] The soul who recognizes her nothingness next to God's All discovers the key to annihilation. Finally, the transformation that leads to annihilation is accomplished not, as traditionally held, through the mediation of the incarnated Savior, but rather through the work of the Holy Spirit within to noble souls. The Holy Spirit, as Love, transforms the soul to become "what God is" by granting to the soul the divine nature it shares as the union of Father and Son. Porete's doctrine of the Holy Spirit as God's goodness, God's will, and God's love is the pivotal element in her understanding of the soul's journey of annihilation, sharing thereby an absolutely unmediated identity with God in the ground of all reality.

Porete's speculations about God range from radically apophatic statements to formulaic assertions about God's absolute qualities. The *Mirror* makes positive assertions about God while maintaining that "God is none other than the one about whom one can understand nothing perfectly. For that one alone is my God, about whom one does not know how to say a word."[7] God is infinitely more than he shares with humanity; therefore, humanity must be content with the "lesser" part of Himself that God shares with the world and accept that His "greater" part is beyond human thought and understanding. The part of God that is unexpressed in creation is that which the soul finds and loves in annihilation. In embodied life, however, the soul cannot understand even the goodness that is God.[8] "This Soul loves better that which is in God, which never was nor is nor will be given, than she [loves] what she has and will have."[9] Triumph in the struggle to name God—which consists in abandoning the struggle entirely—opens the door to annihilation.[10]

Many of Porete's positive descriptions about God are largely formulaic and traditional. God's goodness suffuses all of creation in which He is All in all things.[11] God is a Trinity of power, wisdom, and goodness, related to creatures intimately through bonds of love, which Porete describes with familial metaphors. He is eternal, and He loves souls eternally. He is One, expressed as three. Porete stresses this oneness as the simple one ground of all, as the goal for human souls who attain "simplicity" (*simplece*), which was a central element in courtly mysticism. It is important to note the meaning of this term for Porete. *Simplece* is one of the highest duties of the lover: to remain steadfastly loyal, never duplicitous. The soul in annihilation will attain this simplicity even among worldly temptations.

The implications of this doctrine of God as the ground of all are at once profound and prosaic: a world derived from God is filled with God. Porete emphasizes this divine immanence throughout her book. The Unencumbered Soul reports that "I find Him . . . everywhere, and there He is. He is one Deity, one sole God in three Persons, and this God is everywhere. There, she says, I find him."[12] This recognition is achieved only by those who have jettisoned Reason as their guide and follow only Love. One implication of this immanence is the marginal significance of earthly works designed to "find" God. Those souls who seek God only through masses, sermons, and other worldly means are misled. Porete uses the example of the Sacrament of the Altar as the ultimate instance of this deception. Those in the earthly church might "find" God there; indeed, the Trinity ordains the Sacrament of the Altar "in order to feed and nourish and sustain the [little] Holy Church."[13] Yet the annihilated, glorified Soul knows that God is everywhere, in the Eucharist as without it, and most intimately in the soul. Those who follow Reason and Holy Church the Little seek God in masses and sermons and worldly works, yet the annihilated Soul jettisons these "external" aids.

Another implication of God's immanence is the immanence of goodness throughout creation.

> [The Soul] knows this, says Love, that she always finds Him there, that is, in all things; that one comes to find a thing where it is, and because He is everywhere, the Soul finds Him everywhere. And because of this all things are good to her, because she does not find anything in any part that she does not find God.[14]

God is All in all, thus all that He creates manifests His goodness. This goodness, which is apparent to the annihilated soul, extends to the human body, which, despite its mortal corruption, is created good, as will be shown later in this chapter.[15] Consequently, God's Goodness is our goodness, His Being is our being. Yet, as we shall see, certain souls can surpass derivative goodness and being to embody Goodness and Being.

In Porete's thought, as in the broader Christian tradition, God's absolute immanence is contrasted with God's absolute transcendence. In order to express this idea, Porete invents a new name for the Trinitarian God in relation to the human soul: "Farnear."[16] This relationship is particularly clear in the state of annihilation, in which the soul regains the state of being proper to her before she flowed from God's goodness. In annihilation,

> [God's] farness is greater nearness, because, from nearby, in itself, it better
> knows what is far, which makes [the Soul] always in union with His will,
> without the interference of any other thing that might happen to her. *All
> things are one for her, without a why, and she is nothing in such a One.* Thus
> the Soul has nothing more to do for God than God does for her. Why?
> Because He is, and she is not. She retains nothing more of herself in
> nothingness, because He is sufficient to Himself; that is, He is and she is
> not. She is stripped of all things because she is without being, where she
> was before she was. She has from God what He has, *and she is what God is
> through the transformation of love*, in that point in which she was *before* she
> flowed from God's goodness.[17]

The soul in annihilation achieves a breakthrough to the simple, unified
ground that is God, thereby moving from diversity of works and loves to absolutely undifferentiated unity with God. In this there is no mediator. God
gives all to the soul in His *largesse*.

The following pivotal passage introduces this new name to characterize
its work within the soul as ineffably transcendent and immanent All. The
Trinity is

> shut away and sealed in a secret closure of the most high purity of this ex-
> cellent soul; this closure cannot be opened, nor unsealed, nor closed
> when it is opened, if the gentle Farnear from very far and very near does
> not close and open it, which one alone has the keys, nobody else carries
> them, nor could anyone else carry them.[18]

This Farnear is described here as the Holy Spirit, which flows into the soul in
the "noble" spark of the sixth stage, as described in chapter 2.[19] Farnear is the
means by which the human soul is "moved" from the fifth to the sixth stage in
annihilation.[20] The apparent distance of the Soul from God cloaks an actual
proximity, made manifest by Farnear. Farnear thus resolves the dialectic of
presence and absence, of immanence and transcendence, both of which are illustrated in the opening exempla. Both the maiden and the Soul see God as at
once far away and very close. This tension causes tremendous agony. God,
within all of creation while remaining radically distinct from it, is all in all,
yet all creatures are not God.[21] God remains ineffably other, indescribable by
human words and never contained within His creation. God is not changed
by creating, nor is He controlled nor contained by His creation. And yet God
the Trinity is within the soul. Farnear shows the noble soul that her true being
dwells within her, *virtualiter*.

The Trinitarian nature of this at once immanent and transcendent God
is undoubtedly central to Porete's doctrine of annihilation, though the reader
must reconstruct her understanding of the Trinity from scattered references
throughout the text. Porete succinctly and apparently straightforwardly outlines the particular roles of each of the persons of the Trinity in creation, who

nevertheless create as one: "God willed [creation] by his divine goodness, and all was made in the same moment by his divine power, and all was ordained, in that same hour, by his divine wisdom."[22] Here we see Porete's favored description of God as a Trinity of goodness, power, and wisdom, who creates as one.[23] As we shall see, Porete does not stress the role of the second person of the Trinity as the mediator of creation. Each person of the Trinity is equal in and indispensable to the act of creation.[24]

There are clues throughout the text that indicate that the Holy Spirit, as God's goodness and will and love, is at least as important as the Son in the creation and destiny of the human soul and the world. The foundational text for understanding the relationships that inhere among the persons of the Trinity is found in chapter 67. Again, we see that God the Father is the source without source of creation and of the persons of the Trinity.

> It is true, says Love, that God the Father has the divine power in him, without taking it from anyone. He has the outpouring of his divine power and gives the same that he has in him to his Son. The Son receives it from the Father. The Son is born of the Father and is equal to Him. And from the Father and the Son is the Holy Spirit, one person in the Trinity, who is not born, but is; for the Son is born from the Father, and the Holy Spirit is from the Father and the Son.[25]

God the Father possesses power that is His alone. The Son and the Holy Spirit receive this power derivatively; nevertheless, they are equal to God. This is clearest in the case of the Son, whom Porete describes as begotten of the Father. Yet the Holy Spirit is explicitly *not* born: the Spirit simply "is," mysteriously proceeding from both the Father and the Son. This does not appear to lessen the Spirit's status; in fact, in the *Mirror* the Holy Spirit's equality among the persons of the Trinity is pivotal.

The Son "inherits" his divine nature directly from the Father; as incarnated, the Son becomes the ultimate exemplar in doing the Father's will. Yet how is the Holy Spirit equal to the Father and the Son, if the Spirit is not "born" of either? It is clear throughout the text that the Holy Spirit proceeds from both Father and Son and thereby shares their divine nature. Porete asserts this doctrine in part by resorting to traditional Augustinian formulas. God as Trinity

> is one eternal substance, one pleasing fruition, one loving conjunction. The Father is the eternal substance; the Son is the pleasing fruition; the Holy Spirit is the loving conjunction. This loving conjunction is from the eternal substance and the pleasing fruition by means of divine love.[26]

Again, the Father is the "eternal substance" from which all creatures come. This substance finds its "fruition" in the person of the Son.[27] The Holy Spirit is the union of both the eternal substance and the pleasing fruition. In other words, the Holy Spirit is the meeting of the Father and the Son in Love.

Porete asserts straightforwardly that the Son is equal to the Father, having received divine power from Him by virtue of having been born of Him.
This birth is, of course, a divine birth, in which God imparts all of Himself to
his Son. Porete exalts this divine sonship; however, she takes care to note that
"adoptive" sonship, effected by grace coupled with abandoning the will, is as
salutary as being "begotten" of the Father, as shown when the Soul considers
who can ascend to heaven.

> Truth told me that no one will ascend there except the one who de-
> scended from there, that is, the Son of God Himself. That is to say that
> no one will rise there, *except only those who are Sons of God by divine grace*.
> And because of this Jesus Christ Himself said that my brother, my sister,
> and my mother is the one who does the will of God my Father.[28]

This passage refers specifically to salvation, which will be taken up in more
detail toward the end of this chapter, but it is important to note two pivotal
elements that enable human beings to ascend where only children of God are
permitted: the will, which is properly the will of the Father, and the operation
of grace.[29]

This grace is explicitly Trinitarian. Porete uses the triad of substance,
fruition, and conjunction several times in the *Mirror*; however, she often employs the more traditional designation of Father as power, the Son as wisdom,
and the Holy Spirit as goodness.[30] The following passage presents this traditional triad juxtaposed to another, which discloses one essential facet of the
Holy Spirit.

> [A]nd *the Holy Spirit has in himself the divine nature of the Father and the Son*.
> To believe, to say, to think [this] is true contemplation; it is one power,
> one wisdom, and one will; one sole God in three persons; three persons
> and one sole God. This God is everywhere in his divine nature . . .[31]

Porete defines the Trinity in a traditional way as a unity of power, wisdom, and
goodness. Each of the persons of the Trinity shares the same divine nature
while the Son also possesses humanity, composed of body and soul. In the passage above, however, Porete alters this formulaic description to refer to "one
power, one wisdom, and one will." This substitution of "will" for "goodness" to
describe the Holy Spirit is hardly accidental, as will be shown below.

The first description of creation presented above describes how God
"willed" creation by His "divine goodness." The Holy Spirit, as God's will,
unites the human will to God through goodness. The work of divine Love,
and the work of the creature during life, is to restore "today the first day in the
soul" when God was wholly united to His passive, un-willing creation.[32]
Throughout the *Mirror* one finds the Holy Spirit in the persona of God's
goodness, will, love, or union. These four elements bind creature to Creator.

God's goodness maintains the freedom of the human will while God's love enables union. These elements come to the fore in Porete's descriptions of the
creation and Fall of humanity, which are based in more traditional Christian
anthropology.

THE ROOTS OF A THEOLOGICAL ANTHROPOLOGY

Christian thought in the Middle Ages is perhaps best described as a fusion of
philosophic-religious themes from several somewhat amorphous systems of
thought, including Platonic thought (considered broadly), early Christian
apologetic and patristic writings, and the revelation of the Bible.[33] To put it
very simply, Christian anthropology was largely developed based on certain
themes from Genesis (such as the creation of humanity in God's "image and
likeness" or human dominion over earthly creatures); from the Pauline and
deutero-Pauline books of the New Testament (such as being reformed to the
image of Christ); and from related philosophical ideas. Together these sources
became the foundations of the Christian understanding of human origins, sin,
redemption, and eventual perfection.[34] Porete is heir to this tradition; although the lines of transmission are undetermined and might always remain
so, certain influences from Neoplatonic thought in particular can be found in
her *Mirror*. Notably, she recasts those notions in light of a distinctive re-
reading of the Genesis narrative of creation and fall.

As will be seen more fully in the following chapter, Porete's doctrine of
annihilation is centered on the idea that only certain souls can "realize" their
true identity as direct descendants of the Trinity. This notion is akin to the
the Platonic "spark" of *Nous* (or reason) in the soul that links human and divine. In the Christian tradition, this spark comes to be understood as equivalent to the Christian "image and likeness" referred to in Genesis.[35] The terminology of "image" (Latin *imago*, Greek *eikon*, and Hebrew *celem*) and
"likeness" (Latin *similitudo*, Greek *homoiosis*, and Hebrew *demuth*) in this familiar passage is worth noting, especially since they have traditionally been at
the core of many debates over theological anthropology.[36] Such created "perfection" is possible only because the image dwells within as a latent potential-
ity.[37] Simply put, image is an ontological status; likeness is a moral status. This
moral status is lost in the fall, while the image remains within. This image is
the key to return. For Porete, that image is the soul's nobility. Yet the nature of
the return and the means by which it is achieved admit of many interpretations.

The notion of *Nous* itself (the *nous* from which the soul's spark derives)
as it operates within the universe as the universal Reason forming the world
for the good, was also adopted by later thinkers as the *Logos*, the efficient
cause of creation. In Christian belief, this *Logos* can be identified with the

incarnate Christ. In addition, the Platonic notion of the formation of human-ity and the sensible universe according to a model, as the likeness of a higher reality, finds constant expression in Christian cosmology and anthropology. In both systems, the goal of human life becomes emulation of a virtuous model through virtuous conduct. This doctrine is the source of the practice of *imita-tio Christi*, the imitation of Jesus Christ as the ultimate moral blueprint for Christians. In both systems, whether the Platonic "spark" of *Nous* in the soul or the Christian *imago Dei*, this deposit of the divine within the human soul is posited as the means by which humanity comes to some knowledge of or union with God.

Western thinkers have certainly diverged on the degree to which the inherent powers possessed by the fallen human can effect return to God; nevertheless, almost all emphasize the necessity of a mediator in enabling a return to felicity.[38] Thinkers from Plato onward posited a mediator in cre-ation between divine and human realms; in Christianity, this mediator also becomes the means of return.[39] The presence of this *imago* in the highest part of the soul does not necessarily entail unmediated union with God; in fact, it is most often understood to be derivative of the greater Image of God, or Christ. Moreover, Christian authors tended to describe this spark as merely divinizable, in opposition to pagan and gnostic thinkers who asserted that the spark was truly divine (a tradition with which Porete was sympa-thetic).[40] The underlying assumption is that all created things desire to be like their Creator: for fallen rational souls, the term of this restored likeness is an increasing resemblance to God or, for many Christians, to Christ.[41] For most Western Christian writers, then, knowledge of God must be mediated through the incarnate *Logos*, through the word of scripture, and through the hierarchical church. The system requires an intermediary between creature and Creator.

Other passages from Genesis describing humankind's creation, life in the presence and knowledge of God, and expulsion from God's presence leave later commentators much to work with in developing a coherent Christian account of the role of humanity in the creation of the universe.[42] Yet poten-tially optimistic interpretations of the narrative in Genesis were outweighed by more pessimistic assessments. In general, those writers who focus on the historical actuality of the Fall in the Garden of Eden tend to stress its radically debilitating, inherited consequences. For Augustine and for much of the tra-dition after him, original sin destroyed humanity's ability to choose the good without divine grace. In this line of thought, the Fall of Adam cast humanity in exile from God, into a region of unlikeness to the divine.[43] God, however, chooses to grant his grace to some souls through Christ's mediation, thus em-powering them to struggle against the effects of Adam's sin throughout life. In many of Augustine's writings, for instance, Christian life is depicted as a continuing struggle, a continuous conversion, a constant reordering of the will toward its proper object, God.[44]

The formulation of a distinctly Christian theological anthropology begins in the New Testament and the Pauline letters in particular, in which the image-likeness language used in Genesis is used to characterize both the latent potential of fallen humanity and Christ's saving power. Jesus, as the Image of God, will redeem all and will erase humanity's lowly condition: "Just as we have borne the image of the man of dust, we shall also bear the image of the man of heaven" (1 Cor 15:49; cf. Romans 8:29). Human beings bear the "image" of Adam, an image that will be supplanted by the Image that is Jesus Christ. Christ took on human nature in order to redeem Adam's posterity, thereby exalting wretched humanity. The New Testament thus stresses the recovery of the image-likeness to Christ and God through faith in Christ, who by virtue of his singular sonship redeemed humankind. The human nature of Christ is also central to the New Testament, as it exalts the bodily nature of fallen human beings as the vehicle of reconciliation. For Paul, human beings share a joint sonship in Christ through their bond with Him within the community of the church. A motif of putting off the old self (Adam) and putting on the new (Jesus Christ) appears throughout the Pauline epistles.[45] For this more mainstream Western tradition, the sacramental mediation of the institutional church and the model of Jesus Christ are central. Many Christian authors insist that the goal of human life is to work toward progressive assimilation to God through virtuous conduct and proper orientation of the mind toward its divine source, usually achieved with the salutary aid of grace made available to Christians in the institutional church.

Porete recasts many of these teachings. In a seemingly paradoxical statement, Porete insists the soul received an imprint of the Trinity on what was, prior to sin, "no-thing." This imprint is reciprocal: as the Trinity is imprinted on the soul, the soul is imprinted on Trinity. For Porete, the highest part of soul is eternal and uncreated and capable of lasting union with divinity while still embodied.[46] The fundamental nature of the soul is, in much of Christian thought, destroyed or damaged in humanity's collective turning away from God in the person of Adam. The weight of the tradition thus falls on the tremendous damage done to the original human capacity to do good.[47] Porete stands apart from these thinkers not because she claims that sin infects all, even the most noble, souls; rather, she insists that the very wretchedness brought on through sin is the key to return to God.[48] Moreover, in light of the strong current in the tradition stressing mediation between sinful humanity and God, it is striking that Porete downplays the role of Christ or of any mediating figure or institution in the *Mirror*. For her, there is no mediator in annihilation, just as there is no mediator in creation. There is also no need for works, except at the beginning of the path to God. As described in the previous chapter, the annihilated soul "takes leave of the Virtues," Porete tells us, so that the Virtues do the soul's bidding. It is important to note that she does not dismiss the Virtues entirely, retaining them as necessary for those "lost souls" who will labor throughout their lives on earth. They are always a necessary first stage for those who will advance in spiritual understanding toward the goal of annihilation.[49] This notion of the ability of the soul to take leave of createdness while still embodied derives directly from Porete's teachings about humanity's primeval creation and (ongoing) fall.

CREATION AND FALL OF HUMANITY

Porete often reminds her readers that they must remain mindful of their essential nature, which is nothingness. She insists that "you must not forget your nothingness. That is, you must not forget who you were when He first created you . . ."[50] Returning to this precreational unity is a creature's highest calling, in which the soul "has from God what God has; and *is what God is through the transformation of love*, in that point in which she was, before she flowed from God's goodness."[51] Human beings in their present fallen condition are not divine, but they can become divinized through the transformation of Love, wrought by the Holy Spirit in the Soul. This transformation is accomplished when the Soul gives up her will, created by and for God, and allows the Trinity to work within her, without her, so that the Soul exists "without a why" and without works. Porete insists on the God-given goodness of the paired human natures of body and soul by positing a two-stage "becoming" of humanity from God: the "creation" of the soul and the "formation" of the corporeal body.[52]

Porete's anthropological speculations are best conceived of as two "paths," one of which comprises the whole of the other. The higher path of virtual existence, concerned entirely with the soul's relationship to God, encompasses the lower path of earthly life, concerned with overcoming the sin of Adam and living in the grace ushered in by Christ. In the cycle that leads to annihilation, the soul descends through willing from perfection into imperfection, in order to "unlearn" willing and thus regain perfection.[53] This cycle fully embraces the "earthly" cycle, in which the soul attains salvation through imitation of the works of Christ in the life of grace. Most souls complete only the earthly cycle: those are the lost and sad souls who remain servants of works, encumbered with themselves and with worldly cares. These souls will attain Paradise and salvation. Yet some select, noble, sad souls complete both cycles, achieving annihilation and realizing their true Being in their virtual existence in the Trinity. Thus, Porete sums up her anthropology by pointing toward the possibility of annihilation, as described in the next section of this chapter.

The creation of the soul is accomplished by the Trinity without any involvement from the soul, a passivity that pertains naturally to creation "from nothing" and that is achieved again in annihilation.[54] The creation of the soul is a complete outpouring of God's love, the very moment in which "the true pure seed of divine Love, without creaturely matter, is given by the Creator to the creature."[55] The Holy Spirit gives all to the soul, as promised at creation by the Trinity. All of the persons of the Trinity thus share "all that we have by His goodness in the knowledge of His wisdom without beginning. And so it is right, says the Holy Spirit, that we not hold back from these souls anything which we possess."[56]

As mentioned above, despite this apparently unconditional giving, God retains all within. God does not exhaust Himself in creation. Rather, He overflows all that He has while paradoxically retaining all that He is. Even after creation, God remains

> one eternal goodness who is eternal love, who tends by nature of charity
> to give and to overflow all of His goodness; which eternal goodness
> begets pleasing goodness; from which eternal goodness and from which
> pleasing goodness is loving love from the Lover in the Beloved . . .[57]

This rather complex final phrase reiterates the Trinitarian procession described above. Again we see the pattern of procession within the Trinity, in which each person reveals divine goodness.

It is absolutely essential to note that, in creating the soul, God as Trinitarian unity "sanctified His name within [her] and there the Trinity has her home."[58] Porete here expresses an explicit and reciprocal image doctrine.[59] She asserts that the soul is "engraved in God, and [had] her true imprint maintained through the union of Love. And in the manner that wax takes the form of the seal, so [had] this Soul taken the imprint of this true exemplar."[60] Three essential elements comprise this particular doctrine. First, Porete expressly dismisses the notion of a mediator in creation. The Soul is not created to the image of the Image; that is, to the image of Christ, who is the Image of God. Second, because this image is explicitly Trinitarian, the soul will achieve union with the Trinity through the wills of both the soul and of God, that is, through the Holy Spirit. Third and most importantly, this image is totally reciprocal: the Soul is engraved in God, maintained there by Love, which is the Holy Spirit, and the soul maintains an image of the Trinity within herself. Porete explains that "the greater part of the Soul" exists always in God. This highest portion remains in God, who "loves more the highest part of this soul in God than the lesser part in herself."[61] This image is obscured by sin, as is evidenced by the ignorance and waywardness of all fallen souls, both lost and sad. Both the engraving in God and the engraving of the Trinity within the Soul are eternal and explicitly "maintained" despite the defect of sin.

The divine imprint in the soul is complemented by an eternal and incorruptible image of the Soul within the Trinity.

> Reason, says the Soul, if I am loved without end by the three persons of the Trinity, I have also been loved by them without beginning. For as He will love me without end through his goodness, equally was I in the knowledge of his wisdom that I might be made from the work of his divine power. Thus, as long as God is, who is without beginning, I have been in the divine knowledge, and that I might be without end, since from then he loved the good work that he would do in me from his divine power.[62]

This passage helps to illuminate Porete's understanding of the roles of the persons of the Trinity in creation and to express the sole purpose of human life in doing God's will. The soul has been loved by the Trinity without beginning. The assertion of this Love, a reference to the Holy Spirit, is followed by a declaration that the soul also existed from eternity in the "knowledge of God's wisdom," a reference to the Son. The Soul was, by this account, "made" by God's power. What is most important in this context is that for Porete it is Love (the Holy Spirit), not Wisdom (the Son), that maintains the image of the Soul within God. The Soul is in the Trinity and the Trinity is within the soul, eternally, by the work of Love.

As described above, the Holy Spirit possesses all that God possesses, and the Holy Spirit, as Love, transforms the human soul to this nature in love. Here we see the trinity of eternal substance, pleasing fruition, and loving conjunction as they relate to the human faculties of knowledge.[63]

> Divine love for unity generates . . . eternal substance, pleasing fruition, and loving conjunction. From the eternal substance the *memory* [has] the power of the Father. From the pleasing fruition the *intellect* [has] the wisdom of the Son. From the loving conjunction the *will* [has] the goodness of the Holy Spirit. The goodness of the Holy Spirit conjoins [the will] in the love of the Father and of the Son. This conjunction places the soul in being without being which is Being. Such Being is the Holy Spirit Himself, who is the Love of the Father and the Son.[64]

This memory of God who is power, this knowledge of the Son who is wisdom, and this love of the Holy Spirit who is goodness always exist in the soul.[65] Here Porete seems to dismiss memory and intellect as paths to union, although each provides some way of attaining God's power or wisdom. The goodness and love of the Holy Spirit, as the will of God, unites the human will to God's will in the love shared by Father and Son. Here the noble divinity is united with the noblest part of the soul, the will, which is "one being among the beings, the most noble of all beings."[66]

The soul in annihilation is in "being without being which is Being"; that is, the Soul has become Being through the transformation of Love. In this state, the soul is emptied of creatureliness and filled with God, free from the encumbrance of worldly suffering and striving.[67] The soul realizes that she is nothing but Love, and thus the Soul reports that "I was and I am and I will be always without lack, for Love has no beginning, end, or limit, and I am nothing except Love. How could I have anything else? This could not be."[68] Love is the crucial link, and it works within the will by the work of the Holy Spirit, who is Love. Prior to creation and in annihilation the soul possesses all that God possesses.

A key passage related by the character of the Annihilated Soul shows how utterly dependent the Soul is upon God and also highlights the dialectic of All and nothing that is the key to annihilation:

> I am what I am, by the grace of God. Therefore I am only that which God is in me, and not some other thing; God is the same thing He is in me, for nothing is nothing. Thus He is who is. Therefore I am not, if I am, except what God is, and nothing is beyond God. I do not find anything but God, wherever I might find myself; for He is nothing except Himself.[69]

The personification of Love concurs with this statement, adding that all other (unannihilated) souls do not recognize this true nature, because they "are hidden by Adam's sin through lack of innocence."[70] Yet how does the creature, fallen away from God, come to be what God is and God come to be wholly within the creature, from whom God is utterly distinct?

The two "Petitions of the Soul" presented in chapter 107 provide a useful framework for examining the relationship between God and the human soul at creation, as well as the role of free will in the Fall and in annihilation. In the first entreaty, the Soul appeals for confirmation that she exists virtually in the Trinity. This status ensures the eternal ontological union of the soul with God, despite the defect generated by the Fall. The Soul asks

> that she see herself always (if she sees anything at all) where she was when God created everything from nothing, that she might be certain that she is nothing other than this—when she is of herself—nor will she be eternally [other] because she rebelled against the divine goodness.[71]

This passage contains the kernel of Porete's understanding of the creation of humanity and hints at the enduring lordship of the indwelling Trinity despite the Fall. The fall, as we shall see shortly, has only a minor effect on the potential for the noble, sad soul to advance to annihilation.

In the second petition, the Soul inquires about free will and sin. The Soul asks to be told "what she did with her free will, which God has given to her, so she might see that she has removed her will from God Himself in one sole moment of consent to sin."[72] This passage has multivalent meanings, meant to highlight the nearly universal impulse of human beings to sin and to emphasize the responsibility of each individual soul for the sins she commits.

All pivots on the will. Adam's will was the cause of the universal fall from grace. Jesus Christ, by abandoning his will utterly to God, restores that grace. The complete abandonment of the will accomplished by Jesus thus becomes the supreme model for fallen Christians. Yet the issue is more complex for Porete. Porete departs from tradition in downplaying the role of Christ as exemplar of salvation in His worldly works; rather, she emphasizes His exemplarity in willing God's will, which other noble souls are also capable of accomplishing.

She admits outright that most human beings do not appear capable of accomplishing what Jesus accomplished. They are weighed down, it seems, by two natures: the body and the soul.[73] These two natures, created and formed for union, are split by the will. This occurs both in Adam (who passed on this defect to all of humanity) and in individual souls (who are responsible for every movement of the will away from God). It is unclear in the *Mirror* whether or not Porete understands the formation of the body as a punishment by God for the wayward soul. In several places Porete describes how, by willing contrary to God's will the soul becomes "something"; that is, by using the free will the soul gives up its nothingness to become not-nothing, which is something.[74] Porete describes the soul as a captive in the prison of the body and the created world as schoolroom of sorts, an opportunity for spiritual advancement.[75] For Porete, earthly life prepares the soul for the freeness of willing nothing.[76] Yet the *Mirror* does not dismiss the earthly realm as worthless. As described in the previous chapter, the created world and its virtues and vices are a necessary part of the path to annihilation. Nevertheless, the Soul insists that her "better thing" is beyond time: she possesses time "to attain what is mine from Him. What is mine is that I might be established in my nothingness."[77] These passages seem to point to a conception of the created world as a means to an end, an end that would have been reached at the moment of creation were it not for the will turning away from God. Porete states explicitly that the body, as the locus of *corruption* (not of defect), can never be the source of correction or salvation.[78] Porete thus dismisses bodily works and frees the body from responsibility for the defect with which human beings are encumbered.

Two important elements feed into Porete's understanding of the role of the body in sin. The first is that body and soul were originally united by God in goodness. Adam's willfulness caused a breach in that unity, thereby splitting creatures into two separate "natures." God for Porete is an absolute unity, willing whatever He wills at once. God created humanity to mimic this unity; however, free will, used improperly, forces the creature to become a composite of two and therefore quite unlike God. When the creature overcomes willing and returns to pre-creation, she "makes of two one. But what is this one? This one is when the soul is melted in the simple Deity."[79] The two natures of humanity, body and soul, are melted in annihilation into the simplicity and unity that is God and that was proper to the soul prior to its material formation.

This creation-formation schema does not imply a dualism for Porete; rather, it highlights the eternal indwelling of the soul in God and God in the soul. As shown above, the goodness of God overflows into creation. Porete sees this goodness in all works of creation, even in the corrupt human body. In the following passage, it is apparent that a misguided will, not the body itself, is the source of the defect.

> O God, what pity, when evil has victory over good. And so it is with body and soul. The soul is created by God and the body is formed by God. Thus these two natures are at the same time joined through nature and justice in corruption, in the baptismal font without fault. And these two natures were good by the divine justice that made these two natures.[80]

What is remarkable about this passage is that Porete asserts that both body and soul are accepted in the sacred baptismal font, despite their common "corruption" and mortality, an acceptance that is solely the work of divine justice. The body and soul were made to be united, yet the "defect" of sin causes their estrangement. Simply put, "when imperfection took over this constitution and this creation, who were made by divine goodness, no piety united this creature, however small the imperfection."[81] Nevertheless, these two natures are accepted together in the eyes of the (lesser) Holy Church.

Porete explains that the human body is not *by nature* defective even after the Fall by describing the human birth of Jesus Christ. She addresses an encomium to the Virgin Mary, who was not simply an inert vessel for the savior: she imparted humanity to Christ and thus the natures of both soul and body. Yet Mary is not simply a mediator, because Christ is made from her matter. He is of her lineage in his humanity. Porete writes, "For if He had found in you any kind of lack, . . . He could never have made you His mother. Lady, He could only be what you were, and so He could not be what you were not."[82] The Son of God is everything His Father is in His divine nature and everything His mother is in His human nature (body and soul) by virtue of being "born" of these parents. Yet Jesus Christ, fully divine and fully human, wills the will of the Father and thereby maintains the goodness of both body and soul. The Incarnation of Jesus Christ thus holds a lesson for humanity. Christ's soul, which was without sin, was joined to a human body and glorified at the moment of its creation.[83] Christ's incarnation is evidence that a human soul with a properly oriented will ("without sin") can maintain its purity. When this is so, the body is not an impediment. The soul of Jesus Christ retains its perfection: "It could not have been otherwise: as that soul was joined to divine nature, the body, which was mortal, could not be an encumbrance to [the

Soul]."[84] Christ's body and soul are one; the human body and soul would be one if the will were not misdirected. For Porete, then, the body is only an impediment to the fallen, unannihilated soul, for even a corrupt mortal body is not an impediment to the glorified soul. This concept, which underlies Porete's notion of "taking leave of the Virtues," is one of her most controversial teachings, which we will return to in the final chapter. Yet how can the body be a negligible factor in achieving union of indistinction with God? Porete explains this in part with her doctrines of humanity's "falls" and "returns," thus recasting the traditional "Fall" and "Redemption."

FALL(S) AND RETURN(S)

It is a commonplace in Christian theology that Jesus reopened the gates of paradise to fallen sinners, thus enabling a return to God despite the Fall. Porete agrees with this in principle, as those who are saved by Christ's sacrifice—that is, all human beings, all stained by the sin of Adam—can by Christ's grace ascend to Paradise. Porete uses the word *Paradise* in different ways throughout the *Mirror*; for instance, she describes it as "nothing other than to see God."[85] It is also the realm of the saved, of both good Christians and even of the thieves and murderers to whom Jesus has promised admittance.[86] Porete presents the shocking story of the thief who came to see God at the moment of his ignominious death to show that all are saved. She writes that

> the thief was in paradise, just as soon as the soul departed from his body, although Jesus Christ, the Son of God, did not ascend to heaven until the Ascension, and the thief was in paradise the same day of Good Friday. And how could this be? It was certainly because Christ had promised him. It is true, that he was in paradise that same day. Because he saw God he was in paradise, because nothing else is paradise, except to see God.[87]

Paradise is also the place where Adam was created and fell from grace. It is to this Paradise that many Christians—those guided by Reason—strive to return.[88] It is where humanity is saved and "joined to the person of the Son as well as to the Sacrament of the Altar."[89] Here Paradise is opposed to the fallen earthly realm, where people hide their sins in shame from their neighbors. In Paradise all is known and even sins become glorious. Paradise is thus a place of proper knowledge. "Lord, says the Soul, nobody in this world can understand my sins, as ugly and hideous as they are, except you. But, Lord, in paradise all of those who are there will understand, not to my anguish but to my glory."[90]

Paradise is a wonderful place and the highest vision for most sad and lost souls; nevertheless, Porete makes it clear that Paradise is not the ultimate destination for annihilated souls, because it can be understood as a historical place and experience: it is not no-thing.[91] As a place and an experience it can be desired, and this is reason enough why it cannot be the ultimate destination for the soul. The ultimate "destination" for the soul is no place and nothing: annihilation. The redemption wrought by Jesus Christ plays a critical yet early role in the path to annihilation. Without the redeemer's suffering and death on the cross, human beings could not even begin on the path. Fallen humanity derives its life from Jesus Christ, who ushered in a second "creation"; however, this life is specifically the life of the Virtues, lived by human beings on earth who will achieve salvation by Christ's grace.[92] That grace enables *all* human beings to achieve salvation despite Adam's sin. The annihilated soul moves beyond even this grace. It recognizes a different origin and thus has a different goal.

Porete posits two "types" or degrees of fall, both of which focus on the misuse of free will. Porete makes it clear that by willing the soul abandons nothing to become something. This is a crucial fall away from God, the act of any soul that wills against the divine will. This type of fall takes place continually in earthly life. The other fall—the Fall of Adam—accounts for the universal removal of souls from the realm of nothingness to the earthly realm. Adam's sin is the illustration of this primeval movement away from God. It is the means by which no-thing becomes something; nevertheless, Porete focuses more on its exemplary qualities than on its "historical" significance. For Porete, all sinned in Adam, yet all are furthermore culpable every time they will against God's will. Christ's grace does not remove the "debt" sinners incur each time they move their will away from God. It is will—all human wills, not only Adam's—that distinguishes the soul from God. The soul was "nothing, as long as [she] abandoned nothing of what [God] gave to [her]. Now [she] is another thing, for [she] is less than nothing by however many times [she] has willed something other than [God's] will."[93]

Porete's language here emphasizes the value placed on "nothingness." For Porete, the soul, originating in nothingness and destined to return there, becomes "less than nothing" each time she removes her will from God. That something could be "less than nothing" seems paradoxical; however, a soul that is made from nothing *is*, at its most primal level, nothing. To be less than nothing—to be something—is to refuse or to fail to attain one's true being. The Soul explains to God that only one thing separates them. "If I have the same as you have with the creation you gave me, I would be equal to you except in one particular, that I can exchange my will for another—you would not do this."[94] God's total goodness and absolute justice demand that He never revoke the freedom he bestows, however treacherous the consequences. God grants human beings free will through goodness and goodness safeguards that freedom.

> For God would not be God, if virtue was taken from me in spite of myself.
> . . . And if I will something, why would he not allow it? If he does not
> allow it, his power would deprive me of freedom. But His goodness does
> not allow it to happen that his power might take away my freedom in
> anything.[95]

Here the Holy Spirit, guardian of God's goodness, is the advocate for human
freedom.

Porete uses the story of the fall of the angels to illustrate this idea. God
grants free will to the angels, and some of them, like Adam and his posterity,
inevitably fall from grace through misusing this gift. Porete explains:

> When the divine Trinity created the angels by the courtesy of His divine
> goodness, those who were evil through their perverse choice united
> themselves with the evil will of Lucifer, who willed to have by his nature
> what he could not have except by divine grace. As soon as they willed
> this with their forfeited will they lost being from goodness. Therefore
> they are in hell without being, and without ever recovering the mercy of
> seeing God. And their will made them lose his high vision which they
> would have had for giving their will which they retained. Now see what
> they have come to![96]

The story of the fallen angels is an explicit warning. The angels' sin of willing
caused them to lose "being from goodness" and the vision of God. The fallen
angels willed to follow evil, choosing to attain likeness to Lucifer, who is the
archetype of evil, rather than likeness to God, who is pure goodness. Here evil
is ushered in by a perverse choice, despite the goodness of the original creation. The fallen angels turned their wills away from God and thereby lost
their treasure. Most importantly, however, the solution to this dilemma is not
"simply" turning the will away from evil toward good, with the aid of grace. It
is much more radical. These angels must actually abandon their wills to God
in order to regain the vision of (or proximity to) God.

This pattern pertains as well to Adam and his posterity. Adam is the ultimate exemplar in misusing free will: he sought outside himself for the
knowledge of God which is God's alone. He thus forfeited human innocence
and necessitated law through a single "defect of understanding."[97] Porete asserts that this willfulness was manifest in Adam and that he bequeathed this
defect to his posterity. She claims that all human beings "still hide by the sin
of Adam, except those who are annihilated: those have nothing to hide."[98]
The Fall introduces shame and anxiety and reproach, as evidenced by Adam's
covering his nakedness. It causes human beings to fear God and to hide their
sins and failings from God and their neighbors. These neighbors become impediments on the spiritual journey, as constant sources of torment and anxiety.[99] These themes of shame, dishonor, fear, hiding, and struggle play important roles in the soul's earthly life among the Virtues. In the annihilated life,
however, the soul is free.

It is essential to note that Porete also does not focus on the body as an agent of the Fall. Even Adam's posterity, although weakened by his sin, can resist the body's defect. To explain this, Porete shows how just souls can withstand temptation. Even while contemplating the goodness of God the soul is tempted through the body.

> That is to say that insofar as the will of the just man is totally given over without impediment to contemplate the goodness of God, the body is weak and tends toward defect because of the nourishment of the sin of Adam. And thus it is inclined to give attention to lesser things than the goodness of God. Scripture calls this a Fall, which it is.

The just soul can "fall" through following the body in paying attention to things other than God's goodness. Nevertheless, Porete assures her readers, the will of the just soul "is guarded against consenting to the defect, which could be born from such an inclination."[100] Adam's posterity is not radically bound by sin: a just soul can refuse to acquiesce to the temptations of sin out of the strength of a properly oriented will. The parable of the man who falls seven times each day does not, therefore, illustrate the inevitability of sin; rather, Porete uses this example to show the ability of the just, noble soul to withstand temptation.

Unlike many authors before her, Porete does not focus on temptation, enticement, or the historical actuality of the Fall. She does not focus on Eve or on the Serpent or on the Tree of the Knowledge of Good and Evil. The Genesis account seems to be less a story about temptation or degradation than it is a lesson about willfulness and ignorance. Adam is the type for human willfulness, a negative exemplar. He and his posterity are guilty above all of giving attention to lesser things than the goodness of God in using their free will contrary to God's will. In this, Adam is like all other human beings. For Porete, his tale need not be a historical fact to provide true witness to the human tendency toward willfulness. She does not dismiss the historicity, nor does she ignore the consequences of, the Fall. Nevertheless, her focus on the essential freedom of certain souls before God, based in the virtual existence of the soul in the Trinity, leads her to assert that for some souls, at least, the Fall is no more "damaging" than the discrete "falls" they commit every day. All falls transform what should be "no-thing" into "something."

For Porete, then, the precise reason for Adam's misdirected attention and disobedience is insignificant. It does not matter if a serpent or a woman or the temptations of the body caused Adam to fall, because the ultimate source of Adam's fall was his will. Indeed, he need not ever have been tempted from without to be internally compelled. In essence, the root of Adam's fault was that he had a will with which to sin: if he had no will he could not have sinned.[101] Alienation, ignorance, and "somethingness" are the unfortunate, if inevitable, results of a disordered free will. Adam is thus the ultimate exemplar of willfulness in the *Mirror*, taking on the status of "Everyman" more than the role of archetypal malefactor. The implications of casting Adam in this role are significant. Porete seems to assert that Adam was no better or worse than other human beings. He simply "proved" humanity's tendency to willfulness, which can be seen in all of his ancestors. Adam is not, then, conceived of primarily as the progenitor of the human race. Adam's free will was his downfall, just as it is the downfall of all souls who have not achieved annihilation. God created Adam knowing that his creature would go "the way of pestilence and perdition" and that the debt for this act would be infinite. Recognition of the infinite nature of the debt is a key to the ability of souls to achieve annihilation.

Moreover, every fall, including the Fall of Adam, is a gift from God in the sense that it is made possible through free will, which God grants to human beings out of goodness. God, fully aware that this freedom might cause a fall into wretchedness, included that possibility in the cosmological plan.

> For God sometimes allows some evil to be done, for a greater good gift to be born after. All those who are planted from the Father, and come into this world, are descended from perfect to imperfect, to attain the most perfect. And there the wound is opened, to heal those who are wounded without their knowledge. These folk are humble of themselves. They have carried the cross of Jesus Christ, through the work of goodness, *or they carry a cross of their own*.[102]

This passage is pivotal for understanding the Fall. The Edenic Fall and every subsequent fall are all wounds that must be healed in earthly life, above and beyond the work of Jesus Christ.

It is essential to remember that Porete is less concerned with the fate of the mass of humanity than she is with the fate of certain "elect" individual souls. She insists that those souls who follow Reason are "little on earth and quite little in heaven. They are saved in an *uncourtly* way."[103] God commands no more from these souls, and they fail to see beyond Reason's guidance. Such souls have "forgotten that it would not have been sufficient for Jesus Christ to act on their behalf if He had not done all that humanity could accomplish unto death."[104] Such souls have effectively forgotten Christ's real accomplishments and thus they are classed with the rude "merchants" Porete castigates for shortsighted selfishness. They are excluded from the "secret" of annihilation, in which the soul never forgets "the gift of Christ's suffering, which is always a mirror and an exemplar for them."[105]

The power of Jesus Christ to atone for Adam's sin derives from his fully divine and fully human nature. Christ, the absolutely essential mediator for the mainstream tradition, takes on corruption in order to free humanity from the debilitation of a mortal defect. But for Porete, Jesus Christ is less important as a savior—which He is for all of humanity—than he is as an exemplar of doing God's will, which He is for a select number of annihilated souls. She thus downplays the importance of the unity of "ordinary" humanity and divinity in Christ. Porete would agree that human beings could never make sufficient repayment of the debt of sin, but she asserts that they can make sufficient payment to Jesus Christ in earthly life. Achieving annihilation, however, requires another type of payment.

Porete explains that human beings appear incorrigible in their willful disregard for God's right guidance, despite—or perhaps because of—their apparent alienation from and ignorance of God. God has tried to call human beings back to rightly ordered willing by sending messengers, prophets, and Virtues to guide wayward souls, but his efforts are to no avail. God as Love

> sent Thrones to purify and adorn you, Cherubim to illumine you, and Seraphim to embrace you. By means of all these messengers I called you, that they would have you know my will and the stages of being to which I call you, and you never took account of it. And I vow, says Love, I leave you in your own protection in saving yourselves. And if you had obeyed me, you would have been other, by your own witness. But you will save yourselves well enough, in a life forever encumbered by your own spirit.[106]

Porete here refers to those lost encumbered souls, who, through Christ's grace, will achieve salvation. These followers of Reason remain slaves to the Virtues and to the example of Jesus Christ in his bodily suffering. Porete here rebukes those who do not follow Love's messages, those who choose to "save themselves" through works. These encumbered souls can be saved by Christ's salvific work; however, such souls will never achieve the greatest spiritual heights. Only those who "save themselves" through abandoning the will can achieve annihilation.

Yet although Christ redeems humankind through suffering in his body and soul, Porete consistently downplays the relevance of Christ's human nature for souls seeking annihilation, and focuses instead on Jesus' willing of the divine will. She insists that those who truly love Christ do not cling to his humanity. Porete uses two scriptural examples to buttress this claim, first noting Christ's withdrawal from the apostles, who loved him "too tenderly according to His human nature and too feebly as to His divine nature" and were thus encumbered from receiving the Holy Spirit.[107] John the Baptist did not make this grave mistake. John refused to seek Jesus in the desert, because he had no need to see Christ's humanity; rather, he restrained himself from "grasping on to Jesus Christ in his human person" and clung instead to His divinity.[108] This example shows that human love "impedes the gifts of the Holy Spirit, which can sustain only divine love, pure, without mingling from nature."[109]

For Porete, then, Christ's sacrifice is secondary to the role he plays as exemplar to those following the path to annihilation. Christ's payment of humanity's debt to God does not suffice for souls who wish to achieve annihilation. Human beings incur two "debts" in earthly life: one to Jesus Christ and one to God. Christ's universal salvific work avenges primal sin and helps heal a deep alienation. Yet that does not free certain noble human souls from responsibility for their own path to perfection. The first step is living the life of the Virtues in evangelical perfection, following the example of Jesus Christ. Yet once the soul has

> survived the thrust of the sword in killing the pleasures of the body and in putting to death the desires of the spirit . . . The greater part has delivered her from the debts which she owed to Jesus Christ and therefore she owes him nothing, however much she may have been obligated.[110]

Worldly works suffice to "repay" Jesus Christ for the sacrifice He made on behalf of humanity. Yet, to the soul in the final stages of achieving "nothingness," works are "something" and, therefore, meaningless.

In summary, Porete, unlike many of her predecessors, does not give the second person of the Trinity, the Son, pride of place in creation or in mediation. Her allusions to the Son as God's wisdom are generally formulaic, taking their cue from tradition but not contributing much to her distinctive doctrine. The second person of the Trinity, as Incarnated Savior, redeemed the debt Adam consigned to humanity; however, this does not erase the debt each soul continues to owe to God for each movement of the will away from God. The human will is free to choose between good and evil in embodied life; however, it is most free when it wills God's will. In this Jesus Christ is the supreme exemplar and agent of salvation for those in Holy-Church-the-Little; however, Porete insists that annihilated souls also become saviors. Humanity is apparently different in degree—but not in kind—from Jesus Christ. He saved humankind both through works and through abandoning his will utterly to God. It is the latter "action" that human beings must emulate.

The key to both Fall and annihilation is the will. Each soul is responsible for each movement of the will away from God, its rightful owner.

> Just as God is unfathomable with regard to His power, so equally is this Soul indebted by her incomprehensible nothingness by even one hour of time that she had possessed a will contrary to Him. To Him she owes without subtraction the debt which her will owes, and as many times as she willed to withdraw her will from God.[111]

Jesus Christ knew this and conformed His will to God's will. When Christ was nailed on the cross, He

> had no other consideration in doing this than the will of God His Father alone. And the Son of God is an exemplar for us, and thus we ought to

follow Him in this respect, for we ought to will in all things only the divine will. And thus we will be sons of God the Father, from the example of Jesus Christ His son.[112]

This is true *imitatio Christi* for Porete, the supreme act of abandoning the human will to will the divine will.[113] Christ's example of earthly suffering should be followed early on the ascetic path, although mere mortals are limited in what they can accomplish by this route. Porete dismisses bodily imitation of Christ as the way to achieve union with God, for the soul achieves peace only through repose in the Trinity, which is only attained by annihilating the will.

This is the "peace from peace, and such surprising peace, that the corruption of [the Soul's] constitution could never be the source of correction, if [the Soul] remains in this surprising peace."[114] Asceticism is a means to a limited end. Works are an endless source of frustration and anxiety in a world where all is ultimately "refuse and leftovers" anyway.[115] Porete presents this in an arresting way in the following passage: "One sole encounter or one meeting with that ultimate eternal ancient and ever-new goodness is more worthy than anything a creature might do, or even the whole Holy Church, in a hundred thousand years."[116] Fortunately, God owes as much as he has to the Soul out of divine largesse, consistent with His absolute overflowing of himself in the act of creation and with the motifs of courtly love.[117] Farnear, in His magnanimity and courtesy, ensures the soul's freedom by canceling the soul's debt when the soul recognizes her nothingness and abandons her will. Nothing can owe nothing. Just as the Trinity granted all to the soul in creation, so the Trinity grants all in this "payment" of nothing.

Porete makes a rather bold leap when she suggests that "If [the fault] was in Jesus Christ, this is because of the fault of the human lineage, and if in us, through our own fault."[118] She thus implies that human beings, despite their common corruption *and* defect, can carry their own cross in life. This cross is not, however, the cross of good works and suffering but the cross of abandoning the will. This defect, in fact, brings human beings so low that the weight of the encumbrance can be the cause of disencumbrance. It makes humanity lose the being of God, because even good works, which are the least we can do for God, will not rest alongside God. Human beings are forced by the sin of Adam to work, yet when the soul abandons her will to God, she can finally rest, free of worldly cares.

The greater good that is born from Adam's sin thus seems to be twofold in the *Mirror*: humankind's redemption through Christ as well as the ability of select human beings to "carry their own cross" in order to achieve annihilation. This element of Porete's scheme is essential to understanding the *Mirror*. The Fall is a necessary and inevitable consequence of God's granting humanity a free will to use for good or ill. Porete maintains God's absolute goodness while placing the onus for achieving annihilation and glorification on individual souls. As Adam is the ultimate exemplar of willfulness, Jesus Christ is the ultimate exemplar of abandoning the will. Christ, fully divine and fully human, is a model for Christians on the path to perfection; nevertheless, even Christ's saving sacrifice does not pardon human beings who continually remove their wills from God. The higher path to annihilation hinges on eventual abandonment of all lower earthly things and exemplars, including Jesus Christ.

Porete avoids considering the union of divine and human natures in Jesus Christ, asking "who could sufficiently ponder this?" and "who might ask for such an overabundance?"[119] This unity is the marvelous accomplishment of God's goodness, a marvel she does not try to understand. Porete can never understand Christ's extreme poverty, the torments he bore in life, and the cruel manner of His death.[120] It is enough to know that Christ had both human nature (body and soul) and Love (divine nature) and that He bore tremendous suffering on behalf of Adam's posterity. She acknowledges that Christ was sent to "pay the debt which we had incurred by our forfeited will."[121] She esteems his tremendous suffering and marvels at the power of his blood to redeem humanity.

> The amount of His blessed blood which one could put on the point of a pin would have been sufficient for redeeming one hundred thousand worlds, if there were so many. . . . Because I say that if all the sufferings, and deaths and other torments, whatever they might have been, or are, or will be, from the time of Adam up until the time of the Antichrist, and if all the sufferings above said were gathered as one, truly this still would not be but one point of suffering compared to the suffering which Jesus Christ had . . .[122]

Jesus Christ's ransom of humanity is the ultimate sacrifice, incomparable by ordinary human standards. Nevertheless, for Porete, this does not bear on the attainment of annihilation.

For Porete, the ultimate goal of certain souls on earth is annihilation, in which such souls realize their true being as nothingness and into which the will-less soul falls. This fall reverses the willful Fall in the Garden of Eden by annihilating the will. Adam and his posterity are inclined to sin through means of a disordered free will, but the annihilated soul no longer has a will by which she can move or work.[123] This is not a case of reordering the will but of abandoning the will entirely. Simply put, no soul can live the divine life as long as she possesses will. Certain souls who have traveled through the material world of change and works can attain a state of complete repose from which they cannot fall. This pattern comprises two cycles: creation as nothingness in the Trinity and return thereto, which encompasses a journey of formation and fallenness in the human body and salvation in Christ. Love is the cornerstone of both journeys: "God alone created them and redeemed them, and perhaps many times re-created [them], for the sake of Love in whom they are exiled, annihilated, and forgotten."[124] The next chapter will examine in detail the interplay of nobility and annihilation, the culmination of Porete's doctr ines about the relation of divine and human natures.

✛   CHAPTER FOUR   ✛

NOBILITY AND ANNIHILATION

"God has nowhere to place His goodness," writes Marguerite Porete, "if not in me. He has no dwelling place proper to Him, nor can he establish Himself fully in any place, if not in me. And through this I am the exemplar of salvation, and more, the salvation of every creature and the glory of God."[1] Porete accompanies this extraordinary statement of the power of a single created soul to affect the cosmological scheme with a seemingly contradictory series of statements describing this noble, graced soul as "the height of all evil" and "total wretchedness." This apparent paradox is the key to Porete's doctrine of annihilation as she describes it in her Mirror. Porete's theological and anthropological speculations lead her to assert that certain souls can attain a permanent state of knowing nothing, willing nothing, and having nothing. Such souls are, as she states in several places, "vessels by [God's] election." This "precious election," calling, or chosenness is confirmed in annihilation, the proof on earth that a soul has attained the repose and peace of eternal existence in the Trinity.[2]

Those noble sad souls who are capable of recognizing their own nothingness in comparison to God's All are further ennobled by the transformation wrought within them by Love. Yet Porete insists that "few folk are disposed to receive such a seed."[3] Who are those few? How does Porete define them? How do the characteristics of those souls tie into her doctrine of annihilation? In what ways does Porete step beyond the more traditional theological anthropological model in which Creator and creature remain distinct?

77

This chapter will present Porete's doctrine of annihilation in its properly esoteric vein. First, it will explore the "Three Beautiful Considerations" that
come just before annihilation. It will then examine the soul's achievement
and "experience" of annihilation in the world as well as the implications of
the doctrine, which is based on the fundamental reciprocal imaging of Trinity
and soul described in the previous chapter. It will consider the secondary,
more traditional metaphors Porete employs to describe annihilation, in conjunction with the overarching metaphors of nobility and lineage she has chosen to unite the entire text. It will close with a consideration of the implications of this elitism for Porete and her critics.

THE THREE BEAUTIFUL CONSIDERATIONS

As described in the previous chapter, Porete's descriptions of the unity of the
soul with God in annihilation, which is explicitly a union of identity, emphasize the unmediated, reciprocal, and undifferentiated unity of the noble soul
and the Trinity. The soul in annihilation simply "has neither what nor why."[4]
She becomes no-thing, without works, without knowledge, without her own
"being," as she was before she was. The annihilated soul does nothing, either
for God or for herself: she wills nothing, knows nothing, and has nothing.[5]
The annihilated soul (*âme anientie*) becomes the free soul (*âme franche*) by realizing the "grand nobility" of being ordered by—and established in—nothingness.[6] This free soul has realized the promise of her inborn nobility. Porete
employs three primary adjectives—free, noble, and unencumbered—to describe the soul that has been taken up to the "most noble" sixth stage of
being.[7] These adjectives are pivotal to her program, and they are repeated
throughout the *Mirror*.

> There is nothing lacking to [the Soul], and so she is often carried up to
> the sixth, but this is of little duration. For it is an aperture, like a spark,
> which quickly closes, in which one cannot long remain. . . . The over-
> flowing from the ravishing aperture makes the Soul, after the closing, free
> and noble and unencumbered from all things. This happens from the
> peace of the work of the overflowing and the peace lasts as long as the
> opening of the aperture.[8]

The free, noble, unencumbered soul of the sixth stage experiences nothing
except God, and the soul established in the fifth stage cares no more about
earthly life. The soul in the fifth stage is in "repose and placed in possession of
free being, which gives her rest through the excellent nobility of all things."[9]
She thus transcends the created world and the limits imposed by Adam's fall.
She is no longer weighed down by her body, which stands naked, untouched
by shame or dishonor.

In essence, the whole of the *Mirror* is predicated on the notion of a return to the "beginning," to what the soul was *before* she was in her created, earthly existence, to when the soul dwelt in peace and repose within the Trinity. Yet even this seeing is metaphorical, as the soul that is truly annihilated ceases all such creaturely mediation. The soul in annihilation becomes passive while embodied, one with the Trinity and thus capable of partaking of all created things. This is a radical claim, even within the realm of esoteric speculation. Porete here takes the image doctrine to an extreme in claiming that the annihilation of the human will affects God the Trinity in profound ways. The soul itself, transformed by Love to become "what God is," ushers in her pre-created state while still embodied on earth. This is not a loving union of wills, as depicted so often in the "bridal" mysticism (*Brautmystik* or *Minnemystik*) of both male and female writers, often based on the Song of Songs and positing a union in which the ontological distinctions between God and creature remain. Annihilation is a speculative doctrine more proper to *Wesenmystik*, or the mysticism of being. It is a union of indistinction (*unitas indistinctionis* or *unio sine distinctione* or *differentia*), in which the soul and God are united without difference.[10] *Nobilitas* and *imago* are, for Porete, synonymous.

The words Porete uses to describe this return as it is attained before death by certain souls—like the words she uses to describe the path toward this state and the nature of the created, embodied soul—tell us much about how she conceives of the relationship between the soul and God. Porete's presuppositions regarding the potential of a fruitful relationship between God and the soul are based in a notion that the soul must be of the proper lineage to grasp the Trinitarian indwelling by means of recognizing her own wretchedness. As Bernard McGinn aptly notes, "lineage . . . is the courtly correlative of the theological theme of the soul's preexistence in God."[11] The soul must be "noble" as God is noble, and as such the annihilated soul becomes the embodiment of largesse, courtesy, and courage. Moreover, Porete closely guards the esotericism of her message. There is only one King and only one noble manor to which only the legitimately, purely noble can gain entrance.[12] Human beings, the apex of God's creative work, turned away from God in willfulness, yet the spark of the Trinity within the soul is proof of the soul's lofty calling within the world.[13]

The inner sanctification and eternal indwelling of the Trinity in the soul enables the soul to learn the divine lesson of annihilation. Only the noble souls who can recognize this indwelling can learn its lesson, which "is not written by a human hand but by the Holy Spirit, who writes this lesson in a marvelous manner, and the Soul is the precious parchment."[14] This description of the imprint of the Trinity on the soul focuses appropriately on the role of the Holy Spirit. The Holy Spirit explains that knowing nothing, willing nothing, and having nothing enable [the Soul] to find the treasure, secret and hidden, that is enclosed in the Trinity eternally. *Not, says the Holy Spirit, through divine nature, because that cannot be, but through the force of love, as it must be.* . . . To see, says the Holy Spirit, again that all that I have is from the Father and the Son. And because [the Soul] has all that I have, says the Holy Spirit, and the Father and the Son do not have anything that I do not have in myself, thus this soul has in herself the treasure of the Trinity, secret and enclosed in herself.[15]

The treasure of the soul's true nature is enclosed always within the soul, regardless of the soul's awareness of this indwelling. Yet the way to God is a well-guarded secret, open only to those who recognize that their true and essential heritage is from God (that is, the Trinity) and not from Adam and the created realm. The soul moves only when she acknowledges that "she is not if she is not of Him from whom all things are."[16] This recognition prompts a deep understanding of the Creator's infinite greatness and the soul's absolute wretchedness, which is the soul's assurance of God's ever-present goodness. Yet how does the soul arrive at such a recognition?

Porete describes the essential move to annihilation quite strikingly through a series of dialectical descriptions of the soul and God. Returning to these brings the reader back to the outline of the seven stages of annihilation presented in chapter 2. These "Three Beautiful Considerations," which embolden the soul to endure, are reached through considering the self, God, and the movements of the will. They reflect perfectly the status of both soul and God in creation and the ideal relationship of both afterward, regardless of the Fall. They rely on the understanding that the soul and God share the same "ground," the same imprint that was made on the "first" day of the soul, and they take place in the final moments before annihilation. In these considerations, the Soul states that she does not know God or herself: only God knows these things. She does not know where God comes from, as that is known only by God's power; she does not know what God is, as that is known only by God's wisdom; and she does not know who God is, for that is known only by God's goodness. The Soul goes on to state that only God in his power, wisdom, and goodness comprehends whence, what, and who she, the Soul, is. "Lord," says the Soul, "you are one goodness, by overflowing goodness, and all in yourself. And I am one wretchedness, by overflowing wretchedness, and all in myself."[17]

The Soul goes on to describe God as the supreme Creator: "Lord, you are, and thus everything is perfected through you, and nothing is made without you. And I am not, and thus everything is made without me, and nothing is made through me."[18] God is "one sole God in three persons" while the soul is "one sole enemy in three miseries."[19] These "miseries" are directly contrary to God's power, wisdom, and goodness. The soul is nothing but weakness, ignorance, and wretchedness. The soul's inability to understand even the smallest bit of this leads her to understand that God is all and that she is nothing. Yet how do these pessimistic considerations enable the soul to persist?

The Soul imagines that God poses three imponderable questions. The first is how she would endure if she knew she could love another more than she loves God. The second is how she would endure if she knew God loved another better than He loves her. The third is how she would endure if she knew that someone loved her more than God loves her.[20] At each of these questions, the soul's senses fail her, yet God continually torments her and demands an answer. The soul can neither answer nor will to have these things and thus she is martyred. God would will these things that the soul finds so grievous, and the soul recognizes that if she wills these things she would will no more. Porete here employs a metaphor of growing spiritual maturity and salutary death. The soul reports that her "heart formerly always thought about living love through the desire of good will. Now these two things are dead in me, I who have departed from my infancy."[21]

At this stage the soul abandons her will and desire, becoming truly Christlike. The soul reports emphatically that, despite her wretchedness, the soul becomes the "exemplar of salvation" described at the beginning of this chapter. Porete goes on:

> And I will tell you how, why, and in what. First, because I am the height of all evil . . . I am total wretchedness. And He is the height of all goodness. . . . He is total goodness. . . . Since I am total wretchedness and He is total goodness, I must have all of His goodness before my wretchedness ends. . . . And so I have in me, by His pure goodness through goodness, all of His divine Goodness, which I have had without beginning and will have without end.[22]

When the will has been abandoned and given over to God, God works within the soul. The soul has realized her eternal vocation as no-thing through recognizing her wretchedness in relation to God. The soul then has "no what nor why" nor any work. "This work now belongs to God, who does His work within me. I do not owe Him any work since He works within me. If I should establish my own work there, I would obliterate God's work."[23] Here the soul accomplishes her own "redemption" and becomes the savior of all humanity. As described in the previous chapter, the soul that is truly "nothing" cannot repay any debt. Emptying the soul entirely of will enables God to work within. That, and that alone, is the key to achieving freedom from slavish works and, eventually, annihilation.

Porete taps into an essential theological idea here: the lowest is the most exalted. The most wretched are closest to God through a spiritual nobility that alone enables the soul to recognize its nothingness beside God's All, and only these three considerations can lead the soul along the final painful steps of the journey. The annihilated, unencumbered soul ceases all activity, all searching, all attention to herself or to the created realm and even to God. Such a soul "has nothing more to do with herself, nor with another, nor with God Himself, no more than if she were not; and so she is."[24] The soul realizes that whatever created thing she believed she possessed was never truly hers, including her own will.[25] Annihilated souls must abandon *all* createdness, including their own bodies, reasoning, will, and intellect, while remaining in the world as embodied creatures. They become "folk with feet but no path, hands but no work, mouth but no words, eyes but no vision, ears but no hearing, reason but no reasoning, body but no life, and a heart but no intellect, as long as they are [annihilated]."[26] The body, although continuing to exist, does nothing for the soul in annihilation. Eyes do not see, hands do not work, the tongue is silent. The annihilated soul has not lost her senses and or her body but has utterly lost the *use* of them.[27] Such a soul is

> dead to all feeling from within and without, to the extent that such a soul no longer does any works, neither for God's sake nor for her own. And so she has thus lost all her senses in this practice to the point that she knows not how to seek nor how to find God, nor even how to conduct herself.[28]

The soul gives up her will and lacks, therefore, any agent with which to accomplish any works. This extends even to the will or desire to seek to know or to love God. The annihilated soul is thus

> "without" herself when she has no feeling of nature, no work, nor any interior work, neither shame nor honor, nor any fear of anything which might happen, nor any affection in the divine goodness; nor does she know any longer any indwelling of will, but instead [she] is without will at all moments. Thus she is annihilated, "without" herself, whatever thing God might suffer from her. Thus she does all things without herself, and so she leaves all things without herself. This is no marvel: she is no longer "for" her own sake, for she lives by divine substance.[29]

Such a soul has become what God is.

Yet Porete goes beyond even this to assert that annihilation brings God back to pre-creation. God will then "be of Himself in the goodness which He knew of Himself before she was, when He granted her the goodness by which He made her a lady."[30] The Trinity was stamped upon the soul at creation; the soul was also stamped within the Trinity. Annihilation brings both creature *and* Creator back to pre-creation. The Soul reports that "God gave will to me in order to do His will, to gain Him from Himself."[31] When the soul, created to will God's will, achieves annihilation, God sees himself in the soul as in a mirror. Love explains that "when there is such nothingness [in the soul], God sees Himself in such a creature, without any encumbrance."[32] There is absolutely no creaturely (or divine) mediation in annihilation. When the soul is without will and nothing, she becomes God's perfect mirror. The following passage summarizes the stages of being that culminate in the soul's "clarification."

> [The Soul's] will is [the Trinity's], because she fell from grace into the perfection of the work of the Virtues, from Virtues into Love, from Love into Nothingness, and from Nothingness into clarification by God, who sees Himself with the eyes of His majesty . . .[33]

This "clarification," which enables God to see Himself in the soul, represents the supreme height of annihilation. A clarified soul is a simple soul, an unspotted mirror for God. Porete posits two types of annihilated life: blind and clarified. Both are "royal folk," "very well born," with "excellently noble hearts." Yet those who live the clarified life live "the most noble and most gentle" life, beyond this life "that sustains the [soul's] feet" on earth.[34] Clarified, annihilated souls "see" better than their blind counterparts, and it is in such simple souls that God sees himself.[35] Such a soul is at once most fully abyssed and most exalted. Such a soul is *sans nul pourquoy*.

ANNIHILATION: THE SOUL WITHOUT A WHY

Soul asks Love a pivotal question early in the text of the *Mirror of Simple Souls*. Why did God create humanity for annihilation? Why create something from nothing to return to nothing?

> Now Love . . . tell me why He would be so gracious as to create me and ransom me and recreate me in order to give me so little, He who has so much to give? . . . Now He has taken whatever of value I might have, and He has given me nothing and keeps everything. Ah, Love, for the sake of God, is this the portion of the lover?

Love responds to the Soul that she "knows more than [she] says. And if you have given all to Him, the best part comes to you. And, moreover, you have not given Him anything that was not properly His before you gave it to Him."[36] Quite plainly the Soul "was created for nothing other than to have within the being of pure charity without end."[37] Possessing the "being of pure charity" is doing God's will, which allows the soul to become clarified, naked, and pure.

Annihilation, which is the culmination on earth of the sevenfold spiritual path, is a return of the soul *while in her earthly body* to her prior existence of repose in God, made possible only because of the soul's virtual existence in the Trinity. Annihilation is thus the completion of a spiritual path as well as the permanent status of the embodied soul throughout her earthly life. It is achieved when the soul uncovers its true being in the ground of all by realizing that she and other human souls are properly "nothing because we have nothing of our own: May you see this complete naked nothing by hiding or veiling, and then you would have Him who is his true being in us."[38] In annihilation the soul has only one love, one will, and one work, while giving both body and soul whatever they might need.[39] This soul, unlike the maiden of the first opening exemplum who remains mired in works, has lost all of her practices, dwells with God, and remains dead to the world.

This state is by definition beyond human description, yet Porete is adept at choosing suitable metaphors. In keeping with her theme of the noble soul, she chooses examples that privilege permanence over change and repose over restless searching; that describe nakedness and freedom as opposed to covering and encumbrance; that refer to peace rather than warfare, sufficiency over deficiency, and *largesse* over meanness.[40]

One such metaphor is that annihilation is a "land" to which the exiled, fallen sad soul will return. The soul who has reached this land ceases to have any relationship with God, not even one of love. Porete writes that

> [it] is a very long road from the land of the Virtues, who hold the Sad, to the land of the Forgotten ones, the naked Annihilated ones, the Clarified ones, who are in the highest being, where God is relinquished by them in themselves. Thus He is neither known, nor loved, nor praised by such creatures, except only in this, that one cannot know, nor love, nor praise Him. This is the summation of all their love, the last course of their way: the last accords with the first, for the middle is not discordant. It is right, since [the Soul] has finished the course, that she repose in Him.[41]

To put this passage in theological terms, the soul who has completed this journey has completed the cosmological pattern of *exitus* and *reditus*, coming from God and returning to Him, while still embodied on earth. Porete's most explicit treatment of annihilation is found in chapter 135 and it, too, relies on a geographical metaphor. The soul's nothingness is contrasted explicitly to God's absolute sufficiency in which the soul finds unity in all things, thus resolving the anguish of God's farness and nearness.

The annihilated soul possesses "no comfort, no affection, no hope in creatures, neither in heaven nor earth, but only in the goodness of God. The soul neither begs nor asks anything of any creature."[42] She is a phoenix, living alone in love, alone in God's goodness, as she was before she was created materially. Moreover, in annihilation the will becomes "established" or "planted" in the Trinity. In this state, the soul must "uproot" herself in order to sin, yet she is left without a will by which she could accomplish that feat. Now she is guarded from sin if she leaves her will where it is established, in the One who has given it to her freely from His goodness. Prior to this she had no fertile and restful peace until she was stripped utterly of her will.[43] When planted in the Trinity, the soul becomes fecund.

A crucial element in these reversals is the notion of the dramatic impassivity of the soul in the world. The annihilated soul lives in the world "without reproach."[44] As shown above, freedom from willing engenders freedom from all created things, including reason and the anxiety, fear, and desire ushered in by the Fall. The will is insatiable when it is governed by Reason and Fear. Faith and Love, however, abolish this servitude and place the will in a freedom "without fear of frightening things, without desire for delectable things."[45] Even sin, which was ushered in by Adam, becomes powerless in the face of annihilation; indeed, an annihilated soul can be immersed in a sea of sin and remain untouched. The soul

> swims and bobs and floats, and she is surrounded by divine peace, without any movement in her interior, and without any exterior work on her part. These two things would remove this peace from her if they could penetrate to her, but they cannot, for she is in the sovereign state where they cannot pierce or disturb her about anything.[46]

It is as if the soul were dead and "her ashes [were] thrown into the open sea."[47] Porete also describes a "sea of joy," in which the soul "swims and flows in joy, without feeling any joy, for she dwells in joy and joy dwells in her."[48] Moreover, annihilated souls are unmoved by the judgments of others and thus experience "neither dishonor . . . nor honor, nor the wish to hide or conceal themselves."[49]

This striking contrast, to the point of apathy about one's reputation on earth, might appear shocking, yet Porete finds solid evidence for it in scripture. She describes how Mary Magdalen had no dishonor even when seven demons were expelled from her, because "she concerned herself with no one except Him."[50] St. Peter raised the dead in his shadow despite having denied God three times.[51] St. John the Evangelist fled from captivity; nevertheless, God inspired him to write the Apocalypse.[52] These examples illustrate how a soul living the divine life has no concern for worldly judgment but only for the goodness of God.

In describing annihilation, Porete often uses imagery of inversion of createdness or of the results of the Fall. The annihilated soul takes leave of place and possession and senses: "She does not need hell, nor paradise, nor any created thing. She neither wills nor not-wills anything which might be named here."[53] The annihilated soul is naked and no longer fears temptation.[54] She does not hide herself as Adam did, but rather is hidden by God in God so that "neither the world nor the flesh nor demons are able to hurt her, for they cannot find her in their works."[55] In addition, the soul sheds its fear, which is the result of Adam's sin:

> For even if she should be in the world, and if it should be possible that the world, flesh, devil, the four elements and the birds of the air and the

savage beasts torment and dismember or devour her, she cannot fear anything if God dwells in her.[56]

In essence, the soul has "finished with the world, and the world has taken leave of her and has finished with her" so that "every created thing is so far from her that she cannot feel it."[57]

In annihilation, then, the soul and body remain in their "created" state and the body remains corrupt, yet both are rendered permanently without need for anything beyond themselves. They live free of sin and immersed in joy, without the fear and torment ushered in by the Fall.

> The thoughts of such souls are so divine because they are not impeded with things passing or created, which might conceive anxiety within them, for God is good without containment.[58]

The fallen soul is unable to recognize her true being unless she achieves a state of complete detachment from all createdness, including the created aspects of the soul. This detachment extends most explicitly to the soul's will, which is the element that decisively separates humanity from divinity.

TRADITIONAL MYSTICAL METAPHORS

Several of the themes explored above become prominent elements in Porete's description of the soul's merging with God to "become what God is"; for instance, the impassivity of the soul, the wretchedness of the soul in contrast to God's All, and the reciprocity of the union. Porete thus adopts several traditional metaphors that are particularly suited to illustrating these issues, such as the achievement of spiritual maturity, images of iron in fire, the giving of gifts from lover to the beloved, and intoxication.[59] These metaphors, each with its own intensity, show the perfect consummation of human and divine, in which the soul, different in nature from God, becomes what God is through the transformation of Love, or the Holy Spirit. Her overarching metaphorical references to nobility and lineage will be explored after the following section.

Porete's references to the attainment of maturity are intimately linked to her notion that the soul must undergo several stages of "being" before attaining the repose of "Being." She describes the stages of annihilation as the "seven stages of noble being, from which a creature receives being," stages that must be fulfilled and surpassed before the soul comes to "perfect being."[60] She writes, "It is necessary that an infant possess and perform the works of infancy before he is perfect; thus a man must be ignorant and foolish in his human works before he has the true seed of the being of freeness, which is in the soul by divine practice, without work."[61] One supreme Being eclipses all other stages of being and represents the attainment of the highest spiritual maturity. "For every being, whatever it might be, is but a game of catch or child's play compared to the supreme being of willing nothing . . ."[62] Even the sad souls who can follow the path to the land of freeness must at some early stage live "from milk and pabulum" and in ignorance.[63] Porete explains that the soul who has attained the fifth stage "loses pride and youth, and her spirit has become old, which leaves her being neither enjoying nor charmed any longer . . ."[64] Attainment of maturity, which is the ultimate stage of being in the goodness of God, is the goal. "And this being, of which we speak, the form of which Love gives us of her goodness, restores today the first day in the soul," thereby granting the soul sovereignty in all things, as she was before she was.[65]

Porete explores a similar notion with imagery of iron in fire, by which she shows how "the stronger transforms the weaker into itself."[66] This principle holds throughout the stages of the spiritual path: at each point the soul must be "overtaken" by the next stage in order to advance.[67] The soul becomes "like iron invested with fire which has lost its own semblance because the stronger fire transforms the iron into itself."[68] The soul is thus thoroughly "invested," "nourished," and "transformed" by this greater part, with no account any more of its lesser part.[69] She describes how the annihilated soul is so "enflamed in the furnace of the fire of Love that she has become properly fire, which is why she feels no fire, for she is herself fire, as the power of Love transforms her into the fire of Love."[70] The iron in fire image serves to illustrate the impassivity of the soul in union. The transformation of annihilation places the soul in proper being, in which her "work" is done without her: all that she needs is within her. The soul that burns with this metaphorical fire "sees clearly in all things that she consumes things according to the way one ought to consume things"; that is, without regard to obtaining matter or willing to possess it.[71] Fire doesn't add matter to itself; rather, it transforms matter into itself so that the fire and the matter become one thing.[72]

Porete also employs courtly imagery of gift giving to express the lack of necessity for an intermediary and to emphasize God's *largesse*. Neither the soul nor God desires or requires an intermediary when the soul is free of will.[73] The soul desires that the gifts she receives from God come directly from God: "[I]f He himself would not give it to me properly from Himself, I would lack it forever, because I could not take nor wish to take from any other than from Him."[74] Love exclaims: "How great a difference between a gift from a lover through an intermediary to a beloved and one that is between lovers without an intermediary!"[75] The annihilated soul becomes like the Seraphim, who have no intermediary between their love and divine love.[76] The Virgin Mary is the supreme exemplar in this regard: she willed only the divine will and had, "without any intermediary in her soul, the glorious life of the Trinity in her mortal body."[77] The soul and God have no intermediary between them.

As described above, Porete insists on the reciprocity of annihilation, in which both the soul and God are returned to pre-creation and in which the soul comes to possess all that God possesses. Porete alludes to this reciprocity in a description of taps of divine drink, which illustrates both the infusion of divinity into humanity as well as the high status of humanity.

> In this barrel of divine drink there are without fail several taps. The humanity that is joined to the person of the Son of God knows this, who drinks at the most noble [tap] after the Trinity; and the Virgin Mary drinks at the one after and this noble lady is intoxicated from the most high. And below her drink the ardent Seraphim, on the wings of which these Free Souls fly.[78]

The correctly oriented "free" Soul becomes drunk from what God drinks. It appears that

> the greater part [of the beverage] makes [her] intoxicated, not because she drank the greater part, as it was said, but because her Lover has drunk from it, thus between him and her there is no difference through the transformation of Love, whatever difference there is in natures.[79]

The Soul is filled by the drink she never drinks: "the bouquet alone makes [her] inebriated."[80] The sufficiency of God is infused into the soul that empties itself of will in order to allow God's will to will within. Again, the greater part overtakes and overwhelms the lesser.

As described above, both the soul and God in annihilation are returned to the "first day" by means of reciprocal images that dwell virtually in both God and the soul. Annihilation thus entails the utter transformation and eradication of createdness alongside the seemingly paradoxical freedom of the natural body in the material world. This is only possible because the soul has an innate affinity for God, and God recognizes the soul's nobility.

NOBILITY, LINEAGE, AND ANNIHILATION

Certainly Porete's ultimate goal—annihilation, not salvation—determines her language and rhetoric. She employs a root metaphor of nobility of nature and exploits related themes (such as lineage, inheritance, name, and established place) to illustrate her understanding of both earthly and spiritual status and potential. Porete's interest in lineage is made explicit in many places in her text, while it is implicit in her descriptions of seeds, trees, and fecundity. Her most explicit references to lineage are used to define her audience and thereby to narrow the field of those she feels will understand her message; to insist upon the inalienable inborn characteristics of certain types of souls; and to determine which individuals are the proper heirs of divinity.[81] Her choice of this particular metaphor shapes and enriches her descriptions of annihilation.

Throughout the *Mirror of Simple Souls*, Marguerite Porete privileges nobility of lineage over nobility of merit and thereby counters the tradition of the hierarchical church, which she labels "Holy Church the Little." In favoring the power of lineage, Porete hearkens back to the most "ancient"—indeed eternal—ancestor of humankind: God as Trinitarian ground of all. In adopting this particular perspective, Porete upholds the essential nobility and divinity of certain human souls by positing the possibility of the annihilation of those souls in God. Adam, as exemplar of willfulness, bequeaths fear, anxiety, and constant striving to his progeny. The Trinity, as exemplar of simple unity, dwells eternally in the soul as the soul dwells in the Trinity and bequeaths goodness, largesse, loyalty, and freedom to His rightful heirs. An exalted lineage produces exalted, annihilated souls who are not constrained to "prove" their nobility through works and Virtues.

Porete thus makes a striking departure from her contemporaries who insist on works and sacraments and prayers as the means to attaining a life with God. R. Howard Bloch points out a similar literary strategy adopted by medieval writers, which can be seen as church doctrine. Writers in the later Middle Ages sought to "establish the most ancient ancestry possible and to create the most coherent continuity between [a] mythic beginning and the present."[82] For medieval Christians, the most ancient ancestors of humanity were understood to be Adam and Eve, and the "coherent continuity" between that inauspicious beginning and the present human condition was thought to be apparent in the fallen world. Sinful Adam, the father of a sinful race, passed his sin through the generations. Expiation was to be wrought through works of virtue in this life and in purgatory beyond. This viewpoint formed the backbone of the medieval emphasis on penance and purification.

Yet Porete recognizes two lineages in the world. The mass of humanity, those who will achieve simple salvation through doing earthly works and following Reason, belong to the broadest lineage, which she calls simply the "human race." These folks come to understand God's goodness through mediation, primarily through "Jesus Christ God's son, who is the eternal praise of the father and the ransom of the human creature."[83] The whole human race thus understands God's absolute goodness through His Son. Yet Porete recognizes a higher and more exalted human lineage rooted in virtual existence in God. These souls, noble by birth, are able to become "refined" and achieve "gentility" and spiritual understanding in annihilation, and thereby to dismiss all mediation.[84]

For these two lineages Porete posits two possible paths. One path, the earthly, is derived from Adam and culminates in Jesus Christ's saving sacrifice. The other derives from virtual existence in the Trinity. Those "high-born" souls who can become annihilated and conjoined to divine Love exist in a world apart from those "little ones" who, because of their lowly intellect and misguided attachment to Reason, will never achieve union with the Trinity. An unannihilated base soul is "burdened . . . with these [body and soul], which the unencumbered neither have, *nor are able to have*."[85] Those who can traverse the path of annihilation surpass both body and soul and all createdness.

Porete uses lineage motifs to define her audience and to stress the esoteric nature of her message, which only the high-born can understand. Porete divides the audience for her text—as well as all created souls—into two distinct groups. The *Mirror* was not meant for the simple folk who could not grasp its message; rather, it was written for those souls who are privy to divine secrets by virtue of their nobility. Lineage is the key to esoteric knowledge. Vulgar folk "are kept outside the court of [Love's] secrets, as a peasant would be barred from the court of a gentleman in the judgment of his peers, for no one can be part of the court (certainly not the court of a king) if he is not of the correct lineage."[86] Here, as in numerous other places in her book, Porete invokes a lofty lineage to exclude those who cannot make a claim to it. For Porete, each soul possesses a core identity as noble or non-noble, which which determines both her place in the social hierarchy and her disposition toward others. Nobles are in a class apart, without obligation to those in lower stations.

> This Soul has her allowance of pure freeness, a full measure of it. She responds to no one if she does not wish to, if he is not of her lineage. For a gentleman would not deign to respond to a peasant, even if one would call him or attack him in a battle field.[87]

This passage illustrates the impassive and "above-and-beyond" status of the noble soul. The noble is held apart from the common mass of humanity, dispassionate in the face of others' needs or any threat of danger.

It is apparent that for Porete certain lineages produce certain types of souls and that those souls possess inborn dispositions and abilities. She describes the immutability of a noble nature with a parable of a King's first-born daughter, who possesses gentility even when her behavior is unbecoming. She misbehaves, "and yet, says Love, piety and courtesy are not departed from [her] when time and place require it."[88] Merchants, on the other hand, are crude, selfish "beasts" and "donkeys" who know the base art of mingling in the marketplace. Merchants are lost souls: they might believe that what they are doing is good, but they simply cannot advance in perfection because they are encumbered by their short-sighted worldliness and attachment to reason. They will never receive the "inheritance" of union with God, which is a "gift" and a "treasure" bestowed only on noble descendants of the Trinity.[89] They are base at heart and cannot be reformed. These are inalienable characteristics for Porete: she does not propose that merchants attempt to abandon their ways in this life. Noble sad souls and common lost souls are distinct types. She reiterates the absolute distinction of these two types of souls when she explains why she chooses to talk about each one in turn: when "white and black are next to each other, one sees each better than when each is viewed by itself."[90]

Perhaps the most explicit investigation of a particular lineage is presented in chapter 88, where Love outlines the lineage of the Virtue of Humility, the "mother" of all the Virtues.[91] It is important to note the emphasis on esoteric authority, the obscurity that veils speaking of such an exalted lineage, and the characteristics Humility shares with the annihilated soul.

> This Humility, who is aunt and mother,
> is daughter of Divine majesty and so is born from Divinity.
> Deity is the mother and grandmother of her branches,
> by whom the buds make such great fruitfulness.
> We are silent about it, for speaking ruins them.
> This one, that is, Humility,
> has given the stem and the fruit from these buds,
> because she is there, close
> to the peace of this Farnearness
> who unencumbers her from works,
> and turns away the speaking,
> makes dark there the pondering.
> This Farnearness unencumbers,
> no one encumbers her with anything.
> This one is freed from all service,
> for she lives by freeness.
> Whoever serves is not free,
> whoever senses has not died,
> whoever desires wills,
> whoever wills begs,
> whoever begs has a lack of divine sufficiency.[92]

This passage reiterates the essential characteristics of the annihilated soul: high-born status, proximity to God, freedom from servitude, lack of encumbrance, lack of desire or will, complete sufficiency of life lived in God, and fecundity. Humility is a key to attaining annihilation, because it is the means by which the soul recognizes and embraces her own wretchedness. It is apparent that Humility is as noble, free, and unencumbered as the souls she leads. She is descended in a direct line from Divine Majesty, divinity, Deity.

Porete adopts related seed and reproduction metaphors to underscore this emphasis on lineage. Her use of a seed metaphor seems to conform to the traditional Augustinian emphasis on the necessity of grace, yet her interest lies also with the inherent qualities of the seed itself. She asserts that "all who are planted as seeds from the Father and come into this world, have descended from the perfect into the imperfect, in order to attain the most perfect."[93] God plants human beings like seeds on the earth and allows them to grow freely. The seeds can grow to some extent on their own, but they are limited and grow rather poorly; nevertheless, some retain the ability to grow well. Like Adam, they are granted freedom, but they rely on inherent goodness to achieve perfection. As described in the previous chapter, the descent into imperfection, here analogous to the degeneration of the seed, is a necessary stage in the process of growth. At base, the fate of the seed is determined by the qualities inherent in the core of the seed and the ability of the seed to allow God to work within it. A "noble" seed can grow into what it was meant to be, to fulfill its inherent potential, by allowing God to work within it: a debased seed, wallowing in willfulness, will wither and die. The freedom to grow is attained when willing is abandoned; only then is the soul's inheritance granted. As described above, an exalted lineage is the key to the "inheritance" of esoteric knowledge. Those who are in a particular lineage produce similar "stock" and recognize those who share that lineage. Most importantly, a noble lineage maintained in purity produces truly noble souls.

Porete's insistence on the power of lineage supports her uncompromising views on the inherent nature of people in all social classes. In order to describe the ineffable experience of the soul in annihilation, Porete relies on metaphors related to nobility and lineage, such as servitude and freedom, inheritance, and an established place and name. Nobility language comes into play at pivotal points in the seven stages of the path toward annihilation. The soul cannot climb out of the first stage without a "gentle heart" and "noble courage."[94] Ignoble hearts are too cowardly to advance. When this obstacle is overcome, the soul advances through the stages to the fourth stage, where the soul becomes "impenetrable, noble, and delicate."[95] The soul can become misled at this stage into thinking that there are no higher stages; however, God has made two earthly "greater and more noble" stages beyond this fourth stage. In the fifth stage, the soul is established in repose, freedom, and nobility.[96] Finally, the soul in the sixth stage is free, pure, and clarified, once Love has paid the debt for the soul "through her high nobility."[97] The spark of the sixth stage opens the soul to annihilation. Porete reports that "this work is so preciously noble" that it is beyond the creaturely mediation of speech.[98] Porete describes the union of the soul and God as a "finely noble concord."[99]

The soul in the final stages of annihilation becomes "ennobled" by her progress. Porete demonstrates the noble character of such souls by outlining four particular aspects that "are required in a noble person before he might be called a gentleman and thus of spiritual intellect." She thus establishes an initial nobility required to advance in perfection to the status of "gentleman" and, thereby, to attain union and spiritual understanding (*l'entendement espir-*

ituel).[100] The first aspect is that the soul "has no reproach in her at all, even though she does not do the work of the Virtues"; the second is that the soul has no more will, "no more than the dead in the sepulchres have, but only the divine will"; the third is that the soul believes "that there never was, nor is, nor will there ever be anything worse than she, nor any better loved"; and finally that God "is of Himself in her for her sake" and that she wills nothing other than His will. When the soul is "thus unencumbered in all aspects, she loses her name, for she rises in sovereignty."[101] Porete concludes that whoever could "comprehend the profit of one movement of such annihilation" would be a great lord and supremely free.[102] Yet the soul must be noble to begin the journey.

To become such a great Lord, however, the soul must cease to follow the lead of Reason, and only free souls have the ability to recognize that they can make that step. A soul is a "servant" to herself as long as she wills that she will the will of God with the thought of gain, like a merchant. "To such folk, says Love, God refuses his kingdom."[103] Reason must be abandoned entirely. The soul explains that "as long as I had you, Lady Reason, I could not freely receive my inheritance, what was and is mine. But now I can receive it freely, since I have wounded you to death by Love."[104] The soul hearkens back to its origins to reclaim what is properly her own:

> Now I cannot be . . . what I ought to be until I return to where I was before I departed from Him, where I was as naked as He is who is; to be naked as I was when I was who was not. And it is necessary that I have this, if I wish to receive what is mine. Otherwise I will not have it.[105]

Those who dwell in Love understand the apparent contradiction that embodied souls can live in the world in a state of annihilation, yet Reason's followers are astounded. They do not have the ability to understand Love's message, nor do they dwell with God. Those "who are from the country in which God lives" are not astounded by it at all. Those who marvel at such a magnificent gift are crude. Porete here employs a metaphor of servitude much like that she uses to describe the reversal of servitude of the Virtues and the soul.

> If a King should give one of his loyal servants a great gift, by which gift the servant would be eternally rich, without ever doing any service again, why would a wise man be astounded by this? Without fail, he must not be astounded by it at all, for in doing so he would blame the king and his gift and the liberality of the gift.[106]

A base and unwise soul does not know the "rules" of honor and courtesy. The soul in the service of Love addresses the Trinity and pleads to remain forever in the goodness of God, apart from createdness. "Ah, for the sake of God! Let us not allow anything of ourselves nor of another ever to enter within us for which it would be necessary that God place us outside His goodness!"[107] The noble soul must hold herself apart from all createdness to dwell with God. The soul has become the embodiment of *largesse*, because God works within. Truth praises such souls:

> O emerald and precious gem,
> True diamond, queen and empress,
> You give everything from your fine nobility,
> Without asking from Love her riches,
> Except the willing of her divine pleasure.[108]

The proper inheritance of certain noble souls is thus the realization of an essential likeness to God, based in the reciprocal image imprinted on the highest part of the soul and within God the Trinity. The noble soul seeks nothing outside herself. She asks for nothing, not even Love. Only those who "possess no work through deliberation outside of the will of the spirit and who are worthy heirs will attain proximity to this [state of being] of which we speak."[109] Worthy heirs are those who have maintained the purity of the lineage, *sans bastardise*.[110] Porete insists that God expects nothing less. "Has not the one God made and sustained for us the spirit of life? And what does He desire? Godly offspring. So take heed to yourselves, and let none be faithless to the wife of his youth."[111] Maintaining the purity of the lineage ensures that the esoteric doctrine of annihilation will be passed down to one's progeny by means of the Holy Spirit. The character "God the Father" says that such a loyal soul is "my first-born daughter, heir to my realm, who knows the secrets of the Son through the Love of the Holy Spirit, who has given himself to this soul."[112] This inheritance is absolute: it iş God's giving God's self to the soul. Nothing is therefore lacking to the noble human soul because her "Lover possesses in Himself sufficiency of His righteous nobility without beginning, and will have it without end. And what therefore could be lacking to [the soul]?"[113] Porete thus insists on one noble lineage of "true heirs" of God the Father.

As described in chapter 1, the fixed name and property of a noble family were commonly considered part of the foundations of noble identity. The surname common to those in noble lineage attested to its fixed, landed status. A shared name, which at once describes and categorizes, indicates shared qualities for Porete, while a shared place indicates absolute rootedness and freedom. Porete emphasizes this essential rootedness with the metaphor of a tree that is so firmly rooted it cannot move. Like such a tree, the soul in annihilation is completely passive and weak, enabling God to work within her without encumbrance. The following passage emphasizes the necessity of absolute rootedness of the soul in God. The soul

> plants her will [in the Trinity] so nakedly that she cannot sin if she does not uproot herself. She has nothing to sin with, for without a will no one can sin. Now she is kept from sin if she leaves her will there where it is

planted, that is, in the One who has given it to her freely from His goodness. And thus, by His beneficence, He wills the return of His beloved
nakedly and freely, without a why for her sake, on account of two things:
because He wills it, and because He is worthy of it. And before this she
had no fertile and restful peace until she was purely stripped of her will.[114]

Porete employs this fertile tree metaphor in several places to describe the soul
in its simultaneous rootedness and freeness. When the Soul has attained freeness, she is free, "yet more free, yet very free, yet finally supremely free, in the
root, in the stock, in all her branches and all the fruits of her branches. This
Soul has her share of purified freeness, each aspect has its full measure of it."[115]
Importantly, this freedom is fecund. The soul becomes a creator of sorts, fully
in keeping with "becoming what God is" in annihilation. God is distinguished
by his *largesse*, in which the soul shares absolutely, without works.

> My lover is great who gives me a great gift, and so He is all new and gives
> me a new gift. And so of Himself He is fertile and full of abundance of all
> goodness. And I am pregnant and full and abundantly full of the abun-
> dances of delights from the flowing goodness of His divine goodness,
> without seeking it through the peddling of pain's remedies, which this
> book describes.[116]

Here again Porete dismisses "works" in favor of an unmediated giving of goodness from God to the recipient soul. God's largesse finds its greatest expression
here, in giving All to the soul.

The rooted annihilated soul finds herself in one "place" because she is
unable of her own volition to move. As we have seen, Porete describes this
"place" as an abyss in the fifth and sixth stages; in the sixth stage the soul is
also understood to be carried up to the top of a mountain by the will of God.
Porete favors metaphors of abyss and mountain to describe passivity and the
privileged character of her message; for instance, she describes the soul as "the
very noble rock on the broad plain of truth, alone on the mountaintop except
for those in your domain."[117] Yet this metaphorical language of rootedness and
stasis belies the actual omnipresent state of the soul in annihilation: the noble
soul, like her secular noble counterpart, is free. The soul has received all that
is God's, and therefore God gives "sovereign freeness to [the annihilated soul]
in all places."[118] Once the soul is annihilated, she

> has her peace in all places, for she carries peace with her always, so that,
> on account of such peace, all things and places are comfortable for her.
> Thus such a Soul seats herself on the throne of peace in the book of life,
> without moving, in the witness of a good conscience and in freeness of
> perfect charity.[119]

Here one sees an example of Porete's melding of immanence and transcendence as well as stability and freedom. The soul, having received her rightful

inheritance from God, has all that God has, including his absolute immanence and transcendence. The soul is at once in one place and in all places.
She becomes common to all things in part because she is in the most essential
way removed from all createdness. Porete insists that high spiritual nature
must not become concerned with base earthly materials. This seems to buttress her claim that noble annihilated souls can live in the world without
works or Virtues. She insists that "no one can see the divine things as long as
he mixes himself or mingles with temporal things, that is, with anything less
than God."[120]

Porete thus uses "place," at times dialectically, to explicate both the esoteric nature of her message and the implications of immobility for the freedom of the soul.[121] Porete reports that the annihilated, free, unencumbered
soul is "established" in her nothingness. The annihilated soul dwells in repose
and stability. For Porete stability means freedom: chaining the body frees the
spirit and reaching the fifth stage means freedom from encumbering work or
striving or searching.[122] When the soul is in the supreme state of willing nothing, it remains there, in peace, without moving.[123] Ideally, the annihilated
soul is "imprisoned and held in the country of complete peace," a hostage to
God, in repose and peace, removed entirely from works and striving.[124]

Porete also uses metaphors of naming to describe the state of annihilation, and these expressions refer back to the fixed patronym of the noble family. Porete explains that Love uses the name "soul" in explaining things to
Reason, because unrefined Reason is aided by the use of a "*surnom*," which
can mean either "surname" or "classification." "Soul" is one way of classifying
what Love understands to be more accurately named as "perfectly noble. She
has the name 'pure,' 'celestial,' and 'spouse of peace'."[125] These are the "noble"
names of the soul. Yet like all earthly things, names are simply created (and
thus ultimately disposable) instruments in Porete's system. They are for the
benefit of the "actives" who need such aid in understanding. Names are most
meaningful after they are lost, a loss accomplished only in annihilation.[126]
The Soul loses her name as she rises in sovereignty.

> Thus [the soul] would be like a body of water which flows from the sea,
> which has some name, as one would be able to say Aisne or Seine or an-
> other river. And when this water or river returns into the sea, *it loses its
> course and its name* with which it flowed in many countries accomplishing
> its work. Now it is in the sea where it rests, and thus has lost all labor.[127]

This is a perfect representation of the journey of the soul to annihilation: it
comes from the sea, follows its own path, and eventually finds its way back to
its origin.[128] Porete goes on:

> Now such a Soul is without a name, and because of this she has the name
> of the transformation by which Love has transformed her. So it is with

the waters of which we have spoken, which have the name of "sea" because they are wholly sea as soon as they have entered into the sea.[129]

The soul comes from the sea with a name, returns to the sea having lost her
name as a river (that is, something created), but having gained the "name of
Him into whom she is perfectly transformed."[130] The river, or the soul, is
transformed into the sea (God) and becomes indistinguishable from it. The
only name that matters after this melding is the name that exists virtually in
the soul, the name of God. The soul established in the fifth and sixth stages
loses her name and is with God forever.

As explained in the first chapter, nobility implies a lofty inheritance, a
fixed place of abode, and a distinguished name. Nobility is a proper foundation for attaining the highest stature.[131] Yet the "noble" soul in annihilation is
also no-thing, without status, common to all. The soul's recognition of her
wretchedness, which can be accomplished only by means of this nobility,
leads her to recognize her true being. The once-exalted soul in annihilation

> sees [herself] beneath all creatures, in the sea of sin. And because the
> demons are slaves of sin, and this soul has seen for a long time that she is
> beneath them . . . and in this regard this Soul becomes nothing and less
> than nothing in all of her aspects.[132]

Does this reversal of the soul's apparent "status" imply that nobility is only a
passing condition, jettisoned in annihilation along with name and place and
will? Porete argues that the nobility that enables a soul to approach God and
achieve annihilation is transmuted in annihilation into what must be understood as "divine" nobility: a nobility of absolute largesse, transcendence, immanence, impassivity, immutability, and commonality. The noble soul becomes "gently noble in prosperity, highly noble in adversity, and most
excellently noble in every place she might be."[133] The noble soul achieves
"gentility" in annihilation, becoming "ennobled" by love when it ceases obedience to desire and will.[134]

God's largesse makes the soul common to all, yet unmoved in the face of
change and temptation. In annihilation,

> the soul is not afraid of hardship; she is not detained for consolation, nor
> is she lowered on account of temptation, nor is she diminished by any
> subtraction. She is common to all things through the largesse of pure
> charity and so she asks nothing of anyone on account of the nobility of
> the courtesy of pure good with which God has filled her.[135]

This nothingness is the true nature of the soul, the beginning of a lineage that
finds its noblest expression in annihilated souls in life. The noble seed of divine love enables this nothingness, which entails a completely dispassionate
life within the world, living apart like a true noble.

This brings the reader back to the exempla of love that opened chapter 3. The first exemplum, that of earthly love, tells of a maiden who endures unrequited love for a king. She loves him through her works and through an image she has made to remind herself of his noble qualities. Although she is noble, she does not get beyond worldly works in her love and is thus not ennobled. The second tale focuses on the immanence of God throughout creation and on the solicitude God has for a particular soul. The final sentence of the second tale provides an important clue to Porete's ultimate goal. It is no hindrance that the soul has "His image, for it is not true that I am in a strange land and far from the palace where the very noble friends of this Lord dwell, who are completely pure, perfect, and free through the gifts of this King with whom they remain."

This soul, without struggling and servitude, dwells with those who are in repose, perfection, and freedom. God would allow nothing that is unlike Him to dwell with Him. God cannot live with those who work and strive: "He cannot dwell with this stranger; He is too great to have a strange guest dwell with Him."[136] Souls who have attained this status live in the greatest house and dwell with God.

> Such souls, who are in being, are in sovereignty in all things. For their spirit is in the highest nobility of the orders of created and ordained angels. Thus folks such as these have, on account of this spirit, the highest mansion of all the orders and by nature the most gentle constitution.[137]

The soul that has passed through the six stages of noble being attainable in this life has embraced Being, repose, stability, and the name of the transformation by which Love has transformed her. This immanence of the soul complements the immanence of God. The peace and stability of God become the soul's peace and stability. These souls produce godly offspring. They are "impregnated" by God's largesse, by "the divine seed and Loyal Love," the true being and the ultimate calling of the noble soul.

Porete insists that souls in a noble lineage have the highest calling and the most lofty goal. The soul who is unencumbered of worldly things and is very noble is "gentle in her offspring, which are descended from her, and no rustic is taken in marriage there, and thus she is very noble."[138] Porete ends the *Mirror* with the following injunction:

> And thus I say to you, in conclusion, since God has given you the highest creation and excellent light and singular love, be fertile and multiply this creation without fail, because His two eyes watch you always. Ponder and consider this well, as this seeing makes the Soul simple.[139]

This command to increase and multiply echoes the command made to Adam by God in Genesis. Porete here makes it clear that humanity is the apex of creation and that human beings are constrained to fulfill this "highest" calling. Certain elect, noble souls, however, can go beyond even this exalted calling to attain annihilation and to perpetuate their exalted election in teaching other "simple" noble souls, like Porete herself.

A "SIMPLE" NOBLE SOUL?

The nobility motif infuses Porete's *Mirror* so fully that some readers have remarked that Porete's usage "approaches arrogance."[140] That her apparent elitism got Porete into trouble is clear. What remains less clear, perhaps, are the foundations of this elitism. Edmund Colledge, who was certain that Porete knew herself to be a heretic and thus consciously withdrew from the church and its teachings, claims that Porete did not live out the words she wrote: "The entire book is characterized by a stubborn, willful determination to persist in its opinions, by a spiritual arrogance, which could surely find no place in a truly 'simple soul'."[141] It is true that Porete rebukes those who are base, those who are ontologically inferior to the noble souls. Her thoroughgoing elitism, which Barbara Newman aptly calls "hauteur" and describes as having "carefully defined sets of insiders and outsiders," is embodied in the "personalities" of her personified characters, the most knowing of which (Love and the Soul) seem haughty in the way they answer or dismiss the others.[142] And yet by her definition she was a "simple soul."

Barbara Newman notes in *From Virile Woman to WomanChrist* that many beguines displayed an apparent "contempt for the uncomprehending masses," remarking that "their striking elitism is in part a simple transposition of the courtly ethos into religious terms."[143] Yet it seems that more is at stake here. Porete's elitism is more than a way to set a "cultural barrier raised to compensate for the lost privilege afforded by monastery walls."[144] It is, rather, the manifestation of a soul sure of its own standing as *Imago Dei*. She is not so much creating a "theocratic universe which was the antithesis of the society which she saw around her," but rather using a complex of related metaphors to describe the relationship between the soul and God.[145] She is living out deeply personal experience.

It is important to remember that Porete believes her message will only be understood by those who have the capacity to understand. She insists that "those who live as described in this book understand quickly without it being necessary to explain the glosses."[146] She addresses her readers directly: "You" who understand were born into a noble lineage and

> will recognize [your] practice in this book. And those who are not of this kind, nor were, nor will be, will not feel this being, nor understand it. They cannot do it, nor will they do it. They are not, as you know, of the lineage of which we speak, no more than the angels of the first order are Seraphim, nor can they be, for God does not give them the being of Seraphim.[147]

The ability to understand this message derives from a God-given capacity, without which the Soul is powerless to advance beyond the quest for worldly perfection. Those who understand do so through the "strength of the lineage from which they are and will be" and recognize their fellow noble ones: "And such folk of whom we speak, who are this way and will be, will recognize, as soon as they hear it, the lineage from which they have come."[148] Those who cling to Reason, however outwardly pious they might appear, are misled and will misunderstand Porete's message. She asks

> O my Lover, what will Beguines say,
> and religious folk,
> When they hear the excellence
> of your divine song?
> Beguines say I err,
> priests, clerics, and preachers,
> Augustinians, Carmelites, and the Friars Minor
> Because I wrote about the being
> of the one purified by Love
> I do not make their Reason safe . . .[149]

In several places, then, the reader understands that the *Mirror* is written for those who have the capacity to understand it but may not yet have done so. It is thus not necessarily the province of professional religious; indeed, the passage above may serve to exclude those people. In particular, Porete writes "Not for the sake of those who are this, but for those who are not who yet will be, but who will beg continuously as long as they are with themselves."[150]

It is true that Porete proudly claims the esoteric nature of her thought throughout the *Mirror*.[151] Yet what does she mean by this claim? On one hand, she means secret, arcane knowledge, *understood* by initiates alone. The message might be transmitted through democratizing channels (for her, the vernacular of her region), but it is understood only by those who are capable of understanding. More central to her definition of esotericism is the idea of transmission of a spiritual path from one spiritual guide to others. She has no problem asserting her own authority, for she writes about what she knows, and she knows about annihilation. She is part of an exalted lineage, which is, in the words of Maurice Keen, "the nurse and instructress of nobility, and hence of gentility."[152] This idea was not palatable to her contemporaries, nor does it sit well with modern ideas about egalitarianism and the virtue of hard work. Porete never claims that annihilation will come without work; nevertheless, she does assert that only a few will be able to endure the path. She herself is one of the few. Souls so graced are elected to fulfill the highest spiritual calling: to realize the true status of the soul prior to its creation while "becoming what God is." The annihilated soul has attained the "crown of the perfection of freeness" which was her birthright always.[153]

CONCLUSION

The *Mirror of Simple Souls* is a book of a uncommon insight into the possibility of transformative union between God and individual human souls. That insight proved fatal, yet its author's message endures as testament to a distinctive form of spirituality. This beguine upheld the doctrines she espoused in the *Mirror* without compromise, and the themes that run through her text were played out at her trial: the importance of spiritual lineage and nobility, the temporality of the created world, and the permanence of the soul's union with God due to the soul's virtual existence in the Trinity and the transformation of Love. Porete, a simple, noble soul and thus a worthy conduit for a divine message, has no need of responding to those who would never understand, because she places herself squarely within the select population of "noble" souls. Only such souls share the secret doctrine of annihilation. In addition, by insisting on the power of spiritual lineage and, therefore, of inborn nobility, Porete negates the need for mediation in the return to God, either through the hierarchical church or even through Jesus Christ. This complex of metaphors suits Porete's radical doctrine of annihilation, which gets at the very root of the soul's true identity.

Annihilation can be attained only by those capable of recognizing their true identity as eternally one with God. This is accomplished by virtue of an inborn nobility, which provides the soul with strength and secret knowledge. Annihilation comes only to those souls who divest themselves of *all* createdness, including the will, and thus realize their true nature as images of the

Trinity. The will of the Trinity, in the person of the Holy Spirit, enables the procession of creation from the Godhead as well as the return of creatures to preexistence. Humanity is granted free will, free to turn to good or evil. Yet it is most free, truly free, when it has no will and is thus returned to God. Only then does the Trinity work within it. For Porete, the soul's true nature is as noble heir to God; as such, it derives its identity from the Trinity itself, not from Adam's willful sin. The noble soul is thus not the heir to the Heir (in theological terms, not an image of the Image); she is, rather, the direct descendant and thus the rightful inheritor of the Trinitarian God's goodness and being. For Marguerite Porete, the nobility of the soul is maintained despite (or, perhaps more accurately, "above and beyond") sin. Nobility is a gift, not an earned status: it is a gift from God and thus the highest gift from the most liberal and loyal lover. It is the ultimate grace, surpassing the grace ushered in by Christ to effect salvation, and it requires that the soul recognize its concurrent nobility and absolute impotence to save itself.

Porete's particular association of nobility and theological speculation is unique, but her ideas are not entirely divorced from her contemporary milieu or from the Christian tradition. Themes related to nobility and lineage (which are both also prominent themes in courtly romances) pervade the *Mirror of Simple Souls*. Several themes inform the *Mirror* as well as the texts and authors explored in chapter 1. Secondary motifs, such as the rootedness and impregnability of the noble soul, are echoed in the writings of Hrotsvit of Gandersheim and Hildegard of Bingen, both of whom focus on noble bearing and strength. Hadewijch of Brabant continues this tradition by describing the soul that endures God's absence as "noble" in pain and suffering and thus able to withstand the desolation. Porete adopts these motifs in describing the annihilated soul and the noble soul on the path to annihilation. Yet the "beauty" of such souls is only seen by those who are themselves noble: she would never claim that others, the ignoble merchants, could identify the annihilated souls within their midst.

That nobles are in a class apart is emphasized by Hildegard and Hadewijch, although it is also touched upon by Bernard of Clairvaux when he marvels at the rarity of moral vigor in those who are high-born, indicating a belief in certain traits among those born to a particular station in life. Nevertheless, a particular emphasis on elitism enlivens the writings of Hildegard of Bingen and Hadewijch of Brabant. Both women insist that certain characteristics are inborn, ordained by God and not to be questioned: divine sanction determined stations in life, and the goal of life was to live as well as one could within the confines of one's given status. According to Hildegard, this situation is due to human sin and can be remedied only through living out one's role in a state of impregnable, noble virtue. Hildegard describes this in a practical manner as a way of explaining the differences of status within the world as a whole as well as her restrictive recruitment of only women of noble family stock. Hadewijch uses language very similar to Porete's in putting down the "rustics" and "aliens" who will never know the secrets of union with Love. Porete adopts a similar elitism that completely pervades her text. Throughout her book, Porete takes pains to separate the wheat from the chaff, the sad from the lost, the contemplative from the active, masters from servants, nobles from merchants, and annihilated souls from those souls that remain in will and desire. It is this last that sets Porete apart from the others. She maintains an absolute dichotomy between those who can attain the height of annihilation and those who cannot; between those who can under-stand and those who will never understand; and between those who can dwell in God's kingdom and those who are forever banished from glory. For Porete, certain noble, elect souls can recognize their inborn status and become anni-hilated; base souls cannot and never will. Hildegard and Hadewijch never claimed that any soul could attain such heights.

This gets at the key question for Porete: how is nobility attained? Is it inborn, earned through merit, or a combination of the two? Porete declares that it is explicitly not earned; it is, rather, the identity of the soul in its virtual existence in the Trinity. In this she departs from others. As the comparisons presented in chapter 1 show, earned virtue was often considered the only true "nobility" in the Christian tradition despite the insistence on humanity as the "image and likeness" of God. One possible explanation for this general agree-ment is that each of these authors accepted without question the doctrine of original sin. For each of these thinkers, humanity inherited the sinful deposit of Adam's primeval sin and all must be redeemed by Jesus Christ. All are thus indebted to the "economy of salvation," the mystery of redemption in the per-son of Jesus Christ, and all insist on the value of virtuous works. This does not mean that these thinkers have abandoned the notion that humanity is made in the image and likeness of God; on the contrary, they stress the loss of the likeness which they strive to regain through earthly works and virtues. For each of these thinkers, all are equally sinners before God unless distinctions are made based on virtue and merit. Porete departs decisively from this tradi-tion by dismissing nobility of merit and emphasizing the divine origin of cer-tain noble souls. In short, she relies on a different set of anthropological as-sumptions.

A similar emphasis on works is found in secular literature. Many of the themes presented in the *Roman de la Rose* are found in the *Mirror,* yet the con-trast between the two works is striking. Both distinguish base and noble souls; both insist on the high status of the lover who wishes to do God's will and on the qualities the lover shares with God (or the God of Love); both emphasize the positive aspects of passivity; both downplay the role of reason in love; and both insist that the "true" nature of the individual is found within, not

without. Yet despite their evident similarities, these works diverge on two crucial points. In the *Roman de la Rose*, for instance, nobility is understood more
as a result of virtue than of lineage. All humans are created equal and are
thereafter bound by their willfulness and the operations of Fortune. In the
Mirror of Simple Souls, in contrast, noble annihilated souls exist in a sphere
apart, not bound by willfulness or any other change. In the *Roman*, too, the
attainment of nobility is the highest attainment of the lover. In the *Mirror*,
nobility is a means to an end, not an end in itself. While both stress the value
of imitation of forebears, the *Roman de la Rose* refers to the valiant deeds of
noble ancestors, while the *Mirror* refers to "imitation" in the sense of obliter-
ating the self by doing God's will absolutely.

The closest we come to Porete is Hadewijch of Brabant, whose use of
the notion of spiritual nobility deriving from an exclusive lineage can appear
almost identical to Porete's. Yet the two are separated by a crucial divide.
Hadewijch's mystical writings are most properly considered *Minnemystik* or
love mysticism, which characterizes the union with God as one of fervent reciprocal love. Nobility is, for Hadewijch, an ontological status that is fully realized through love of Jesus Christ. For Porete, on the other hand, nobility is an
ontological status fully realized through recognizing one's own wretchedness.
She is thus a proponent of *Wesenmystik*, or mysticism of being, leaving behind
the notion of passionate love for an intermediary to go directly to the essential
identity of the soul. Porete stands alone in her adoption of spiritual lineage
and nobility as the keys to esoteric knowledge and spiritual heights.

This study aims to counter the weight of scholarship which has, hereto-
fore, avoided extended consideration of women's speculative treatises. Porete
in particular is difficult to tackle because she exists outside of so many accepted frames of reference. Yet she is an outstanding thinker, not only for her
speculative mystical doctrines but for what she represents within the broader
Christian tradition. For Porete, as for thinkers before her, the soul's true nature—even in its fallen state—is pivotal. Yet she stands alone in insisting that
that true nature can be regained by the fallen soul even while it remains embodied in the material world. The original character of Porete's thought is
rooted in a particular ontological principle: the virtual existence of the Trinity
in the soul and, reciprocally, of the soul in the Trinity. For her, then, the *imago
Dei* is the soul's nobility, recognizable by only a few souls. No author before
her professed such a strong sense of reciprocality or of permanent identity between Creator and creature.

Porete departs from the mainstream Christian tradition in other ways.
For instance, her anthropological speculations lead her away from the doctrine that return to God is achieved through the mediation of the church, imitation of Christ, and the merit of increasing likeness to God. Even in mystical treatises, the soul and God remain distinct. Yet Porete presents her readers

with a distinctive anthropology, based on a cycle of creation, fall, redemption, and return to a "precreational oneness" with God. Indeed, she posits two "cycles" of created life lived by two types of souls within the embrace of two churches, one earthly and guided by Reason, one spiritual and guided by Love. For Porete, all human souls are descended both from the Trinity and from Adam. All things are thus both eternal (by way of the virtual existence of the soul in the Trinity and the Trinity in the soul) and made (by way of creation in time). All creation, all "lost" and "sad" souls, will pass through the mundane cycle of Fall, redemption, and return within the arms of Holy Church the Little. Certain souls *by virtue of an inborn nature* can return to the original state of no-thingness, to a pre-creational, everlasting union without distinction, which entails rejection of the church-sanctioned merit-based system of spiritual advancement.

Each soul thus possesses a core nature that determines its place in the created hierarchy and its relation to other embodied souls. That core nature, which is never earned, is either noble or debased; that is, it is either capable of achieving annihilation or it is destined to remain a lost soul, following the Virtues and the teachings of Reason. Nobility and lineage language is particularly suited to Porete's message in two essential ways: it enables her to establish and define an audience for her esoteric message, and it provides a strong set of metaphors for the soul who can become or is annihilated. "Annihilation," an embodied spiritual state of "knowing nothing, having nothing, and willing nothing," is achieved without worldly works. In contrast to mainstream church teaching, Porete insists that certain souls realize this exalted status before God not through ascetic and sacramental practices but through an inborn nobility that enables a recognition of the soul's true nature. This, in turn, enables a return to the nothingness from which the soul originated. In this annihilated state, the soul realizes the promise of unmediated union with God, the one ground of all. No other writer before Porete had so boldly dismissed these elements as mere "steps" on the path to God. No writer had dared to assert that an embodied, fallen human being could exist within the world without sin, without cares, without attachment to works, and "without a why."

Porete also departs from the tradition in the manner in which she writes her treatise. Rather than relying on a topos of feminine humility, Porete establishes herself and her readers as truly noble souls and thus privy to a certain cache of knowledge and power. Certainly, Porete's assertive writing brings out a tension that is rarely seen in work by other women, who traditionally relied on humble claims to divine inspiration, whether through visions or spoken messages, to legitimate their authority. Like many of her contemporaries, Porete employs secular imagery to express and develop her ideas about the transcendent experience of annihilation and union. Yet she departs from many of the established models and authorities. She rarely quotes from scripture, rarely mentions Christ or His suffering, and rarely brings the text down from a speculative mode. Unlike her contemporaries, she presents herself as a conduit for divine truth without giving any authorizing visions or apologizing for her lowly status or for her gender. She does not use the bridal or erotic language so common with other women writers of her time. Porete also downplays traditional claims to authority and even reproves learned theologians, actives, and contemplatives as ignoble—and therefore unworthy—recipients of her lofty message. She does not apologize for being a "lowly woman" because she is writing primarily for fellow noble souls. She writes as an equal to striving equals. In short, Porete rejects many of the expected "feminine" literary formulas, because her interests lie elsewhere. These interests surely sparked more controversy than her gendered images or her own status as a woman. It is indeed difficult to avoid the conclusion that the awkward boundary status of many beguines made them appear suspect to the (male) church hierarchy and (male) secular authorities. Porete's elitism, which is based on her distinction between noble and non-noble souls, was certainly influential in prompting church authorities to take action against her.

Porete's twin pivots—nobility and annihilation—can both be summed up with one word: simplicity. God is simple, a simple Trinitarian unity, the divine ground of all in which the soul finds repose. Simplicity is not diversity and change (as life is for the "common" folk) but rather repose and permanence (as it is for the "noble"). Simplicity is also the courtly ideal of loving the beloved entirely, without duplicity. This sort of simplicity in love is attainable only by the soul that endures all the trials that God sends her on the path to annihilation. On a spiritual level, the uncreated part of the soul that dwells in the Trinity is eternally simple, and repose in that simplicity even within embodied life is attained only by souls who can recognize the mark of the Trinity within. Simplicity is the union without difference of the (created) human will and the (uncreated) Trinitarian image of God within the soul. In the simplicity of annihilation the soul "becomes" God. Simplicity is, at base, absolute unity with God, indifference to the created world, and an ineffably rooted freedom. It is attainable only by the noble lover, who lives apart from the common herd.

In conclusion, by positing the power of an inborn nobility in the achievement of lasting and complete union with God, Porete asserts that closeness to God is not measured by the degree of effort given to religious exercises. For Porete, positing a return of the soul to its pre-created state—described as a state of not-willing, not-knowing, and not-having—entails rejection of a merit-based system of advancement; accordingly, her seven stages on the path to annihilation are predicated on increasing detachment from createdness. The soul advances as it sheds not only works but the necessity and desire for works. The soul realizes high status before God not through ascetic and sacramental practices but through an inborn nobility that enables a recognition of the soul's true nature as at once the highest of creation and (as fallen) the most wretched. Certain souls can recognize and return to their primal state of no-thingness in order to realize the promise of unmediated union with God, the one ground of all with whom they are properly one.

APPENDIX

Following are three texts related to Marguerite Porete's condemnation. The first is an account of her questioning and censure, followed by the extant articles from the Paris condemnation. The third is an excerpt of the decree *Ad nostrum*, which condemned both "Free Spirit" and beguine doctrines.

> Here is the case in question. From the time that Marguerite Porete was suspected of heresy, she refused, remaining in rebellion and insubordination, to take the oath and to respond to the inquisitor about everything pertaining to his office as inquisitor. The inquisitor initiated a process against her anyway, and by the deposition of many witnesses he learned that the said Marguerite had composed a book containing heresies and errors. The book had been publicly condemned as heresy and solemnly burned. . . . The bishop had ordered in an official letter that if she dared again to propagate by word or writing such things as were contained in this book, he would condemn her and give her over to the judgment of the civil court. The inquisitor learned next that she had acknowledged . . . that she still had in her possession, even after the condemnation mentioned above, the said book and other books . . . and that after the condemnation of the book had sent a similar book containing the same errors . . . to the bishop, but also to many other simple persons . . . as if it were good.[1]

THE PARIS CONDEMNATION

The Paris condemnation of Marguerite in 1309 included the following two articles (the first and fifteenth):

1. That the annihilated soul is freed from the virtues and nor is she any longer in the service, because she does not have them as far as their practice is concerned, but the virtues obey according to her good pleasure.
15. That such a soul has no concern for the consolations of God nor for his gifts, and she neither ought nor is able to care, because her total intent is toward God, and otherwise her efforts toward God would be impeded.[2]

AD NOSTRUM

1. That man in the present life can acquire so great and such a degree of perfection that he will be rendered inwardly sinless, and that he will not be able to advance farther in grace; for, as they say, if anyone could always advance, he could become more perfect than Christ.

2. That it is not necessary for man to fast or pray after he has attained such a degree of perfection; because then his sensuality is so perfectly subject to the spirit and to reason that man can freely grant to the body whatever it pleases.

3. That those who are in the aforementioned degree of perfection and in that spirit of liberty are not subject to human obedience, nor are they bound to any precepts of the Church, because as they assert "where the spirit of the Lord is, there is liberty". (2 Cor. 3:17)

4. That man can so attain final beatitude according to every degree of perfection in the present life, as he will obtain in the blessed life.

5. That any intellectual nature in itself is naturally blessed, and that the soul does not need the light of glory raising it to see God and to enjoy Him beatifically.

6. That it is characteristic of the imperfect man to exercise himself in acts of virtue, and the perfect soul gives off virtues by itself.

7. That a woman's kiss, since nature does not incline to this, is a mortal sin. But the carnal act, since nature inclines to this, is not a sin, especially when the one exercising it is tempted.

8. That in the elevation of the body of Jesus Christ they ought not to rise nor to show reverence to it, declaring that it would be characteristic of the imperfection in them if from the purity and depth of the contemplations they should descend to such a degree as to think about other things regarding the minister or the sacrament of the Eucharist of the passion of the humanity of Christ . . .

We with the approval of the Sacred Council condemn and disapprove completely that sect together with its past errors, restraining more strictly lest anyone in the future hold, approve, or defend them.[3]

Notes

Chapter One

NOBILITY AS HISTORICAL REALITY AND THEOLOGICAL MOTEL

1. Georges Duby, *The Three Orders: Feudal Society Imagined* (Chicago: University of Chicago Press, 1980). This type of classification can be found in sources from as early as the tenth century. This particular scheme is found in the early eleventh century in *Carmen ad Rotbertum regem* by Adalbero of Laon. For more on Adalbero's ideas, see Claude Carozzi, "Les fondements de la tripartition sociale chez Adalbéron de Laon," *Annales: Économies, sociétés, civilisations* 33 (1978): 683–702.

2. Giles Constable, "The Orders of Society," in *Three Studies in Medieval Religious and Social Thought* (Cambridge: Cambridge University Press, 1995), 249–360. Other useful sources on social categorizations include D. A. Bullough, "Early Medieval Social Groupings: The Terminology of Kinship," *Past and Present* 45 (1969): 3–18.

3. Maurice Keen, *Nobles, Knights, and Men-at-Arms in the Middle Ages* (London: Hambledon, 1996), 203.

4. The term *nobility*, as used by these authors, is likely shaped by each writer's own (very often noble) education and upbringing. All of the authors examined in this chapter are said to have come from noble stock. This is not surprising, since education was generally reserved for the elite, and the church and the nobility had strong ties in many regions. On this see, for instance, John Howe, "The Nobility's Reform of the Medieval Church," *American Historical Review* 93 (1988): 317–339; the review essay by Constance B. Bouchard, "Community: Society and the Church in Medieval France," *French Historical Studies* 17, No. 4 (Fall 1992): 1035–1047; Bouchard's chapter on "Nobility and the Church," in *'Strong of Body, Brave and Noble': Chivalry and Society in Medieval France* (Ithaca: Cornell University Press, 1998); and Elizabeth J. Gardner, "The English Nobility and Monastic Education, c. 1100–1500," in *The Cloister and the World*, ed. John Blair and Brian Golding (Oxford: Clarendon, 1996).

5. Considering this theme more widely must be reserved for a separate monograph. This particular survey is limited in scope because Porete's theology is its primary focus. Nevertheless, other authors and texts worth considering in this context include, but are not limited to, Meister Eckhart, the "Schwester Katrei" treatise, Johannes Tauler, and John Ruusbroec, the much-considered late twelfth century *Art of Courtly*

111

Love attributed to Andreas Capellanus, the thirteenth century prose Lancelot, and the writings of Bartolus of Sassoferrato.

6. In many cases they received their educations and wrote within institutions that were often founded, supported, and largely inhabited by members of the secular nobility. It is easy to dismiss this as a fact of little significance, since monastics gave up their worldly identities in exchange for the humble identity of servant of Christ. Yet personal experiences and education certainly shape their understandings, and thus their use of certain terms is bound to be self-serving and even paradoxical at times.

7. This exploration largely overlooks the tradition of "courtly love" literature in favor of examining a broader theme that can be found in courtly literature but that was also a working term and status in the "real" world. On this, see especially Barbara Newman, *"La mystique courtoise:* Thirteenth-Century Beguines and the Art of Love," in *From Virile Woman to WomanChrist: Studies in Medieval Religion and Literature* (Philadelphia: University of Pennsylvania, 1995), 137–167. See also, for instance, Elizabeth Wainwright-deKadt, "Courtly Literature and Mysticism: Some Aspects of their Interaction," *Acta Germanica* 12 (1980): 41–60 and Edmund Reiss, "Fin'Amors: Its History and Meaning in Medieval Literature," *Medieval and Renaissance Studies* 8 (1979): 74–99.

8. Others have disagreed. Alessandro Barbero insists that the term *noble* as found in vernacular imaginative literature refers neither to birth nor social class and Emilie Zum Brunn, noting Porete's distinction of noble and non-noble, remarked that "though resorting to feudal symbolism, [this categorization] has nothing to do with social, ecclesiastical, or religious hierarchy." See Barbero, *L'aristocrazia nella società francese del medioevo. Analisi delle fonti letterarie* (secoli X-XIII) (Bologna, 1987) and Zum Brunn, "Self, Not-Self, and the Ultimate in Marguerite Porete's *Mirror of Annihilated Souls,"* in *God, the Self and Nothingness: Reflections Eastern and Western,* ed. Robert E. Carter (New York: Paragon House, 1990), 84.

9. Maurice Keen, *Nobles, Knights, and Men-at-Arms,* 204.

10. On this situation generally, see several older but reliable sources: R. W. Southern, *Western Society and the Church in the Middle Ages* (Baltimore: Penguin, 1970); Lester K. Little, *Religious Poverty and the Profit Economy in Medieval Europe* (Ithaca: Cornell University Press, 1983); and M.-D. Chenu, *Nature, Man, and Society in the Twelfth Century: Essays on New Theological Perspectives in the Latin West* (Chicago: University of Chicago Press, 1968).

11. On these see especially Constable's *Three Studies.*

12. Peter Brown notes that "one of the unconsidered strengths of Christianity in the late fourth century was the sensitivity with which it could replicate, in its model of relations with the other world, the social experience of the contemporary Roman Empire" in his *The Cult of the Saints: Its Rise and Function in Latin Christianity* (Chicago: University of Chicago Press, 1981), 62.

13. Wayne Meeks, *The First Urban Christians* (New Haven: Yale University Press, 1983). See also John S. Kloppenborg, "Egalitarianism in the Myth and Rhetoric of Pauline Churches," in *Reimagining Christian Origins* (Valley Forge, Pa.: Trinity Press, 1996), 247–263.

14. Paul reiterates this point in Colossians 3:11 and in 1 Corinthians 12:13. The texts are, respectively, "Here there cannot be Greek and Jew, circumcised and uncir-

cumcised, barbarian, Scythian, slave, free man, but Christ is all, and in all." And "For by one Spirit we were all baptized into one body—Jews or Greeks, slaves or free—and all were made to drink of one Spirit" (RSV).

15. Both are quoted in David Herlihy, *The Social History of Italy and Western Europe, 700–1500* (London: Variorum, 1978), 623.

16. Very little work has been done recently on the interplay of theology and nobility. See, for instance, an old but useful essay by Ernst Benz, "Über den Adel in der deutschen Mystik," in *Deutsche Vierteljahrsschrift für Literaturwissenschaft und Geistesgeschichte* XIV, No. 4, ed. Paul Kluckhorn and Erich Rothacker (Halle: Niemeyer, 1936), 505–535, in which the author explores primary sources from Meister Eckhart, Marguerite Ebner, Mechtild von Magdeburg, and others. John W. Baldwin's *Masters, Princes, and Merchants: The Social Views of Peter the Chanter* (Princeton: Princeton University Press, 1970) considers social structures from a monastic viewpoint. C. Stephen Jaeger's *The Envy of Angels: Cathedral Schools and Social Ideals in Medieval Europe, 950–1200* (Philadelphia: University of Pennsylvania Press, 1994) provides thorough background for this study. Finally, Burcht Pranger's brief consideration of this connection in "The Rhetoric of Mystical Unity in the Middle Ages: A Study in Retroactive Reading," in *Journal of Literature and Theology* 17, No. 1 (March 1993): 13–49 is also worth considering for the connections between Porete and Meister Eckhart and the theme of nobility.

17. Gabrielle M. Spiegel, "Genealogy: Form and Function in Medieval Historical Narrative," *History and Theory* 22 (1983): 48. See also her "History, Historicism, and the Social Logic of the Text in the Middle Ages," *Speculum* 65 (1990): 59–86. Dominique Barthélemy's "L'état contre «le lignage»: une thème a développer dans l'histoire des pouvoirs en France aux Xie, XIIe, et XIIIe siècles," in *Medievales* 10 (1986): 37–50, provides a solid view of the political dimensions of this development. Georges Duby, "French Genealogical Literature of the Eleventh and Twelfth Centuries," in *Chivalrous Society*, trans. Cynthia Postan (Berkeley: University of California Press, 1977), 149–157 is also a good source.

18. Maurice Keen notes in *Chivalry* (New Haven: Yale University Press, 1984) that families hearkened back to mythical founding figures if they could not establish a true noble forebear (33). On the relationship between family and rising "state" power, see Barthélemy, "L'état contre le «lignage»."

19. Peter Dembowski explains the semantic difficulties inherent in certain binomial constructions, such as *noble* and *gentil, noble* and *franche,* or *noble* and *courtoise.* See Peter F. Dembowski, "Vocabulary of Old French Courtly Lyrics: Difficulties and Hidden Difficulties," *Critical Inquiry* 2 (1975/6): esp. 773ff.

20. J. F. Niermeyer, *Mediae Latinitatis Lexicon Minus* (Leiden: Brill, 1976). One interesting article on related definitions is Jacques Monfrin, "A propos du vocabulaire des structures sociales du haut Moyen Age," *Annales du Midi* LXXXX (968): 611–620.

21. See Robert Fossier, *Enfance de l'Europe,* Volume 2 (Paris, 1982): 965. For one view of the church's use of such language, see Constance B. Bouchard, *Sword, Miter, and Cloister: Nobility and the Church in Burgundy, 980–1198* (Ithaca: Cornell University Press, 1987).

22. An example of this can be found in Andreas Capellanus's *Art of Courtly Love* when he describes the order of clerics. Among his many assertions related to the

relations between three orders of individuals (*plebeia, nobilis,* and *nobilior,)* Capellanus insists that "The order of clerics is also a sort of nobility, coming from God rather than from birth." Clerics are a higher order of nobility than those of mere "mundane" nobility. See page 117 of the translation by John J. Parry (New York: Columbia University Press, 1960).

23. Useful, if dated, overviews of the state of the question include Bernard S. Bachrach, "Some Observations on *The Medieval Nobility:* A Review Essay," *Medieval Prosopography* 1 (1980): 15–33, and T. N. Bisson, "Nobility and the Family in Medieval France: A Review Essay," *French Historical Studies* 16, No. 3 (Spring 1990), 597–613. Léopold Genicot has also written several useful bibliographical essays: "La noblesse médiévale: Pans de lumière et zones obscures," *Tijdschrift voor Geschiedenis* 93 (1980): 341–356; "Recent research on the Medieval Nobility," in *The Medieval Nobility,* ed. and trans. Timothy Reuter, volume 14 of *Europe in the Middle Ages, Selected Studies* (New York: North-Holland Publishing, 1979), 17–36 (first published as "Les recherches relatives à la noblesse médiévale," *Bulletin de l'Académie Royale de Belgique,* classe de lettres, 5e série, 1975, 45–68); and "La noblesse médiévale: Encore!" *Revue d'histoire ecclésiastique* 88 (1993): 173–201.

24. Bloch's work draws heavily upon that of Paul Guilhiermoz before him. The seminal texts for this debate are Paul Guilhiermoz, *Essai sur l'origine de la noblesse en France* (Paris: n.p., 1902) and Marc Bloch, *La Société féodale,* 2 vols (Paris, 1939–40), translated by L. A. Manyon as *Feudal Society* (Chicago: University of Chicago Press, 1961).

25. See, for instance, Georges Duby, *La société aux Xie et XIIe siècles dans la région mâconnais;* Gerd Tellenbach, "Zur Erforschung des hochmittelalterlichen Adels (9.–12. Jahrhundert)," in *XIIe Congrès international des sciences historiques.* Vol. 1. Vienna: 1965; Martin Heinzelmann, "La noblesse du haut moyen âge (VIIIe-Xie siècles)," *Le Moyen Âge* 83 (1977), 131–144; Theodore Evergates, "Nobles and Knights in Twelfth-Century France," in *Cultures of Power: Lordship, Status, and Process in Twelfth-Century Europe,* ed. Thomas N. Bisson (Philadelphia: University of Pennsylvania Press, 1995), 11–35; and Karl Ferdinand Werner, *Naissance de la Noblesse: L'essor des élites politiques en Europe* (Paris: Fayard, 1998), which pulls together much of his life's work on this subject.

26. For a consideration of theoretical approaches to this subject, see Stephen Rigby, "Approaches to Pre-Industrial Social Structure," in *Orders and Hierarchies in Late Medieval and Renaissance Europe,* ed. Jeffrey Denton (Toronto: University of Toronto Press, 1999), 6–25, and Georges Duby, "The Diffusion of Cultural Patterns in Feudal Society," *Past and Present* 39 (1968): 3–10.

27. An encyclopedic source on all elements of noble life in the twelfth and thirteenth centuries is Joachim Bumke's massive *Courtly Culture: Literature and Society in the High Middle Ages,* trans. Thomas Dunlap (Berkeley: University of California Press, 1991). Constance Bouchard's *Strong of Body, Brave and Noble* also provides fascinating descriptions of everyday noble life.

28. Bouchard, unlike Bloch, asserts that these "new" nobles were not new at all but found their origins in Carolingian noble families. See her "Origins of the French Nobility," *American Historical Review* Nos. 1–3 (1981): 501–532. See also Léopold Genicot, "La noblesse au moyen âge dans l'ancienne 'Francie'," *Annales* 17 (1962): 1–8; P. Bonenfant and G. Despy, "La Noblesse en Brabant au XIIe et XIIIe siècles," *Le*

Moyen Age 64 (1958): 27–66; and Jane Martindale, "The French Aristocracy in the Early Middle Ages: A Reappraisal," *Past and Present* 75 (1977): 5–45. David Herlihy adds to these findings with evidence showing the unexpected rates of social mobility—usually downward—of medieval society. See Herlihy, *Social History,* 625. Thomas Evergates has shown the difficulty of maintaining a noble lineage in the face of early deaths and lack of heirs. He concludes that a "broader conception of lineage that sees all noble-born children as entitled accords far better" with the evidence he uncovered. See his "Nobles and Knights," 28.

29. See, for instance, Georges Duby, *La société aux Xie et XIIe siècles dans la région mâconnais* and Dominique Barthélemy, "Qu'est-ce que le servage, en France, au Xie siècle?" *Revue historique* 582 (1992): 233–284.

30. *Convivio,* 193. The text used here is Dante Alighieri, *Il Convivio,* trans. Richard H. Lansing (New York: Garland, 1990). On Dante's social views, see especially Spencer Pearce, "Dante: Order, Justice, and the Society of Orders," in *Orders and Hierarchies,* 33–55.

31. *Convivio,* 197.

32. *Convivio,* 236.

33. *Convivio,* 206. See also 166, where Dante explains that simply being the son of a famous man does not make one famous, particularly if one does not deserve the honor.

34. Compare, for instance, the point of view of Andreas Capellanus's popular (if thoroughly ironic) *Art of Courtly Love.* This treatise, which ostensibly explores the social and romantic relations among commoners *(plebeia),* the simple nobility *(nobilis),* the high nobility *(nobilior),* and clerics, continually exalts excellence of character over high birth. "For since all of us human beings are derived originally from the same stock and all naturally claim the same ancestor, it was not beauty or care of the body or even abundance of possessions, but excellence of character alone which first made a distinction of nobility among men and led to the difference of class." See *The Art of Courtly Love,* 35, also 38 and 49.

35. *Convivio,* 167.

36. See, for instance, Antonio DiSalvo, "Ramon Lull and the Language of Chivalry," *Mystics Quarterly* 14 (December 1998): 197–206, where he examines Lull's insistence on the acquisition of nobility through virtuous conduct

37. See Paolo Cherchi's excellent study *Andreas and the Ambiguity of Courtly Love* (Toronto: University of Toronto Press, 1994), 32ff.

38. See, for instance, Karl Ferdinand Werner, "Adel: Fränkisches Reich, Imperium, Frankreich," in *Vom Frankenreich zur Entfaltung Deutschlands und Frankreichs* (Sigmaringen, 1984), 12.

39. Maurice Keen, *Chivalry,* esp. 144–146. Robert Lucas also asserts that nobility was essentially a closed caste in the century beginning around 1250 in his "Ennoblement in Late Medieval France," *Mediaeval Studies* 39 (1977): 239–260. See also Georges Duby, *The Chivalrous Society,* esp. 8 and 79; Joachim Bumke, *The Concept of Knighthood in the Middle Ages* (New York: AMS Press, 1982); and Joseph R. Strayer, *Feudalism* (Princeton: Princeton University Press, 1965). Elizabeth A. R. Brown calls for reconsidering the usefulness of the feudal model in "The Tyranny of a Construct: Feudalism and Historians of Medieval Europe," *American Historical Review* 79 (1974):

1063–1088. See also Alessandro Barbero, "Noblesse et chevalerie en France au Moyen Age: une réflexion," *Moyen Age* 97 (1991), 431–437. It is interesting to note that twenty years before Porete was executed, Philip the Fair granted the first charter of nobility of his reign. See Jan Rogozinski, "Ennoblement by the Crown and Social Stratification in France, 1285–1322: A Prosopographical Survey," in *Order and Innovation in The Middle Ages: Essays in Honor of Joseph R. Strayer*, ed. William C. Jordan et al. (Princeton: Princeton University Press, 1976), 273.

40. Basing his argument on nonliterary sources, Jean Flori has shown a large chasm between knighthood (profession of arms) and nobility (birthright) in both *L'essor de la chevalerie, Xie-XIIe siècles* (Paris, 1986) and "Chevalerie, noblesse et lutte de classes au Moyen Age," *Le Moyen Age* 94 (1988): 257–279. He argues that "chivalry" was a twelfth-century innovation that admitted of a range of interpretations rather than followed a single, well-defined standard. As Georges Duby remarks in "The Nobility in Eleventh- and Twelfth-Century Mâconnais," "The knighthood of the year 1000 was the former 'nobility' now supplied with a shape and a definition, crystallized around the profession of arms and the legal privileges brought with it." As quoted and translated in an excerpt by Fredric L. Cheyette in *Lordship and Community in Medieval Europe* (New York: Holt, Rinehart, and Winston, 1968), 149. See also two historiographical surveys: Tony Hunt, "The Emergence of the Knight in France and England, 1000–1200," *Forum for Modern Language Studies* 17 (1981): 93–114 and Giovanni Tabacco, "Su nobiltà e cavalleria nel medioevo: Un ritorno a Marc Bloch?" *Rivista storica italiana* 91 (1979): 5–25.

41. See Jan Rogozinski, "Ennoblement by the Crown."

42. This was a commonplace in romance literature. See Elspeth Kennedy, "The Quest for Identity and the Importance of Lineage in Thirteenth Century Prose Romance," in *The Ideals and Practice of Medieval Knighthood*, ed. Christopher Harper-Bill and Ruth Harvey (Dover, N. H.: Boydell Press, 1986), 70–86.

43. According to Bradford Broughton in the *Dictionary of Medieval Knighthood and Chivalry: Concepts and Terms* (New York: Greenwood Press, 1986), 344–345, to be noble in the Middle Ages was "to count among one's ancestors no one who has been subject to slavery," which was attested to perhaps most powerfully by the established name and residence of the noble family. As Constance Bouchard notes, peasants rarely had surnames before the fourteenth century. See *Strong of Body*, 70.

44. Duby, *The Chivalrous Society*, 102, and Bouchard, *Strong of Body*, 70.

45. See Genicot, "Recent Research on the Medieval Nobility," 17–36.

46. Thomas Evergates's "Nobles and Knights" notes that in France just before Porete's time, the nobility was considered largely a closed, elite, ruling class.

47. Genicot, "The Nobility in Medieval *Francia*: Community, Break, or Evolution?" in *Lordship and Community in Medieval Europe*, 131–132.

48. The term *amour courtois* was likely coined in 1883 by Gaston Paris, who identified it as a topos first appearing in twelfth-century French literature, known to contemporaries as *fin amor*. The utility of this term, once generally accepted, has recently been questioned. A fascinating study of courtly love is Paolo Cherchi's *Andreas and the Ambiguity of Courtly Love*. A more general introduction to the term can be found in *The Meaning of Courtly Love*, ed. F. X. Newman (Albany: State University of New York Press, 1968). See a recent reconsideration of the usefulness of this term in Don A.

Monson, "The Troubadour's Lady Reconsidered Again," *Speculum* 70 (1995): 255–274. C. Stephen Jaeger provides a compelling interpretation of the roots of chivalry in his *The Origins of Courtliness: Civilizing Trends and the Formation of Courtly Ideals, 939–1210.* (Philadelphia: University of Pennsylvania Press, 1985). In contrast, John F. Benton has remarked on page 120 of "Clio and Venus: A Historical View of Medieval Love" that the term has no specific content, is not originally medieval, and has "no useful meaning, and it not worth saving by redefinition." He calls for banning its use altogether. See this essay in *Culture, Power, and Personality in Medieval France,* ed. Thomas N. Bisson (London: Hambledon Press, 1991), 99–121. In a similar vein, see D. W. Robertson Jr.'s "The Concept of Courtly Love as an Impediment to the Understanding of Medieval Texts," in F. X. Newman's *Meaning of Courtly Love,* 1–18.

49. This, as Paolo Cherchi points out, is the courtly motif of *amor de lonh,* a topos inspired by the writings of Jaufre Rudel but reaching back to antiquity. Cherchi calls this love a "purely noetic" form of pure love. See Cherchi, *Andreas,* 60. Porete employs this most explicitly in the opening exempla, which are discussed in chapter 3.

50. The writings of Hrotsvit (also Hrotsvitha, Roswitha, or Rosvide) were "rediscovered" in 1501 by Conrad Celtes. The best of the few existing studies is Katharine M. Wilson, "The Saxon Canoness, Hrotsvit of Gandersheim," in *Medieval Women Writers,* ed. Katherine Wilson and trans. Gwendolyn Bryant (Athens: The University of Georgia Press, 1984). The most accessible volume of Hrotsvit's work can be found in *Hrotsvit of Gandersheim: A Florilegium of Her Works,* translated with introduction, notes, and essay by Katharine M. Wilson (Rochester, N.Y.: Boydell and Brewer, 1998). I will follow Wilson's translation here, referred to hereafter as *Hrotsvit.*

51. Hrotsvit repeatedly refers to individuals as she does to one Pelagius "of illustrious descent." See *Hrotsvit,* 33. She was likely of noble Saxon descent herself and she spent her life in a royal institution that accepted as recruits only those of noble descent. On this, see Peter Dronke, *Women Writers of the Middle Ages: A Critical Study of Texts from Perpetua (d. 203) to Marguerite Porete (d. 1310)* (New York: Cambridge University Press, 1985), 55–56. See Dronke's interpretation of Hrotsvit's place in the history of women's writing in *Women Writers,* 55–83.

52. Jan Ziolkowski, "Avatars of Ugliness in Medieval Literature," *Modern Language Review* LXXIX (1984): 1–20.

53. Moreover, the usage of this particular term leads to a simple confusion, as the title of "noble" can be merely honorific and, in that sense, "empty" of meaning about actual social status. That word (and associated modifiers) was part of the standard language of praise used in late antiquity, in early Christian martyrologies, and in hagiographical works from the early church through the later Middle Ages. In ancient Rome, for instance, a person who could lay claim to lineage and property was afforded honor and social capital, based on what Karen J. Torjesen calls "the collective honor of the past generations." See Karen J. Torjesen, "In Praise of Noble Women: Gender and Honor in Ascetic Texts," *Semeia* 57 (1992): 43.

54. *Hrotsvit,* 103. Similarly, she hails the founder of Gandersheim Abbey, Liudulf the Duke of Great Saxony, as "He, born of noble stock and illustrious parentage / Proved himself worthy of his great family / In his noble conduct and deeds of virtue," after which she adds that he was very handsome and surpassed his forefathers "in rank and in honors." Cf. 108.

55. *Hrotsvit*, 45.

56. *Hrotsvit*, 83–84.

57. *Hrotsvit*, 84.

58. References here will be to the *Corpus Christianorum: Continuatio Medievalis* edition of her *Scivias*, volumes 43 and 43A (Turnholt: Brepols, 1978), referred to herein as *Scivias* and accompanied by part, vision, and line numbers. Translations from her letters are from *The Letters of Hildegard of Bingen*, Volume 1, translated by Joseph L. Baird and Radd K. Erman (Oxford: Oxford University Press, 1994), hereinafter referred to as *Letters*.

59. Hildegard's theology certainly shaped her understanding of human capacities for sin and moral attainment. Julia Dietrich explores this issue in "The Visionary Rhetoric of Hildegard of Bingen," in *Listening to Their Voices: The Rhetorical Activities of Historical Women*, ed. Molly Meijer Wertheimer (Columbia, S. C.: University of South Carolina Press, 1997), 199–214.

60. Important general works on Hildegard include Sabina Flanagan, *Hildegard of Bingen, 1098–1179: A Visionary Life* (New York: Routledge, 1989) and Barbara Newman, *Sister of Wisdom: St. Hildegard's Theology of the Feminine* (Berkeley: University of California Press, 1987). Peter Dronke also provides an interesting essay in his *Women Writers of the Middle Ages*.

61. *Scivias*, part 1, vision 2, line 602 and part 1, vision 3, line 152. Hildegard equates moral goodness (e.g., virginity) with "nobility," a usage that was applied to her as well. Letter 40 reads that "Odo of Paris . . . sends his prayers and whatever else may be considered worthy of such saintliness and nobility of person to the lady Hildegard, the remarkable virgin of Christ." *Letters* 40, 109–110.

62. *Scivias*, part 3, vision 10, lines 560–564: "uirilem et nobilem uultum habens: quia ipse fortissimus leo *destruxit mortem*, nobili facie sine peccato scilicet uisibilis ueniens natus ex Virgine, pallidi tamen coloris exsistens: quoniam cum terrenis terrenum honorem non quaesiuit, sed humillimus, modicus et pauper in sancta humilitate apparuit."

63. This parallel is explicit throughout her work, both for Jesus Christ and for the Virgin Mary.

64. Cf. *Scivias*, part 3, vision 9, line 417 as well as her reference to the "noble" edifice of the church in Letter 18. In *Scivias*, part 2, vision 6, she describes the strengthening of the early church through the noble virtue of priestly chastity.

65. *Scivias*, part 3, vision 10, line 880: "in se nobilissimos lapides." Peter Dronke notes in *Women Writers* (161) that Hildegard learned this motif "from the second-century poetic treatise *Pastor Hermas*."

66. *Scivias*, part 1, vision 5, lines 109–11: "quia magnitudinem diuinorum praeceptorum suscipiens munitionem et defensionem nobilis et electae ciuitatis praenuntiauit . . ."

67. *Scivias*, part 3, vision 6, lines 254–255: "Exuo uetus testamentum et induo nobilem Filium Dei cum iustitiis eius in sanctitate et ueritate."

68. See, for instance *Scivias*, part 2, vision 1, line 385 and part 3, vision 3, line 111.

69. An emphasis on social ranking is found throughout Hildegard's *Scivias*, as well as in her many letters. Her insistence on placing people in proper place in a social

hierarchy allowed her to control the "quality" of novitiates in her convent and to place herself in positions of importance. Yet these ideas also proved divisive, as described below.

70. *Letters* 52r, 129.

71. An important examination of Hildegard's social ideas is Sabina Flanagan, " 'For God Distinguishes the People of Earth as in Heaven': Hildegard of Bingen's Social Ideas," *The Journal of Religious History* 22, No. 1 (February 1998): 14–34. Flanagan shows that Hildegard's apparent elitism is based on a nuanced view of the social world as she experiences it.

72. On this see Flanagan, "For God Distinguishes," 32–34.

73. *Scivias*, part 2, vision 6.

74. *Scivias*, part 2, vision 3, lines 396–399: "Sed quia Adam praeceptum meum transgressus est, sine lege cum genere suo fuit usque ad tempus illud quod nobilitatem Filii mei praenuntiauit." See also part 2, vision 3 and part 3, vision 6.

75. *Letters* 38r, 107. Cf *Scivias*, part 2, vision 3, lines 588–593: "Quoniam ut fur qui nobilissimam et pretiosissimam pecuniam regis furatur, furtiue subintrat, sic tortuosa conceptio in ingluuie diaboli deceptiose surrepsit, ita quod ipse dilectissimam gemmam sanctae innocentiae et castitatis in quibus Spiritus sanctus habitat nequiter abstraxit, unde nunc in santificatione ablutionis emundanda est."

76. *Scivias*, part 2, vision 7, lines 225–228: "hunc qui illud infideliter subsequitur, de noblissimo opere digiti Dei et ab omni honore et a beatitudine supernae uisionis abicit, atque eum exulem faciens a uiuente fructu et a radice iustae arboris abscidit."

77. *Scivias*, part 3, vision 8, lines 679–681: "orta scilicent de radice Iesse, id est ab illo qui quasi fundamentum erat regalis prolis de qua eadem illibata Mater nata processit."

78. *Scivias*, part 3, vision 8, lines 116–118: "Formato autem homine—o, o, o—nobilissimum granum et—o, o, o—dulcissimum germen, Filius Dei propter hominem in fine temporum natus est homo."

79. See, for instance, *Scivias*, part 3, vision 2, lines 205–213 and part 2, vision 6, lines 304–307.

80. Hildegard recognized that some nobles would use their status unfairly to intimidate others. In Letter 16r, she warns the Archbishop of Cologne against terrorizing subordinates "with awesome words stemming from your office as bishop and the aristocracy of your birth . . ."

81. *Scivias*, part 2, vision 5, line 287–8: "passionem Filii mei propter supernam dilectionem, quam in corde suo fideliter habuit, imitando."

82. *Scivias*, part 3, vision 8, lines 648–650: "quatenus sole fulgentiora Christi membra capiti suo in lucidis acquisitionibus nobilissime perfecta coniungantur."

83. See, for instance, *Scivias*, part 3, vision 6, line 176: "O fortissime et nobilissime Deus, attende!"

84. *Scivias*, part 3, vision 6, lines 443–446: "Quia in saecularibus causis sunt nobiles et nobiliores, sunt et famulantes atque obsequentes. In spiritualibus uero sacramentis sunt praecellentes et superiores, sunt et oboedientes atque corripientes."

85. *Scivias*, part 3, vision 6, lines 400–409: "Sic uidelicet quod Deus abstulit nimietatem et iactantiam illam quod populus populum non honoraret, ita quod unusquisque

faceret quod sibi placeret, si hoc Deus inaestimabili sapientia consilii sui non prostrauisset, sed ipse discreuit populum inter populum, minorem scilicet cum ministratione oboedentiae maiori suo subiacere, maiorem uero in omni utilitatis regimine sollerter et deuote minori subuenire, sicut etiam in accensione Spiritus sancti datum est Iacob per patrem suum quod esset dominus fratrum suorum, ut supra dictum est."

86. Hildegard is referring here to Apoc. 7.3. (38). Her use of "sealed" might refer to the clergy to distinguish them from those who are simply baptized.

87. Letter 52, 127–128. Sabina Flanagan, in "For God Distinguishes," points out that the Riesenkodex version of this passage differs from that found in the Stuttgart manuscript. See Flanagan, fn. 6.

88. Letter 52r, 129.

89. See also her reference to the noble virgin who is surrounded by those like her in *Scivias*, part 2, vision 5.

90. Dronke, *Women Writers*, 200.

92. These letters have been the subject of some debate among scholars. I will present one response here, since it is pertinent to the scandal that surrounded Porete. Peter Dronke points out that while Tengswich "succinctly showed that the myth of classes was not compatible with *primitiva ecclesia*, Hildegard's analogies rest on the fallacious assumption that humanity comprises separate species." According to Dronke, "Here [Hildegard] has deluded herself into thinking that the political myth of the ruling class of her day is a divine truth: deluded in the sense that she imagines this myth to be consistent with the teachings of Christ, about which in principle she has no doubts whatever, but which she had not consulted on this point. She is here in full accord with the dominant social beliefs of her class and time (just as, from the twelfth century to the fourteenth, we know of only the fewest people who believed, or argued, that crusading was an activity irreconcilable with Christ's teachings)." See Dronke, *Women Writers*, 166–167.

92. See Emilie Zum Brunn and Georgette Epiney-Burgard, *Women Mystics in Medieval Europe*, trans. Sheila Hughes (New York: Paragon, 1989), 6.

93. For more general considerations of Bernard as a mystic and theologian, see Etienne Gilson, *The Mystical Theology of St. Bernard* (London: Sheed & Ward, 1940) and chapter 5 of Bernard McGinn, *The Growth of Mysticism: Gregory the Great through the 12ᵗʰ Century* (New York: Crossroad, 1994), 158–224. I will here use the translations in *Bernard of Clairvaux: Selected Works*, trans. G. R. Evans (New York: Paulist Press, 1987), hereinafter referred to as *Bernard*, as well as *The Letters of St. Bernard of Clairvaux*, trans. Bruno Scott James (Kalamazoo, Mich.: Cistercian Publications, 1998), hereinafter referred to as *Letters*. Bernard's full works can be found in *Sancti Bernardi Opera*, ed. J. Leclercq, C. H. Talbot, and H. M. Rochais, 6 vol. (1957–).

94. Jean Leclercq, *Monks and Love in Twelfth-Century France: Psycho-Historical Essays* (Oxford: Clarendon, 1979), 92.

95. Bernard, *Letters* 273, 346. Bernard, letters 155, 223, and 356, 433, and 412, 481.

96. *Sancti Bernardi opera, Sententiae*, 3: 8b:234: "In natura enim, nullus inferior, nullus superior; nullus anterior, nullus posterior; nemo nobilis, nemo ignobilis; sed omnes aequales nos ipsa natura semper creat."

97. *Sancti Bernardi opera, De laude nova militiae*, 4: 3:220

98. Bernard, *Letters* 443, 508.

99. Bernard, *Letters*.

100. Bernard, *Letters* 105, 152.

101. Bernard, *Letters* 111, 168.

102. Bernard, *Letters* 112, 169. See this theme reiterated on the occcasion of a youth's conversion in *Letters* 278, 449.

103. Bernard, *Letters* 24, 58–59.

104. Bernard, *Letters* 116, 174–175.

105. Ibid.

106. Ibid.

107. *Sancti Bernardi opera, De laude nova militiae*, 4: 3:220: "Persona inter eos minime accipitur: defertur meliori, non nobiliori."

108. Porete's *Mirror* seems to follow de Lorris's more idealistic approach to love; the erotic *Brautmystik* of de Meun is absent in her work.

109. Here I will use my own translations and will cite the original text as given by Ernest Langlois, *Le Roman de la Rose, par Guillaume de Lorris et Jean de Meun, publiè d'après les manuscrits*, 5 vols. (Paris: Librairie Ancienne Honoré Champion, 1914–24). References will be to line number throughout. The body of critical work on the text, beginning in the mid-nineteenth century and continuing unabated to the present day, is dauntingly vast. Heather Arden provides a succinct and useful overview of the critical history of the text in *The Romance of the Rose* (Boston: Twayne, 1987), 87–102. See also her extensive annotated bibliography: *The Romance of the Rose: An Annotated Bibliography* (New York: Garland, 1993).

110. See, for instance, line 18978.

111. Lines 16816–19.

112. Lines 16730–36 and 16740–46: "Quant il trés beaus fist cet beau monde, / Don il portait en sa pensee / La bele fourme pourpensee / Toujourz en pardurableté / Ainz qu'ele eüst dehors esté, / Car la prist il son essemplaire, / E quanque li fu necessaire; . . . Con nule rien dehors n'eüst; / Car de neient fist tout saillir / Cil en cui riens ne peut faillir; / N'onc riens ne l'esmut a ce faire, / Fors sa volenté debonaire, / Large, courteise, senz envie, / Qui fontaine est de toute vie."

113. See, for example, lines 19061–62; lines 19087–88: lines 19107–08; lines 19091–92; and lines 19215–16.

114. Line 19053: "C'est uns petiz mondes nouveaus"; and 18597–18602: "Par mei naissent semblable e nu / Fort e feible, gros e menu; / Touz les met en equalité / Quant a l'estat d'humanité; / Fortune i met le remanant . . ."

115. Lines 19240–48.

116. Lines 17464–72: "Si la veit Deus des maintenant / Ausinc con s'el fust avenue; / E de toujourz l'a il veüe / Par demontrance veritable / A son miroer pardurable, / Que nus, fors lui, ne set polir, / Senz riens a franc vouleir tolir. / Cil miroers c'est il meïsmes, / De cui comencement preïsmes."

117. Lines 17551–52.

118. See for instance lines 17725–26.

119. See lines 17868–71.

120. Lines 1941–54: "Senz faille il i a poine e fais / En moi servir, mais je te fais / Enor mout grant, e si doiz estre / Mout liez don tu as si bon maistre / Et seignor de si haut renon, / Qu'Amors porte le gonfanon / De Cortoisie e la baniere; / Si est de si bone maniere, / Si douz, si frans et si gentis / Que, quiconques est ententis / A li servir e enorer, / Dedenz lui ne puet demorer / Vilanie ne mesprison / Ne nule mauvaise aprison."

121. Lines 2026–27: "E te metrai en haut degré, / Se mauvaistié ne le te tost . . ."

122. Lines 1985–88: "Li cuers est vostres, non pas miens, / Car il covient, soit maus ou biens, / Que il face vostre plaisir: / Nus ne vos en puet dessaisir; . . ."

123. Line 4208: "Je ne m'en sai plus entremetre."

124. Lines 1920–23.

125. See for instance lines 18635–76.

126. See, for instance, lines 18677–78 and lines 18731–39.

127. Lines 18615–17: "nus n'est gentis / S'il n'est a vertuz ententis, / Ne n'est vilains fors pour ses vices."

128. Lines 18619–34: "Noblece vient de bon courage, / Car gentillece de lignage / N'est pas gentillece qui vaille / Par quei bonté de cueur i faille; / Par quei deit estre en li paranz, / La proëce de ses parenz, / Qui la gentillece conquistrent / Par les travauz que granz i mistrent. / E quant dou siecle trespasserent, / Toutes leur vertuz emporterent, / E laissierent aus eirs l'aveir, / Qui plus ne porent d'aus aveir. / L'aveir ont, riens plus n'i a leur, / Ne gentillece ne valeur, / S'il ne font tant que gentill seient / Par sens ou par vertuz qu'il aient." The Old French *cuer/coer/cor* could mean either heart or courage.

129. See lines 18755–59. Compare this to the similar perspective presented in the fourth treatise of Dante's *Convivio*.

130. Lines 19779–82: "Souviegne vous de voz bons peres / E de voz ancienes meres; / Selonc leur faiz les voz ligniez; / Gardez que vous ne forligniez." See also lines 19701–02 and 19753–54, as well as line 19792.

131. See the examples of kings Arthur and Alexander as archetypes of the good noble soul in lines 6588–89 and 12664–75. These two kings are outstanding above all in their embodiment of the courtly virtue of *largesse*. Porete employs this motif in the opening of her book, here presented at the outset of chapter 3.

132. Lines 2216–17: "Onques on rien d'amer ne sot / Cui il n'abelist a doner."

133. See lines 5243–48.

134. See, for instance, lines 4983–84 and lines 5071–72.

135. Except perhaps where it is shown to be the one test of true friendship. Note the extended diatribe against mendicant and other orders professing "poverty" as a rule of life in lines 11003–12380. Inborn nobility was a courtly, not a clerical, motif. Clerical emphasis was placed on earning merit and nobility.

136. Lines 4924–27.

137. Lines 5082–90: "Il bee a beivre toute Seine, / Don ja tant beivre ne pourra / Que toujourz plus en demourra. / C'est la destrece, c'est l'ardure, / C'est l'angoisse qui toujourz dure, / C'est la douleur, c'est la bataille / Qui li detrenche la couraille / E le destreint en tel defaut: / Quant plus acquiert, plus li defaut."

138. Lines 5330–38 and 5341–42: 'Trop as meilleur chose e plus chiere: / Touz les biens que dedenz toi senz, / E que si bien les quenois enz, / Qui te demeurent senz

cessier, / Si qu'il ne te peuent laissier / Pour faire a autre autel servise: / Cil bien sont tien a dreite guise. / Es autres biens, qui sont forain, / N'as tu vaillant un viez lorain; . . . / *Car sachiez que toutes voz choses / Sont en vous meïsmes encloses; . . .*" Emphasis mine.

139. For this claim, see Wilhelm Breuer, "Mystik als alternative Lebensform. Das 37. Strophische Gedicht der Suster Hadewijch," *Zeitschrift für deutsche Philologie* 103 (1984): 110. See also Tanis M. Guest, *Some Aspects of Hadewijch's Poetic Form in the 'Strofische Gedichten'* (The Hague: Martinus Nijhoff, 1975), 166–167 where the author goes so far as to note that "Love here seems to be regarded not merely as noble, but as of such high nobility that Hadewijch may do homage to her without endangering her own rank; surely such emphasis suggests one conscious of her own high birth."

140. I will cite here from the most accessible English translation of her works: *Hadewijch: The Complete Works*, trans. Mother Columba Hart (New York: Paulist, 1980), hereinafter referred to as *Hadewijch*, followed by an indication of passage type (e.g., Stanzaic poem), section number, and page number in that volume.

141. Tanis M. Guest, *Some Aspects*. See also Marieke van Baest, *Poetry of Hadewijch*, Studies in Spirituality Series, Supplement 3 (Leuven: Peeters, 1998) and Saskia Murk-Jansen, *The Measure of Mystic Thought: A Study of Hadewijch's Mengeldicten* (Göppingen, 1991).

142. *Hadewijch*, Letter 6.191, 60.

143. Luke 15:11–20.

144. *Hadewijch*, Letter 18.63, 86.

145. Hadewijch, Letter 6.344, 63.

146. *Hadewijch*, Stanzaic 22.2, 186. See also, for example, Stanzaic 4.9, 139.

147. *Hadewijch*, Letter 10.26, 67.

148. *Hadewijch*, Stanzaic 14.2, 162. See also Stanzaic 20.7, 181.

149. *Hadewijch*, Letter 4, 1, 53.

150. *Hadewijch*, Letter 6.361, 63.

151. *Hadewijch*, 19.46, 90.

152. *Hadewijch*, Stanzaic 4.7, 138.

153. *Hadewijch*, 18.51, 86.

154. *Hadewijch*, Stanzaic 43. 8, 252.

155. *Hadewijch*, Letter 2.150, 51.

156. *Hadewijch*, Letter 18.13, 85.

157. *Hadewijch*, Stanzaic 32.7, 220.

158. *Hadewijch*, Letter 18.130, 87.

159. *Hadewijch*, Stanzaic 12.6, 159.

160. *Hadewijch*, Stanzaic 17.13, 174–75.

161. *Hadewijch*, Letter 18.112, 87.

162. See, for instance, *Hadewijch*, Stanzaic 9 and 11.

163. *Hadewijch*, Stanzaic 9.3, 150.

164. *Hadewijch*, Stanzaic 9.4, 150.

165. *Hadewijch*, Letter 18.1, 85, cf. also 19.27, 89.

166. *Hadewijch*, Letter 6.86, 58.

167. *Hadewijch*, Letter 10.1, 66.

168. *Hadewijch*, Letter 1.8, 47.

169. R. Howard Bloch, *Etymologies and Genealogies: A Literary Anthropology of the French Middle Ages* (Chicago: University of Chicago Press, 1983), 33.

170. Ibid., 82.

Chapter Two

THE "BEGUINE CLERGERESSE" AND HER *MIRROR*

1. The sources pertaining to Marguerite's inquisitorial trial have been assembled by Paul Verdeyen in "Le Proces d'inquisition contre Marguerite Porete et Guiard de Cressonessart (1309–1310)," *Revue d'histoire ecclesiastique* 81 (1986): 47–94. Verdeyen insists that Marguerite was brought to trial primarily because of unfortunate political circumstances determined by the suppression of the Templars. Other sources pertaining to the trial include Paul Fredericq, ed., *Corpus documentorum inquisitionis haereticae pravitatis neerlandicae*, 2 volumes (Ghent: The Hague, 1889–1906); *Les grandes chroniques de France*, Vol. VIII, ed. J. Viard (Paris: n.p., 1934), 273; as well as Henry C. Lea, *A History of the Inquisition in the Middle Ages*, Vol. II (New York: n.p., 1887).

2. This supporter was Guiard de Cressonessart, a beghard, who recanted and was given a life sentence for his support of Marguerite's heresy. See Robert E. Lerner, "An Angel of Philadelphia in the Reign of Philip the Fair: The Case of Guiard of Cressonessart," in *Order and Innovation in the Middle Ages: Essays in Honor of Joseph R. Strayer*, ed. William C. Jordan, Bruce McNab, and Teofilo F. Ruiz (Princeton: Princeton University Press, 1976), 343–364 and 529–540. For a report of Marguerite's conduct during her questioning, see the Appendix.

3. These events cannot be divorced from their political contexts, although those are not central to this investigation. The king of France, Philip IV (the Fair), had developed a system of centralized authority that relied heavily on the alliance of papal and secular authorities in his affairs. By doing so, the king may have accomplished much politically by executing Marguerite, such as showing support for the mendicant orders in their suppression of the Knights Templar (with whom Porete was thought associated) and thus portraying himself as a defender of the faith.

4. For the historical background of the text and its circulation, see Kurt Ruh, "Le *Miroir des Simples Ames* de Marguerite Porete," *Verbum et Signum* 2 (1975): 365–387 and Ruh's "Le miroir des simples âmes' der Marguerite Porete," in *Kleine Schriften*, II, ed. Volker Mertens (Berlin: De Gruyter, 1984), 212–236. Also good on the complexities of the manuscripts is Povl Skarup, "La langue du *Miroir des simples âmes* attribué à Marguerite Porete," in *Studia Neophilologica* 60 (1988): 231–236. Edmund Colledge and Romana Guarnieri explore a redaction of the work in "The Glosses by 'M.N.' and Richard Methley to 'The Mirror of Simple Souls'," *Archivio Italiano per la Storia della Pietà* 5 (1968): 357–382. On English reception of the work, see Michael G. Sargent, "Le *Mirouer des simples âmes* and the English Mystical Tradition," in *Abendländische Mystik im Mittelalter*, ed. Kurt Ruh (Stuttgart: Metzler, 1986): 443–465. Nicholas Watson provides a brief but substantive account of the history of the manuscripts in "Melting into God the English Way: Deification in the Middle English Version of Marguerite Porete's *Mirouer des simples âmes anienties*," in *Prophets Abroad: The*

Reception of Continental Holy Women in Late-Medieval England, ed. Rosalynn Voaden (Boston: D.S. Brewer, 1996), 20–27. See also Elisabeth Gössman, "Ein Wissen, das Frauen nicht zukommt'. Die Geschichte der 1310 hingerichteten Mystikerin Marguerite Porete," *Orientierung* 52.4 (Feb. 28, 1988): 40–43, as well as Ulrich Heid, "Studien zu Marguerite Pòrete und ihrem Miroir des simple âmes," in *Religiöse Frauenbewegung und mystische Frömmigkeit im Mittelalter*, ed. Peter Dinzelbacher and Dieter R. Bauer, *Archiv für Kulturgeschichte* 28 (Vienna: Böhlau, 1988), 185–214.

5. See Franz-Josef Schweitzer, "Von Marguerite von Porete (d. 1310) bis Mme. Guyon (d. 1717): Frauenmystik im Konflikt mit der Kirche," in *Frauenmystik in Mittelalter*, ed. P. Dinzelbacher, and D. Bauer (Stuttgart: Schwabenverlag, 1985).

6. See Bernard McGinn, *Flowering of Mysticism: Men & Women in the New Mysticism—1200–1350*. Vol. 3 of *The Presence of God: A History of Christian Mysticism* NY: Crossroad, 1998, 141–142 and 199.

7. See, for instance, E. W. McDonnell, *The Beguines and Beghards in Medieval Culture, with Special Emphasis on Belgian Scene* (New Brunswick, N. J.: Rutgers University Press, 1954), 523, as well as chapters 2 and 3 of Robert E. Lerner, *The Heresy of the Free Spirit in the Later Middle Ages* (Berkeley, University of California Press, 1972). The two sides of the debate are perhaps best represented in the following two works. For Marguerite as heretic, see Edmund Colledge, "Liberty of Spirit: 'The Mirror of Simple Souls'," in *Theology of Renewal*, ed. L. K. Shook (Dorval, Quebec: Palm Publishers, 1968). For Marguerite as orthodox, see J. Orcibal, "Le 'Miroir des simples âmes' et la «secte» du Libre Esprit," *Revue de l'Histoire des Religions* 1 (July-September 1969): 35–60. More conciliatory are Eleanor McLaughlin, "The Heresy of the Free Spirit and Late Medieval Mysticism," *Medievalia et Humanistica* 4 (1973): 37–54 and Winfried Corduan, "The Gospel According to Margaret," *Journal of the Evangelical Theological Society* 35/4 (December 1992): 515–530, both of whom recognize the official heretical aspects of Porete's *Mirror* but focus on her contributions. A very good overview is provided by Franz-Josef Schweitzer in "Von Marguerite von Porete (d. 1310) bis Mme. Guyon (d. 1717): Frauenmystik im Konflikt mit der Kirche."

8. On Porete's apophatic and paradoxical language, see, for instance, Michael Sells, "The Pseudo-Woman and the Meister," in *Meister Eckhart and the Beguine Mystics*, ed. Bernard McGinn (New York: Continuum, 1994), 114–146; Sells's *Mystical Languages of Unsaying* (Chicago: University of Chicago Press, 1994), especially chapters 5 and 7; Amy Hollywood, *The Soul as Virgin Wife: Mechtild of Magdeburg, Marguerite Porete, and Meister Eckhart* (Notre Dame: University of Notre Dame Press, 1995), chapters 4 and 7; and Zum Brunn, "Self, Not-Self, and the Ultimate in Marguerite Porete's *Mirror of Annihilated Souls.*" For Porete in light of postmodern throught, see Maria Lichtman, "Negative Theology in Marguerite Porete and Jacques Derrida," *Christianity and Literature* 47, No. 2 (Winter 1998): 212–227 and Thomas A. Carlson, "The Poverty and Poetry of Indiscretion: Negative Theology and Negative Authority in Contemporary and Historical Perspective," same journal and volume: 167–193. Fascinating interpretations can be found in Luisa Muraro, "La Filosofia mistica di Margherita Porete: Il concetto di ragione," *Rivista di spiritualità e politica* 13 (June 1993): 67–80; Michela Pereira, "Fra Raison e Amour: il Miroir des simples âmes di Margherita Porete," in *Filosofia Donne Filosofia*, ed. M. Forcina et al. (Lecce: Milella, 1994); and Catherine Randall, "Person, Place, Perception: A Proposal for the Reading of Porete's *Miroir des âmes simples et anéanties*," *Journal of Medieval and Renaissance Studies* 25, No. 2 (Spring 1995): 229–244.

9. In this category I include the following (limited) sample: Catherine Müller, *Marguerite Porete et Marguerite d'Oingt de l'autre côté du miroir* (New York: Lang, 1999) and her "Writing as Mirror in the Work of Marguerite Porete," *Mystics Quarterly* (under the name Bothe) 20, No. 3 (1994): 105–112; Geneviève Souillac, "Charisme et prophétisme féminins: Marguerite Porete et le *Miroir des simples âmes,*" *Australian Journal of French Studies* 35, No. 3 (December 1998): 261–278; as well as two works by Maria Lichtman: "Marguerite Porete and Meister Eckhart: The *Mirror for Simple Souls* Mirrored," pp. 65–86, in *Meister Eckhart and the Beguine Mystics,* and "Marguerite Porete's *Mirror for Simple Souls:* Inverted Reflections of Self, Society, and God," *Studia Mystica* 16, No. 1 (1995): 4–30. For a more general view, see also Béatrice Acklin Zimmerman, "Mittelalterliche Frauenmystik: 'Feministische Theologie des Mittelalters' als Korrektiv an der herrschenden Theologie?" in *Frauen zwischen Anpassung und Widerstand: Beiträge der 5. Schweizerischen Historikerinnentagung,* ed. Regula Ludi et al. (Zürich: Chronos, 1990), 13–21. Other recent studies include Marie Bertho, *Le Miroir des âmes simples et anéanties de Marguerite Porète. Une vie blessée d'amour* (Paris: Larousse, 1993); Giovanna Fozzer, " 'Parfaicte franchise n'a nul pourquoi.' Notizia sullo 'Specchio delle Anime Semplici' di Margherita Porete," *Revista di Ascetica e Mistica* (1991): 375–395; and Louise Gnädinger, "Margareta Porete, eine Begine," in *Der Spiegel der Einfachen Seelen* (Zürich: Artemis, 1987), 215–239.

10. McGinn, *Flowering of Mysticism,* 12.

11. *Les Grandes Chroniques de France* refer to Porete as a "beguine clergeresse" (as quoted in Verdeyen, "Le Procès d'inquisition," 91, cf. 60; Guillaume de Nangis and Géraud de Frachet both label her a "pseudo-mulier" (Verdeyen 87 and 90).

12. On this see JoAnn McNamara, "*De Quibusdam Mulieribus:* Reading Women's History from Hostile Sources," in *Medieval Women and the Sources of Medieval History,* ed. Joel Rosenthal (Athens: University of Georgia Press, 1990), 237–258.

13. See E. W. McDonnell, *Beguines and Beghards,* 367.

14. On women in medieval society generally, see, for instance, Joel Rosenthal, *Medieval Women and the Sources of Medieval History;* and Brenda Bolton, "Vitae Matrum: A Further Aspect of the *Frauenfrage,*" in *Medieval Women,* ed. Derek Baker (Oxford: Blackwell, 1977). On women mystics and visionaries more specifically, see especially Caroline Walker Bynum's groundbreaking *Holy Feast and Holy Fast: The Religious Significance of Food to Medieval Women* (Berkeley: University of California Press, 1987); Ulrike Wiethaus, ed., *Maps of Flesh and Light: The Religious Experience of Women Mystics* (Syracuse: Syracuse University Press, 1993); Emilie Zum Brunn and Georgette Epiney-Burgard, *Women Mystics in Medieval Europe;* Peter Dinzelbacher, "Europäische Frauenmysik des Mittelalters: Ein überblick," in *Frauenmystik im Mittelalter* (Stuttgart: Schwabenverlag, 1985), 11–23.

15. For the classic history of this *Frauenbewegung,* see Herbert Grundmann's masterful work that was recently translated into English by Steven Rowan as *Religious Movements in the Middle Ages* (Notre Dame: University of Notre Dame Press, 1995). R. W. Southern gives a brief and useful history of the Beguines in *Western Society and the Church in the Middle Ages.* Until recently, the most extensive (yet poorly organized) work in English was E. W. McDonnell's *The Beguines and Beghards in Medieval Culture.* Other general studies include Dennis Devlin, "Feminine Lay Piety in the High Middle Ages: The Beguines," in *Medieval Religious Women,* ed. John A. Nichols and Lillian

Thomas Shank, Volume 1 (Kalamazoo: Cistercian Publications, 1984), 185–196; Alcantara Mens, "Les béguines et béghards dans le cadre urban de la culture mediévale," *Le Moyen Age* 64 (1958): 305–315; Dennis Devlin, "Feminine Lay Piety in the High Middle Ages: The Beguines;" and Penelope Galloway, " 'Discreet and Devout Maidens': Women's Involvement in Beguine Communities in Northern France, 1200–1500," in *Medieval Women in Their Communities*, ed. Diane Watt (Toronto: University of Toronto Press, 1997), 92–115. Also useful is Walter Simons, "The Beguine Movement in the Southern Low Countries: A Reassessment," *Bulletin de l'Institut Historique Belge de Rome* 59 (1990): 63–105. One interesting study involves the influence of art on beguine communities: Joanna Ziegler, "Reality as Imitation: The Role of Religious Imagery Among the Beguines of the Low Countries," in *Maps of Flesh and Light*, ed. Ulrike Wiethaus (Syracuse: Syracuse University Press, 1993), 112–126.

16. See especially Robert E. Lerner, *The Heresy of the Free Spirit in the Later Middle Ages*, and Franz-Josef Schweitzer, "Von Marguerite von Porete (d. 1310) bis Mme. Guyon (d. 1717): Frauenmystik im Konflict mit der Kirche." On heresy in the Middle Ages, see especially Malcolm Lambert, *Medieval Heresy: Popular Movements from the Gregorian Reform to the Reformation*, Second Edition (Cambridge, Mass.: Blackwell, 1992), xi, which defines heresy as "whatever the papacy explicitly or implicitly condemned during the period." See also Gordon Leff's two volume *Heresy in the Later Middle Ages: The Relation of Heterodoxy to Dissent c. 1250–1450* (New York: Barnes and Noble, 1967); R. I. Moore, *The Formation of a Persecuting Society: Power and Deviance in Western Europe 950–1250* (New York: Blackwell, 1987) as well as Moore's *Origins of European Dissent* (New York: St. Martin's Press, 1977); and two works by Jeffrey Burton Russell: *Dissent and Reform in the Early Middle Ages* (Berkeley: University of California Press, 1965) and *Dissent and Order in the Middle Ages: The Search for Legitimate Authority* (New York: Twayne, 1992).

17. The origin of the term *beguine* is unclear. Scholars have suggested the following etymologies: after Lambert Le Begue (d. 1177), an early leader; after the grey, undyed woolen habit worn by these women; after the German "beggen"; or after St. Begga. The most commonly accepted etymology derives from the label "Albigensians," a heretical sect. On this last, see J. van Mierlo, "Béguinages," in *Dictionnaire d'histoire et de géographie ecclesiastique*, 7:457–473, as well as Van Mierlo's "Béguins, béguines, béguinages," in *Dictionnaire de spiritualité* (Paris: Beauchesne, 1937), 1:1341–52; Alcantara Mens, "Beghine, Begardi, Beghinaggi," in the *Dizionario degli Instituti di Perfezione* 1:1165–80; and Robert E. Lerner, "Beguines and Beghards," in the *Dictionary of the Middle Ages* 2:157–163.

18. One example of the "old school" of thought is McDonnell's *Beguines and Beghards*, 120. For the other side of the debate, see especially Carol Neel, "Origins of the Beguines," *Signs* 13, No. 2 (1989)": 333. Joseph Greven first proposed possible parallels in *Anfänge der Beginen* (Münster: Aschendorff, 1912), 112. This idea is perhaps most ably adopted by Brigitte Degler-Spengler in "Die religiöse Frauenbewegung des Mittelalters: Konversen - Nonnen - Beginen," *Rottenburger Jahrbuch für Kirchengeschichte* 3 (1984): 75–88. Other sources include Joanna E. Ziegler, "Secular Canonesses as Antecedents of the Beguines in the Low Countries: An Introduction to Some Older Views," *Studies in Medieval and Renaissance History* 13 (Old Series Vol. 23, 1992); Simone Roisin, "L'efflorescence Cistercienne et le Courant Féminin de Piété au

XIIIe Siècle," *Revue d'Histoire Ecclésiastique* 39 (1943): 342–378; and Brenda Bolton, "Some Thirteenth-Century Women in the Low Countries: A Special Case?" *Nederlands Archief voor Kerkgeschiedenis* 61, No. 1 (1981): 7–29.

19. Robert Arbrissel founded Fontevrault and Norbert of Xanten founded Premontré, both in the twelfth century and both with the aim of providing alternatives for religious women to live in community with some degree of autonomy. On these these movements, see especially essays in John A. Nichols and Lillian Thomas Shank, *Medieval Religious Women* Vol. 1: *Distant Echoes*. Cistercian Studies Series 71 Kalamazoo: Cistercian Publications, 1984; Brenda Bolton, "*Vitae Matrum:* A Further Aspect of the *Frauenfrage*"; and Bolton, "*Mulieres Sanctae,*" in *Women in Medieval Society,* ed. Susan Mosher Stuard (Philadelphia: University of Pennsylvania Press, 1976), 141–158.

20. See Janet I. Summers's exploration of this aspect of the Cistercian sisterhood in "The Violent Shall Take it by Force: The First Century of Cistercian Nuns, 1125–1228" (University of Chicago Dissertation, 1986) and John B. Freed, "Urban Development and the *Cura Monialium* in the Thirteenth Century," *Viator* 3 (1972): 311–327. Other interesting studies include Penelope Johnson, *Equal in Monastic Profession: Religious Women in Medieval France* (Chicago: University of Chicago Press, 1991) and Michael Parisse, *Les religieuses en France au XIIIe siècle* (Nancy: Presses Universitaires de Nancy, 1985).

21. E. W. McDonnell and other scholars have adopted the schema proposed by L. J. M. Philippen, which posits a four-stage development toward increasing claustration. See L. J. M. Philippen, *De Begijnhoven, Oorsprong, geschiedenis, inrichting* (Antwerp: n.p., 1918), 40–126, adopted later by McDonnell in *Beguines and Beghards*, 157; Little in *Religious Poverty*, 130; and Southern in *Western Society*, 324–325. The basic pattern runs as follows: 1) small groups of women or individuals living uncloistered religious lives, often ecstatic and living free of community; 2) after 1215, semireligious associations of disciplined beguines, often with obedience to superior, working within the community; 3) nearly enclosed communities, frequently following a rule; and, 4) communities formed into autonomous parishes with residing clerics. This particular arrangement of stages seems to imply at least one trend: the increasing hostility of authorities toward individual aspirations to spiritual life, answered by increasing claustration.

22. For a sampling of local studies, see Bernard Delmaire, "Les beguines dans le Nord de la France au premièr siècle de leur histoire (vers 1230-vers 1350)," in *Les religieuses en France au XIIIe siècle*, ed. Michel Parisse, 121–162; Dayton Phillips, "Beguines in Medieval Strassburg: A Study of the Social Aspect of Beguine Life" (Stanford dissertation, 1941); Frederic Stein, "The Religious Women of Cologne, 1120–1320" (Yale University dissertation, 1977); and the much older "Les Béguines de Paris" by Léon Le Grand, in *Mémoires de la Societé de l'Histoire de Paris et de l'Ile de France* 20 (Paris: Champion, 1893): 295–357. Jean-Claude Schmitt's analysis of the disintegration of the Strasbourg Beguines (*Mort d'une hérésie: L'Église et les clercs face aux béguines et aux béghards du Rhin supérieur du xiv.e au xv.e siècle* [Paris: École des Hautes Études en Sciences Sociales, 1978]) should be read with caution. See Robert E. Lerner's review of Schmitt's work in *Speculum* 54 (1979): 842–844.

23. See one "Rule for Beguines," published in Karl Christ, ed., "*La regle des fins amans.* Eine Beginenregal aus dem Ende des XIII Jahrhunderts," in *Festschrift für*

K. Voretzsch (Halle: n.p., 1927): 192–206, as well as Léon Le Grand's "Les Béguines de Paris."

24. Gilbert of Tournai, in *Collectio de scandalis ecclesiae*, ed. Ignaz von Döllinger, *Beitrage zur politischen, kirchlichen, und Culturegeschichte*, vol. 3 (Vienna: Manz, 1882), 197, as cited in Carol Neel, "The Origins of the Beguines," 323.

25. Richard Kieckhefer, *Repression of Heresy in Medieval Germany* (Philadephia: University of Pennsylvania Press, 1979), 21.

26. See Robert E. Lerner's refutation of this attribution in *The Heresy of the Free Spirit in the Later Middle Ages*, 71. See also Romana Guarnieri, "Frères du Libre Esprit," in *Dictionnaire de Spiritualité* 5:1241–1268 (Paris: Beauchesne, 1964). For an older view of the Free Spirit movement, see Norman Cohn, *The Pursuit of the Millenium* (New York: Oxford University Press, 1970).

27. See the text of the *Ad nostrum* decree in the Appendix.

28. See Lerner, *Heresy of the Free Spirit*, 145.

29. One such example is Robert D. Cottrell, "Marguerite Porete's *Le Mirouer des simples âmes* and the Problematics of the Written Word," *Medieval Perspectives* 1, No. 1 (1986): 151.

30. The text is in Fredericq, *Corpus documentorum*, 2:63–64: "primus talis est: 'Quod anima adnichilata dat licentiam virtutibus nec est amplius in earum servitute, quia non habet eas quoad usum, sed virtutues obediunt ad nutum.' Item decimus quintus articulus est: 'Quod talis anima non curat de consolacionibus Dei nec de donis ejus, nec debet curare nec potest, qui tota intenta est circa Deum, et sic impediretur ejus intentio circa Deum'." I will capitalize "Virtue" throughout this work when it is used in this sense.

31. Excerpts of these decrees can be found in the Appendix. On the Vienne decrees, see Jacqueline Tarrant, "The Clementine Decrees on the Beguines: Conciliar and Papal Versions," *Archivum Historiae Pontificae* 12 (1974): 300–308.

32. On the *vita apostolica* specifically, see M.-D. Chenu, *Nature, Man and Society*, 202–269; R. W. Southern, *Western Society and the Church in the Middle Ages*; Brenda Bolton, "*Paupertas Christi*: Old Wealth and New Poverty in the Twelfth Century," in *Renaissance and Renewal in Christian History*, ed. Derek Baker, Studies in Church History, Volume 14 (Oxford: Blackwell, 1977): 95–104; and Giles Constable, *The Reformation of the Twelfth Century* (Cambridge: Cambridge University Press, 1996).

33. Among several fine sources on this topic, see N. Bérion, "La prédication au béguinage de Paris pendant l'année liturgique 1272–3," *Recherches Augustiniennes* 13 (1978): 105–229.

34. In 1957 Jean Leclercq published *The Love of Learning and the Desire for God: A Study of Monastic Culture* as a corrective to the received view that all medieval theology was scholastic in form and content. Leclercq identified a distinctly monastic theology by examining a corpus of nonscholastic texts to show their distinct literary character and their contemplative, mystical orientation. His work has led the way toward establishing a tripartite division of medieval sources: scholastic, monastic, and vernacular. See *The Love of Learning*, trans. Catharine Misrahi (New York: Fordham University Press, 1988).

35. On this see McGinn, "The Abyss of Love," in *The Joy of Learning and the Love of God: Essays in Honor of Jean Leclercq*, Cistercian Studies Series 160, ed. E. Rozanne Elder (Kalamazoo: Cistercian Publications, 1995): 95–120.

36. The first critical edition of the text appeared in *Archivio Italiano per la Storia della Pieta*, ed. Romana Guarnieri (Rome: n.p., 1965): 513–635. Here, references will be to the critical edition published as *Corpus Christianorum: Continuatio Medievalis*, Volume 69, ed. R. Guarnieri and Paul Verdeyen (Turnholt, Belgium: Brepols, 1986), which gives the Guarnieri text juxtaposed to Verdeyen's edition of the Latin (hereinafter referred to as CCCM). The best English translation is by Ellen Babinsky in the Classics of Western Spirituality Series (New York: Paulist Press, 1993). There are two other partial and unreliable English translations (Downside, 1927, and Crossroads, 1981). I will follow Babinsky's translation with modifications where noted. The bibliography of this work provides a list of other translations.

37. Chapter 96, lines 20–24, CCCM, 268: "Et ainsi escripsit ceste mendiant creature ce que vous oez; et voult que ses proesmes trouvassent Dieu en elle, par escrips et par paroles. C'est a dire et a entendre, qu'elle vouloit que ses proesmes fussent parfaitement ainsi comme elle les diviseroit."

38. Chapter 52, lines 3–5, CCCM, 152: "O tres bien nee, dit Amour a ceste precieuse marguerite, bien soiez vous entree ou seul franc manoir, ouquel nul ne entre, se il n'est de vostre lygnage, sans bastardise." NB: The Old French "marguerite" means "pearl"; Marguerite is surely playing with her name in this passage. See also the parable of the pearl in Mark 13:45–46.

39. The use of this word throughout the book indicates that it was likely intended to be read aloud, if not enacted.

40. Chapter 1, lines 6–7, CCCM, 10: "et peut estre adnientifs par vraie amour . . ."

41. Chapter 68, lines 16–18, CCCM, 192: "qu'il m'esconvient pour leur rudesse taire et celer mon langage, lequel j'ay aprins es secrez de la court secrete . . ."

42. See chapters 69 and 103.

43. Chapter 69, lines 35–40, CCCM, 194 and 196: "Telz gens, dit ceste Ame, que je appelle asnes, quierent Dieu es creatures, es monstiers par aourer, en paradis creez, en paroles d'ommes, et es escriptures. Hee, sans faille, dit ceste Ame, en telx gens n'est pas nez Benjamin, car Rachel y vit; et il convient mourir Rachel en la naissance Benjamin, ne jusques ad ce que Rachel soit morte ne peut Benjamin naistre." See Richard of St. Victor's *The Twelve Patriarchs* (especially chapters XIV, XVIII, LXXIII, LXXIV, and LXXXII) for a parallel use of the Rachel and Benjamin motif. For Richard, Rachel (Reason) must die to allow Benjamin (contemplation) to live. *Richard of St. Victor. The Twelve Patriarchs. Mystical Ark. Book Three of the Trinity*, trans. Grover Zinn (New York: Paulist Press, 1979).

44. Chapter 12, lines 29–30, CCCM, 50: "Vous prenez la paille et laissez le grain . . ." and cf. chapter 17.

45. Chapter 140, lines 26–29, CCCM, 407: "Sed bene dixit quod non consulebat quod multi eum viderent. Quia, ut dicebat, possent dimittere uitam suam ad quam sunt uocati, aspirando ad istam ad quam forte numquam peruenirent." This passage survives only in Latin and Middle English translations.

46. Prologue and chapters 11, 13, 14, 16.

47. Chapter 9, lines 31–33, CCCM, 34: "maistres de sens de nature, ne tous les maistres d'escripture, ne tous ceulx qui demourent en amour de l'obedience des Vertuz, ne l'entendent et ne l'entendront, la ou il fait a entendre."

48. Chapter 9, line 35, CCCM, 34: "celluy qui Fine Amour demande."

49. Chapter 7, lines 9–11, CCCM, 26: "car l'Escripture ne le prent, - ne sens d'omme ne le comprent, - ne travail de creature ne desert l'entendre-ne comprendre."

50. Watson, "Melting into God the English Way," 28.

51. Nicholas Watson, "Misrepresenting the Untranslatable: Marguerite Porete and the *Mirouer des simples ames*," *New Comparison* 12 (1991): 124–125. Watson goes on to claim (29–30) that Porete only comes to understand her own message in the last part of the book.

52. Watson, "Melting into God," 30.

53. Throughout this exploration of Marguerite's text, the words of Soul or Love will be understood as the words of those who understand and convey Marguerite's message, with sensitivity to context and ironic overtones. Amy Hollywood's *Soul as Virgin Wife* is very useful in this context.

54. Chapter 21, lines 44–45, CCCM, 82: "Je suis Dieu, dit Amour, car Amour est Dieu, et Dieu est Amour . . ." cf. Jn. 4:16. Cf. also Augustine's *De Trinitate* 8.7.19 (PL 42:957).

55. Chapter 21, lines 45–47, CCCM, 82: "et ceste Ame *est* Dieu par condicion d'amour . . . et ceste Ame l'est par droicture d'amour." My emphasis.

56. The text attests to a tension between two attitudes related to authorship: Porete seems to cast herself as one of the characters in this drama (specifically, "Soul") while also professing divine inspiration, understood as the work of the Holy Spirit within the soul (Love). At times she divests herself of all claims to human authorship, yet part of her message is predicated on her wretched humanity, as will be explained in the following chapters.

57. Chapter 69, lines 22–25, CCCM, 194: "que a celluy seul, dit ceste Ame, qui est si fort qu'il ne peut jamais mourir, duquel la doctrine n'est mie escripte ne par oeuvres d'exemples ne par doctrine de hommes, car le don de luy ne peut on donner fourme."

58. Chapter 13, lines 33–43, CCCM, 56: "Car mon entendement et mon sens et tout mon conseil est pour le mieulx que je sçay conseiller, que on desire despiz, pouvreté, et toutes manieres de tribulacions, et messes et sermons, et jeunes et oraisons, et que on ait paour de toutes manieres d'amour, quelles qu'elles soient, pour les perilz qui y pevent estre, et que on desire souverainement paradis, et que on ait paour d'enfer, et que on refuse toutes manieres de honneurs, et les choses temporelles, et toutes aises, en ostant a nature ce que elle demande, fors sans plus ce sans quoy elle ne pouroit vivre, a l'exemple de la souffrance et passion de nostre seigneur Jhesuchrist."

59. Chapter 13, lines 57–65 and 67–68, CCCM, 58: "que telles Ames, lesquelles Fine Amour demaine, ont aussi cher honte comme honneur, et honneur comme honte, et pouvreté comme richisse, et richesse comme pouvreté, et tourment de Dieu et de ses creatures comme confort de Dieu et de ses creatures, et estre amee comme hayé, et hayé comme amee, et en enfer comme en paradis, et en paradis comme en enfer, et petit estat comme grant, et grant estat comme petit, pour elles ne pour leur personnes . . . car telles Ames n'ont point de voulenté, fors ce que Dieu veult en elles . . ."

60. Chapter 55, lines 10–17, CCCM, 158 and 160: "Les ungs sont qui du tout mortiffient le corps, en faisant o<e>uvres de charité; et ont si grant plaisance en leurs oeuvres qu'ilz n'ont point cognoissance qu'il soit nul meilleur estre que l'estre de oeu-

vres de vertuz et mort de martire, en desirer de perseverer en ce par l'aide d'oraison remplie de prieres, en multipliance de \<bo\>n vouloir, tousjours pour la t\<en\>ue que telles gens ont ad ce, et que ce soit le meilleur de tous les estres qui pevent estre."

61. See chapters 16 and 24.

62. Chapter 57, lines 5–6, CCCM, 164: "qui sont sers et marchans; mais ilz font plus saigement que les periz ne font."

63. Chapter 74, line 18, CCCM, 208: "Martha, ce sachez, est trop empeschee, et ne le scet mie."

64. Chapter 86, lines 52–53, CCCM, 246: "Marie n'a que ung seul esperit en elle, c'est assavoir une seule entente, qui luy fait avoir paix . . ."

65. Chapter 85, lines 20–21, CCCM, 242: "Ceste, qui telle est, ne quiert plus Dieu par penitance ne par sacrement nul de Saincte Eglise . . ."

66. Chapter 134, lines 3–5, CCCM, 394: "Telle Ame, dit Amour, est en la plus grant parfection de l'estre, . . . quant Saincte Eglise ne prent point d'exemple en sa vie."

67. See chapter 43.

68. Chapter 1, lines 2–5, CCCM, 10: "Ame de Dieu touchee . . . est montee par divines graces . . . ouquel estat l'Ame a le plain de sa parfection par divine fruiction ou païs de vie."

69. Marguerite rarely explains this final stage, remarking only that nobody knows how to speak of it.

70. See chapters 60 and 62.

71. See chapters 21 and 118.

72. Chapter 63, line 24, CCCM, 185: "uiuunt uita diuina." This passage is extant in Latin only.

73. Chapter 61, lines 2–7, CCCM, 176: "ilz sont sept estaz, de plus hault entendement assez les ungs que les aultres, sans comparaison; car d'autant comme il y a a dire d'une goute d'eaue envers toute la mer, qui est moult grant, autant a il a dire du premier estat de grace envers le second, et ainsi des aultres, sans comparaison."

74. Chapter 58, lines 6–7, CCCM, 168: "Ceste Ame . . . qui est ytelle, n'est perie ne marrie. Ainçoys est en esbauts ou cincquiesme estat avec son amant."

75. Chapters 3 and 8. Annihilated souls continue to practice the virtues, although they have no need of them. This doctrine will be examined in more detail in chapter 6.

76. Chapter 60, lines 8–10, CCCM, 172 and 174: "qu'il ne demoure en elle ne coulour ne savour ne odour de chose nulle que Dieu deffende en la Loy . . ."

77. Chapter 118, lines 32–34, CCCM, 318 and 320: "en oeuvre de mortiffiement de nature, en desprisant richesses, delices et honnours, pour accomplir la parfection du conseil de l'Euvangile, dont Jhesucrist est l'exemple."

78. Chapter 69, lines 7–12, CCCM, 192: "et Jhesucrist l'exaussa de son propre corps, qui voioit la bestialité de ceulx qui en ce travail se sauveroient, et pource leur convenoit il certaineté. Et Jhesucrist, qui ne les vouloit mie perdre, si les a de luy mesmes affiez par sa mort, et par ses Euuangiles, et par ses escritures, la ou gens de labour se radressent."

79. See chapter 94.

80. Chapter 78, lines 39–42, CCCM, 220: "ilz se travailloient chacun jour avec eulx d'amplir la parfection des apostres par estudie de voulenté, si ne seroient ilz mie descombrez d'eulx (nul ne s'i attende), ne d'eulx mesmes, c'est assavoir de corps et de ame."

81. Chapter 124, lines 44–46 and 49, CCCM, 352 and 354: "Mais quant le sage laboureur a sa terre fouyé, et houee, et mis le froment dedans, toute sa puissance n'y peut plus aider . . . et ce povez vous veoir par sens de nature."

82. Chapter 124, lines 52–56, CCCM, 354: "Comment ce grain pourrist, et comment il revient, dont il porte fruit au centiesme par grant multipliance, ne scet nul fors Dieu, lequel tout seul fait ceste oeuvre, aprés ce que le laboureur a fait ce qui est en luy, et non point plus tost." Mk. 4:3–8.

83. Chapter 124, lines 32–33, CCCM, 352: "adonc se repousa Marie sans faire oeuvre d'elle, et Dieu fist la sienne gentilment en Marie, pour Marie, sans Marie."

84. See McGinn, "The Abyss of Love." McGinn notes seventeen references in the *Mirror* to "abyss".

85. Chapter 56, lines 21–22, CCCM, 162: "Qui pouvre seigneur sert longuement, pouvre loyer en atend et petite souldee."

86. Chapter 118, lines 51–53, CCCM, 320: "car nulle mort ne luy seroit martire, fors l'abstinance de l'oeuvre que elle ayme, qui est le delit de sa plaisance et la vie de voulenté, qui de ce se nourrist."

87. Chapter 118, line 76–79, CCCM, 322: "que il n'est point de plus haulte vie, que de ce avoir, dont elle a seigneurie; car Amour l'a de ses delices si grandement resasié, que elle ne croit point que Dieu ait plus grant don a donner a ame ycy bas, . . ."

88. Chapter 118, lines 103–105, CCCM, 324: "espant la divine Bonté par devant ung espandement ravissable du mouvement de divine Lumiere . . ."

89. The text is in Fredericq, *Corpus documentorum*, 2:63: "primus talis est: 'Quod anima adnichilata dat licentiam virtutibus nec est amplius in earum servitute, quia non habet eas quoad usum, sed virtutues obediunt ad nutum.' "

90. See, for instance, chapter 94.

91. Chapter 80, lines 6–10, CCCM, 226: "Ceste Ame a apparceu par divine lumiere l'estre du pays dont elle doit estre, et a passé la mer, pour succer la mouelle du hault cedre. Car nul ne prent ne n'ataint a ceste mouelle, s'il ne passe la haulte mer, et se il ne noye sa voulenté es ondes d'icelle." Ezechiel 17:3. "Estre" refers to a state or condition of the soul.

92. See chapter 91.

93. Chapter 3, lines 5–8, CCCM, 16: "Dyeu, qui nous commende que nous l'aymons de tout nostre cueur, de toute nostre ame et de toute nostre vertu; et nous mesmes ainsi comme nous devons; et nos proesmes ainsi comme nous mesmes."

94. Chapter 3, lines 18–19, CCCM, 16: "Ces commendemens sont à tous de necessité de salut: de maindre vie ne peut nul avoir grace." See chapter 8 in which Reason insists that the Virtues enable one to live in the life of grace and that whoever possesses them cannot be deceived. Reason wonders who would be crazy enough to abandon such assistance. Those who follow Reason are hard pressed to give up the certainty of grace in this life of obedience.

95. See chapter 21.

96. Chapter 8, lines 17–19, CCCM, 28: "Quant elles demourerent en l'amour et en l'obedience de vous, dame Raison, et aussi des aultres Vertuz; et tant y ont demouré, qu'elles sons devenues franches."

97. Chapter 5, lines 6–14, CCCM, 18 and 20: ".i. une ame / .ii. qui se saulve de foy sans oeuvres, / .iii. qui soit seulement en amour, / .iv. qui ne face rien pour Dieu, / .v. qui ne laisse rien a faire pour Dieu, / .vi. a qui l'en ne puisse rien aprandre, / .vii. a qui l'en ne puisse rien toullir / .viii. ne donner, / .ix. et qui n'ait point de voulenté."

98. Chapter 3, lines 21–24, CCCM, 16: " 'une chouse te fault faire, se tu vieulx estre parfait. C'est: va et vens toutes les chouses que tu as et les donne aux pouvres, et puis si m'ensuis, et tu auras tresor es cyelx.' "

99. Chapter 4, lines 3–19, CCCM, 18: "Charité n'obbeist a chose creee fors que a Amour. Charité n'a point de propre, et pouse qu'elle ait aucune chose, si ne dit elle point qu'il soit a luy. Charité laisse sa propre besoigne et vait faire celle d'autruy. Charité ne demande point de loyer a nulle creature, pour quelque bien ou plaisir qu'elle face. Charité n'a honte, ne paour, ne mesaise; elle est si droite qu'elle ne peut flechir pour quelque chose qui luy adviengne. Charité ne fait ne ne tient compte de chose qui soit dessoubz le soleil; tout le monde n'est que son relief et son demourant. Charité donne a tous ce qu'elle a vaillant, ne elle mesmes ne se retient elle mie, et avec ce promet souvent ce qu'elle n'a mie, par la grant largesse d'elle, en esperance que qui plus donne plus luy demoure. Charité est si saige marchande, qu'elle gaigne partout, la ou les autres perdent, et se eschappe des lyens ou les autres se lient, et ainsi elle a grant multipliance de ce qui plaist a Amour."

100. Chapter 49, lines 11–12, CCCM, 146: "grans arrerages de moultipliances d'amour."

101. Note that Meister Eckhart makes this distinction clear in Sermon 52. Eckhart distinguishes "external" poverty, manifested in practices for love of Christ, and "inward" poverty of wanting, knowing, and having nothing.

102. Chapter 134, lines 6–7, CCCM, 394: "et si est *oultre* l'oeuvre de Pouvreté et *dessus* l'oeuvre de Charité." Emphasis mine.

103. Chapter 16, lines 30–33, CCCM, 66: "n'a mesaise de peché qu'elle fist oncques, ne de souffrance que Dieu ait souffert pour elle, ne des pechez ne des mesaises esquieulx ses proesmes demourent."

104. Chapter 118, lines 133–135, CCCM, 326: "que elle n'y trouve ne commencement ne mesure ne fin, fors une abysme abysmee sans fons." On this see McGinn, "The Abyss of Love."

105. Chapter 118, lines 143–144, CCCM, 328: "C'est profondesse d'umilité qui la siet en la chaere, qui regne sans orgueil."

106. Chapter 53, lines 3–4, CCCM, 154: "O tres doulce abysmee, dit Raison, ou fons sans fons d'entiere humilité . . ."

107. Chapter 74, lines 9–10, CCCM, 206: "Car elle se siet ou fons de la vallee, dont elle voit le mont de la montaigne . . ." Porete tells us that certain souls can attain the top of the mountain, which is spared wind and rain; that is, it is spared the shame and honor and fear human beings experience in the earthly places below the summit. This is fully in keeping with Porete's esoteric doctrine of annihilation.

108. Chapter 5, lines 3–4, CCCM, 18: "Or y a il une autre vie, que nous appellons paix de charité en vie adnientie."

109. Chapter 44, lines 8–10, CCCM, 136: "c'est une grant guerre et perilleuse! . . . on doit bien telle vie d'estude appeller languour et vie de guerre."

110. Chapter 5, lines 10–25, CCCM, 24: "Vertuz, je prens congé de vous a tousjours, / Je en auray le cueur plus franc et plus gay; / Voustre service est troup coustant, bien le sçay. / Je mis ung temps mon cueur en vous, sans nulle dessevree; / Vous savez que je estoie a vous trestoute habandonnee; / Je estoie adonc serve de vous, or en suis delivree. / J'avoie en vous tout mon cueur mis, bien le sçay, / Dont je vescu ung tandis en grant esmay. / Souffert en ay maint gref tourment, mainte paine enduree; / Merveilles est quant nullement en suis vive eschappee; / Mais puis que ainsi est, ne me chault: je suis de vous sevree, / Dont je mercie le Dieu d'en hault; bonne m'est la journee. / De voz dangers partie sui, ou je esté en maint ennuy. / Oncques mais franche ne fui, fors de vous dessevree; / Partie suis de voz dangers, en paix suis demouree."

111. Chapter 66, lines 12–15, CCCM, 188: "elle print leçon a vostre escole par desirer des oeuvres des Vertuz. Or est elle maintenant si entree et seurmontee en divine leçon, que elle commence a lire la ou vous prenez vostre fin."

112. Chapter 36, lines 4–6, CCCM, 116: "car la noblesse de la courtoysie de mon espoux ne me daigneroit plus lesser en vostre servaige . . ."

113. Chapter 56, lines 6–7, CCCM, 162: "nous le tendrions a bougre et a mauvais crestien."

114. See chapter 77, lines 28–29, and chapter 78, lines 20–21.

115. Chapter 134, line 8, CCCM, 394: "qu'elle ne pourroit entendre leur langage."

116. See chapter 7.

117. See chapter 19.

118. Chapter 17, lines 39–41, CCCM, 72: "faulte d'innocence et enconbrier de paix, en laquelle ceste Ame se repouse de toutes choses."

119. Chapter 17, lines 41–50, CCCM, 72: "Qui est celluy qui doie faire conscience de prendre son besoing des .iiij. elemens, comme de la clarté du ciel, de la chalour du feu, de la rousee de l'eaue, et de la terre qui nous soustient? Nous prenons le service de ces .iiij. elemens en toutes les manieres que Nature en a besoing, sans reprouche de Raison; lesquieulx elemens gracieulx sont faiz de Dieu, comme aultres choses; et aussi telles Ames usent de toutes choses faictes et creees, dont Nature a besoing, en autelle paix de cueur, comme elles font de la terre sur quoy elles marchent."

120. Chapter 43, lines 48–50, CCCM, 134: "Et ainsi que nous avons en nous, dit le Saint Esperit, ce que nous avons, par nature divine, et ceste Ame l'a de nous en elle par droicture d'amour."

121. Chapter 108, lines 23–24, CCCM, 292: "fust ores aussi riche comme Dieu est."

122. Chapter 116, line 5.

123. Chapter 11, lines 58–59.

124. Chapter 43, lines 40–41 and 47–48, CCCM, 134: "sans vouloir nul guerdon en ciel ne en terre, mais seulement pour nostre seule voulenté . . . par droitture d'amour."

125. Chapter 79, lines 14–15, CCCM, 222: "Car qui tout donne, tout a, et aultrement non."

126. Chapter 52, lines 38–44, CCCM, 154: "Ceste Ame lesse les mors ensevelir les mors et les marriz o<e>uvrer des vertuz, et se repose du moins ou plus, mais elle <se> sert de toutes choses. Ce plus luy monstre son nient, nu, sans couverture; lequel nu luy monstre le Tout Puissant, par la bonté de divine droicture. Ces regars la font parfonde, large, haultaine et seure, car ilz la font tousdis nue, toute et nulle, tant comme ilz <l'>ont en leur tenue."

127. Irving Singer, *The Nature of Love*, Volume 2 (Courtly and Romantic) (Chicago: University of Chicago Press, 1984).

128. Chapter 24, lines 11–12.

129. On the use of "Mirror" in medieval titles and imagery, see Rita Mary Bradley, "Backgrounds of the Title 'Speculum' in Medieval Literature," *Speculum* 29 (1954): 100–115, and Herbert Grabes, *The Mutable Glass: Mirror Imagery in Titles and Texts of the Middle Ages and English Renaissance* (Cambridge: Cambridge University Press, 1982). Catherine Müller also discusses these issues in her *Marguerite Porete et Marguerite d'Oingt*.

Chapter Three

GOD, THE SOUL, AND NO-THINGNESS

1. Chapter 1, lines 16–44, CCCM, 10, 12, and 14: "*Exemple:* Il fut ung temps une damoyselle, fille de roy, de grant cueur et de noblesse et aussi de noble courage; et demouroit en estrange païs. Si advint que celle damoiselle oit parler de la grant courtoisie et noblece du roy Alixandre, et tantost sa volenté l'ama, pour la grant renommee de sa gentillesse. Mais si loing estoit ceste damoiselle de ce grant seigneur, ouquel elle avoit mis son amour d'elle mesmes, car veoir ne avoir ne le povoit; par quoy en elle mesmes souvent estoit desconfortee, car nulle amour fors que ceste cy ne luy souffisoit. Et quant elle vit que *ceste amour loingtaigne, qui luy estoit si prouchaine ou dedans d'elle,* estoit si loing dehors, elle se pensa que elle conforteroit sa masaise par ymaginacion d'aucune figure de son amy dont elle estoit souvent au cueur navree. Adonc fist elle paindre ung ymage qui representoit la semblance du roy, qu'elle amoit, au plus pres qu'elle peut de la presentacion dont elle l'amoit et en l'affection de l'amour dont elle estoit sourprinse, et par le moyen de ceste ymage avec ses autres usages songa le roy mesmes.

"*L'Ame:* Semblablement vrayement, dit l'Ame qui ce livre fist escrire, au tel vous dis je: je oÿ parler d'ung roy de grant puissance, qui estoit par courtoisie et par tres grant courtoisie de noblece et largesse ung noble Alixandre; *mais si loing estoit de moy et moy de luy, que je ne savoie prandre confort de moy mesmes,* et pour moy souvenir de lui il me donna ce livre qui represente en aucuns usages l'amour de lui mesmes. Mais non obstant que j'aye son ymage, n'est il pas que je ne soie en estrange païs et loing du palais ouquel les tres nobles amis de ce seigneur demourent, qui sont tous purs, affinés et franchix par les dons de ce roy, avec lequel ilz demourent." I here depart from Babinsky in explicitly differentiating the two tales.

2. This is the courtly motif of *amor de loigne*, which Porete uses to describe part of the soul's relationship to God or "Farnear."

3. This "exemplum" is a version of the popular tale of Candace and Alexander the Great. It must be noted that in the context of the whole *Mirror* this King does not seem to refer to Jesus Christ, who is the traditional lover in allegorical courtly tales. This King is God Himself. Yet this "king" has been variously interpreted in modern scholarship. Robert Cottrell, for instance, claims the king is Jesus Christ, "wholly immanent, a product, in fact, of her own love." See Cottrell, "Marguerite Porete's *Le Mirouer des simples ames* and the Problematics of the Written Word."

4. See a fascinating study by C. Stephen Jaeger, *Ennobling Love: In Search of a Lost Sensibility* (Philadelphia: University of Pennsylvania Press, 1999), in which Jaeger shows that the love of kings was a spiritualized love that responded to the virtue, charisma, and the saintliness of the beloved. This book also includes a good appendix of translated texts. See also Stephen Kaplowitt, *The Ennobling Power of Love in the Medieval German Lyric* (Chapel Hill: University of North Carolina Press, 1986), in which the author argues based on a study of "the entire body of lyric poetry from the beginning through the works of Walther von der Vogelweide" (167), that the theme of ennobling love in German lyric poetry has been exaggerated in scholarship.

5. Recent work on Porete's theology includes Paul Mommaers, "La Transformation d'Amour Selon Marguerite Porete" *Ons geestelijk erf* 65 (1991): 89–107; Louise Gnädinger, "Die Lehre der Margareta Porete von der Selbst- und Gotteserkenntnis. Eine Annäherung," in *Denkmodelle von Frauen im Mittelalter*, ed. Béatrice Acklin-Zimmermann (Fribourg, Switzerland: Universitätsverlag, 1994), 125–148; and Alois Haas's brief "Marguerite Porete," in *Geistliches Mittelalter*, ed. Alois Haas (Fribourg, Switzerland: Universitätsverlag, 1984), 407–409. Some older views include Charles V. Langlois, "Marguerite Porete," *Revue Historique* 54 (1894): 295–299.

6. A parallel can be drawn here to the though of Eriugena, for whom the Fall of humanity manifested the ultimate reach of God in *emanatio*, the farthest procession into the greatest multiplicity, and the key to the return of all things to their causes. But because this "metaphysical" Fall involves dispersion and ignorance, it threatens to disrupt the return and has deleterious consequences for embodied humanity. Most importantly, however, the Fall for Eriugena is not a "historical" event. The Paradise to which Christians strive to return is rather a purely intelligible future reality. Adam "fell" through ignorance of his true nature. Christ, as the universal Reason, restores humanity's knowledge and enables the return of all of *natura* to its causes. Porete stands in this line of thought. Adam's Fall was more a lesson about willfulness and ignorance than an ineluctable fact of human history. For Porete, every human being struggles against its willful, blind nature, at first with the aid of grace and then, for noble souls, on their own.

7. Chapter 11, lines 114–115, CCCM, 44: "Car aultre Dieu n'est que celluy dont on ne peut rien cognoistre parfaictement. Car celluy tout seul est mon Dieu, de qui l'en ne scet mot dire . . ."

8. Chapter 52, line 34, CCCM, 154: "C'est mon tout et mon meilleur"; and chapter 16, lines 51–2, CCCM, 68: "Dieu est bon sans comprennement."

9. Chapter 11, lines 77–79, CCCM, 42: "Ceste Ame ayme mieulx ce qui est en Dieu, qui oncques ne fut donné ne ja donné ne sera, qu'elle ne fait ce qu'elle a et qu'elle auroit . . ."

10. As Michael Sells notes in "The Pseudo-Woman and the Meister," Porete uses apophatic language to "keep both the deity and the human from falling into categories

of being, substance, and entification." See Sells in *Meister Eckhart and the Beguine Mystics*, 114. On apophatic thought more generally, Denys Turner, "The Art of Unknowing: Negative Theology in Late Medieval Mysticism," *Modern Theology* 14, No. 4 (October 1998): 474–488.

11. Chapter 30, line 6–7 as well as chapter 16, line 28.

12. Chapter 69, lines 51–53, CCCM, 196: "Je le trouve . . . partout, et la est il. Il est une Deité, ung seul Dieu en trois Personnes, et cil Dieu est partout tout; la dit elle, le trouve je."

13. Chapter 15, lines 39–40, CCCM, 64: "pour Sainte Eglise repaistre et nourir et soustenir." Porete is here referring to Holy Church the Little, the earthly church.

14. Chapter 30, lines 8–13, CCCM, 98: "Ce scet elle, dit Amour, car la le trouve elle tousjours, c'est assavoir en toutes choses; car il convient a trouver la chose la ou elle est, et pource qu'il est tout partout, le trouve ceste Ame partout. Et pource luy sont toutes choses convenables, car elle ne trouve chose nulle part que elle n'y trouve Dieu."

15. It follows, as will become clear in the discussion of God's creation of humanity, that God does not create evil. Evil is the result of a perverse choice of the free will of God's creatures.

16. The Old French has "Loingprès" and the Latin "longe propinquum."

17. Chapter 135, lines 8–19, CCCM, 397: "Longinquum huius est magis propinquum, quia cognoscit magis de prope illud longinquum in seipso, quod continue facit eam esse in unione uelle eius, absque taedio alterius rei quae eueniat ei. *Totum est sibi unum sine propter quid, et est nulla in tali uno.* Tunc nichil habet plus facere de Deo quam Deus de ea. Quare? Quia Ipse est et ipsa non est. Ipsa nichil plus retinuit in nichilo sui ipsius, quia istud est sibi satis, scilicet quod Ipse est et ipsa non est. Tunc est omnibus rebus nuda, quia ipsa est sine esse, ubi ipsa erat, antequam esset. Et ideo habet a Deo id quod habet; *et est id quod Deus est per mutationem amoris,* in illo puncto in quo erat, antequam a Dei bonitate fluxisset." Emphasis mine. This passage survives in Latin and Middle English only; however, the chapter title is preserved in Old French.

18. Chapter 98, lines 7–12, CCCM, 272: "qui est enfermé et seellé en la secrete closture de la plus haulte purté de telle excellente Ame; laquelle clousture nul ne peut ouvrir, ne desseeler, ne clorre quant elle est ouverte, se le gentil Loingprés de tres loing et de tres pres ne la clost et ouvre, lequel tout seul en a les clefz, ne aultre ne les porte, ne aussi porter ne les pourroit."

19. Chapter 58, lines 13–14. William of St. Thierry uses similar "spark" language in his *Golden Epistle*, 2.257.

20. See chapter 61.

21. Those who claim that Porete taught pantheism seem to neglect this rather prominent aspect of her thought.

22. Chapter 101, lines 32–34, CCCM, 278: "Il le voult de sa divine bonté, et tout ce fut fait en ce mesmes moment de sa divine puissance, et tout ordonné, en celle mesmes heure, de sa divine sapience." The multivalence of the Old French *ordener/ordonner* renders this passage difficult. This short passage contains what appears to be a disjunction between God's power and will—creating together "en ce mesme moment"—and God's wisdom, who creates with the others but "en celle mesmes heure." Interpretation of this passage hinges on this translation: is the second description to be

taken literally as "in that same hour" or as the more colloquial "at the same time"? The author may have simply altered her phrasing to suit the ear, relying on her readers' colloquial understanding. Yet the modern reader cannot give temporal precedence or assert absolute unity to any of these three creative elements on the basis of this passage. There is enough evidence in the rest of the text, however, to support unity over differentiation in the acts of the Trinity to assume that creation happened all at once.

23. This is the Abelardian triad of power (*potentia*), wisdom (*sapientia*), and goodness (*bonitas*). See Peter Abelard, *Apologia contra Bernardum* (chapter 12); *Commentaria in epistulam Pauli ad Romanos* (Book 1, Chapter 1); and *Theologia Christiana* (Books 1 and 4).

24. This could be characterized as an Augustinian emphasis. In this particular passage, the second person of the Trinity is reported to have "ordained" all of creation, while creation was "made" by God's power and "willed" by God's goodness. The Old French *ordonné* (*ordener, ordonner*) has multivalent connotations that can significantly alter the meaning of this passage. Here it is translated most literally as "ordained," perhaps suggesting to modern readers a sanctification or consecration. The Son is thereby granted the role of sanctifying God's creation. "Ordained" can also be understood in the sense of "decreed" or "ordered," thus making the Son, who is referred to as God's wisdom, the rational force in the universe. This is faithful to the doctrine of the Son as *Logos*, as seen in earlier writers. That appellation could be buttressed by another possible interpretation of "ordonné" that relates to prior knowledge: the Son foreordained or foreknew creation as it manifests itself in the material world. These translations lend different levels of authority to the person of the Son and thus lead to very different understandings of the role of the second person of the Trinity in creation. Other passages posit the eternal existence of all things in God's wisdom.

25. Chapter 67, lines 13–20, CCCM, 190: "C'est verité, dit Amour, car Dieu le Pere a la divine puissance de luy, sans la prendre de nully; car il a de la deffluence de sa divine puissance, et donne a son Filz ce mesmes qu'il a de luy, et le Filz le prent du Pere. Si que le Filz naist du Pere et si est egal a luy. Et du Pere et du Filz est le Saint Esperit, une personne en la Trinité: non mye naist, mais est; car aultrement naist le Fils du Pere, et aultrement est le Saint Esperit et du Pere et du Filz."

26. Chapter 115, lines 3–7, CCCM, 308: "Il est une substance permanable, une fruiction aggreable, une conjunction amiable. Le Pere est substance permanable; le Filz est fruiccion aggreable; le Saint Esperit est conjunction amiable. Laquelle conjunction amiable est de substance permanable et de fruiction aggreable par la divine amour."

27. This perhaps supports the translation of "ordonné" as "ordered" and giving the Son the role of *Logos*.

28. Chapter 128, lines 23–29, CCCM, 370: "Et Verité me dist que nul n'y montera, sinon celluy seul qui en descendit, c'est assavoir le Filz de Dieu mesmes. C'est a entendre, que nul n'y peut monter, *sinon seulement ceulx qui sont filz de Dieu par divine grace. Et pource dit Jhesucrist mesmes que cil est mon frere, ma seur, et ma mere, qui fait la voulenté de Dieu mon Pere." Emphasis mine. Cf. John 3:13; Mt. 12:50; and Mk. 3:35.

29. Nevertheless, the preponderance of Porete's rhetoric dismisses the sort of grace mediated through the sacraments in the path toward annihilation.

30. See, for instance, chapters 11, 14, 52, and 92.

31. Chapter 14, lines 3–18, CCCM, 60 and 62: "Elle scet, dit Amour, par la vertu de foy, que Dieu est tout puissant et toute sapience et parfaicte bonté, et que Dieu le Pere a fait l'oeuvre de l'incarnacion, et le Filz aussi, et le Saint Esperit aussi; ainsi que Dieu le Pere a joinct nature humaine a la personne de Dieu le Filz, et la personne de Dieu le Filz l'a joincte a la personne de luy mesmes, et Dieu le Saint Esperit l'a joincte a la personne de Dieu le Filz. Si que le Pere a en luy une seule nature, c'est assavoir nature divine, et la personne du Filz a en luy trois natures, c'est assavoir celle mesme nature divine que le Pere a, et nature de ame et nature de corps, et est une personne en la Trinité; *et le Saint Esperit a en luy celle mesmes nature divine laquelle a le Pere et le Filz*. Ce croire, ce dire, ce penser est vraie contemplacion; c'est ung povoir, ung savoir, et une voulenté; ung seul Dieu en trois personnes; trois personnes et ung seul Dieu. Ce Dieu est partout en sa divine nature . . ." Emphasis mine. Porete here shows that the attributes of power, wisdom, and will are appropriated by each of the persons of the Trinity.

32. Chapter 94, line 25, CCCM, 264: "ramaine en l'ame le premier jour a celluy d'uy . . ."

33. Of the huge corpus of works on the "Platonisms" that influenced medieval thought, see especially the Introduction to Stephen Gersh, *Middle Platonism and Neoplatonism: The Latin Tradition*, Volume 1 (Notre Dame: University of Notre Dame Press, 1986), 1–50; Dominic O'Meara, ed., *Neoplatonism and Christian Thought* (Albany: State University of New York Press, 1982); and Raymond Klibansky, *Middle Platonism: The Continuity of the Platonic Tradition during the Middle Ages* (London: Warburg Institute, 1939).

34. The most commonly invoked scriptural account of the creation of humanity is found in the Book of Genesis (1:26): "Then God said, 'Let us make man *in our image, after our likeness*; and let them have dominion over the fish of the sea, and over the birds of the air, and over the cattle, and over all the earth, and over every creeping thing that creeps upon the earth.' So God created man in *his own image*, in the image of God he created him; male and female he created them." The Latin for the first sentence of this passage reads: "Faciamus hominem ad imaginem et similitudinem nostram." See also 2 Cor 3:18. This passage from Genesis presents humanity as created in "our" image and after "our" likeness, taken by later commentators to indicate the Trinitarian nature of the one God. This plural pronoun is abandoned toward the end of the passage, where God is referred to by a singular pronoun. The significance of this shift is minor for commentators after the Council of Nicea in 325, which set the stage for establishing the doctrinal consubstantiality of the Trinity and rendered "his" and "our" equivalent in this context.

35. For an overview of Plato's thought and his influence on later thinkers, see Frederick C. Copleston, *A History of Philosophy*, Volume 1 (New York: Doubleday, 1993).

36. The scholarship on this topic is vast and spans all of Christian history. For more information on the use of *imago* in the Bible, see G. Söhngen, "Die biblische Lehre von der Gottenbildlichkeit des Menschen," *Münchener Theologische Zeitschrift* II (1951): 52 ff.; W. Hess, "Imago Dei (Gen. 1.26)," *Benediktinische Monatsschrift* 29 (1953): 371 ff; and Gunnlaugur A. Jónsson, *The Image of God: Genesis 1:26–28 in a Century of Research* (Lund: Almquist and Wiksell International, 1988). See also two essays on this topic in *Christian Spirituality: Origins to the Twelfth Century*, ed. Bernard McGinn and John Meyendorff (New York: Crossroad, 1985), 290–330: Lars Thunberg, "The Human Person as Image of God: I. Eastern Christianity" and Bernard

McGinn, "The Human Person as Image of God: II. Western Christianity." For this theme as it emerges in the Middle Ages and Renaissance, see especially Robert Javelet, *Image et ressemblance au douzième siècle: De Saint Anselme a Alain de Lille*, 2 volumes (Paris: Letouzey et Ané, 1967) and "Image et ressemblance," in *Dictionnaire de spiritualité* 7:1341–53; Marie-Louise Lamau, "L'Homme a l'Image de Dieu chez les Théologiens et Spirituels du XIIe siècle," *Melanges de Science Religieuse* 48 (Jan.-June 1991): 203–213; Stephan Otto, *Die Funktion des Bildesbegriffes in der Theologie des 12. Jahrhunderts* (Münster: Aschendorff, 1963); and Charles Trinkaus, *In Our Image and Likeness: Humanity and Divinity in Italian Humanist Thought*, 2 volumes (Chicago: University of Chicago Press, 1970). For a modern feminist perspective, see the collection of essays edited by Kari Elisabeth Borreson, *The Image of God and Gender Models in Judaeo-Christian Tradition* (Atlantic Highlands, N. J.: Humanities Press, 1991).

37. The actual location of this image and likeness "within" is not made explicit in this passage from Genesis but is worked out by later commentators and placed within the highest part of the soul.

38. Even William of St. Thierry, who grants tremendous power to the individual soul to effect its own salvation, insists strongly on the necessity of salvation and grace. He exhorts his readers to imitate Jesus Christ, who has attained the "being" of God, the goal of human life

39. The "terms of return" for thinkers in the tradition vary. For Origen, for instance, proper reading of scripture and emulation of the incarnate *Logos*, at once the locus of creation and salvation, are the only means by which fallen souls can return to God. Christ is the exemplar of proper Christian life, to be imitated by those who seek to return to God. For Augustine, the Word Incarnate grants the grace of salvation, the only hope for desperately fallen humanity. If in Adam all fell, in Christ all are saved. There is thus one salvation and one church for all, and the mediation of these two is essential.

40. Perhaps the foremost representative of what became "mainstream" Western Christian teaching on this issue is Augustine of Hippo. For Augustine, the image of God in the soul enables all human beings to remain capable of God (*capax Trinitatis*) even in their fallen state. Augustine held that knowing oneself as an image of the Trinity is the beginning of the path to transformative knowing and loving God. With the aid of grace, the human soul, properly oriented toward God in memory, understanding, and will, can attain increasing—if necessarily imperfect—knowledge of the Trinitarian God. Augustine teaches that humans enjoy *participation* in the nature of God, but he insists that creatures remain essentially unlike their Creator. For Augustine and for most of the mainstream Western Christian tradition, creatures can find rest in God, but they never become God.

41. The Western Christian tradition as a whole came to distinguish image and likeness as interrelated but functionally distinct faculties after a fall from an original perfection of both image and likeness. Due to that fall, "likeness" was obliterated or destroyed, and the goal of human life became the restoration of the essential likeness, which is the perfection of the image. A thoroughly virtuous, just, and good person is as "like" God as a mortal human can be because that person has perfected the image of God within and has achieved likeness or resemblance to God. A sinful person is no longer at all "like" God, because that person cannot even begin to approach the qualities displayed by God in creation.

42. For more on the influence of the Genesis narrative on Christian thought, see Elaine Pagels, *Adam, Eve, and the Serpent* (London: Weidenfeld and Nicholson, 1988).

43. This was a common theme in theological writing. See, for instance, Etienne Gilson, "*Regio Dissimilitudinis* de Platon á Saint Bernard de Clairvaux," *Mediaeval Studies* 9 (1947): 108–130; Gervais Dumeige, "Dissemblance," in *Dictionnaire de spiritualité, ascetique et mystique, doctrine et histoire* 3:1330–1346 (Paris: Beauchesne, 1957); and A. E. Taylor, "Regio Dissimilitudinis," in *Archives d'histoire doctrinale et littéraire du moyen âge*, Volume 9 (1934): 305–306.

44. This theme of spiritual maturation is also found in other writers, notably Hadewijch of Brabant. In similar fashion, William of St. Thierry employs numerous metaphors relating to the healing of sickness, return from exile, or the increasing maturity of the soul who longs to live with God.

45. For instance, Col. 3:10 and Eph. 4:24.

46. A possible source for such an assertion can be found in the ninth-century Irish author John Scottus Eriugena. For Eriugena, the only true existence of humanity is as an idea in God's mind. Eriugena duplicates the divine ideas in humanity, thereby positing humanity as a pivotal part of the cosmological scheme of *exitus* and *reditus* and making humanity co-creator of sorts. For both Porete and Eriugena, the essential nothingness or true intelligibility of humanity is the key to union with or return to God. This idea did not enjoy wide currency in the history of Christian thought nor are the links of transmission absolutely clear, but it appears that Eriugena and Porete share similar theological ideas.

47. Some thinkers, such as Origen of Alexandria and John Scottus Eriugena, maintained that even fallen human souls had the capacity to do good or evil. For instance, Origen described Adam's Fall as more an archetypal instance of humanity's neglect of God than an infectious illness that damages all capacity for good.

48. In that way, her thought resembles Origen's and Eriugena's, both of whom insist that the Fall—whether truly historical or essentially ahistorical—is a pivotal step toward greater perfection.

49. Porete is not entirely alone making such an assertion. William of St. Thierry, for example, insists that surpassing the virtues was the natural consequence of deification in Christ within in the community of the church. For William, certain advanced souls can pass beyond the ministrations of the church and scripture in pursuing contemplation of God, though they would never reject those mediating elements in their ascent to God. Yet despite his insistence on the essential spiritual liberty (the *libertas spiritus* of 2 Corinthians 3:17) of the soul, William remains true to tradition in insisting on obedience as the supreme virtue in this quest. The Virtues continue to dwell within the soul for William, as they do for Porete.

50. Chapter 34, lines 14–16, CCCM, 112: "pourtant ne devez vous pas oblier vostre neant. C'est a dire que vous ne devez mie oblier qui vous estiez, quant il vous crea premierement . . ."

51. Chapter 135, lines 17–19, CCCM, 397: "Et ideo habet a Deo id quod habet; *et est id quod Deus est per mutationem amoris*, in illo puncto in quo erat, antequam a Dei bonitate fluxisset." This passage survives only in Latin and Middle English versions.

52. Genesis 2:7.

53. One interesting study of this aspect of Porete's thought is Emilie Zum Brunn, "Non Willing in Marguerite Porete's 'Mirror of Annihilated Souls,'" *Bulletin de l'Institut Historique Belge de Rome* 58 (1988): 11–22.

54. See chapter 111.

55. Chapter 18, lines 9–11, CCCM, 72 and 74: "le vray noyau affiné de divine Amour, qui est sans matere de creature, et donné du Creatour a creature . . ." This seed metaphor will be examined in detail in chapter 6.

56. Chapter 43, lines 31–34, CCCM, 132 and 134: "octroyé de sa bonté ou savoir de sa sapience sans commancement, tout ce que nous avons; et si est bien droit, dit le Saint Esperit, que nous ne retenons contre telles Ames chose que nous ayons."

57. Chapter 112, lines 3–7, CCCM, 304: "Il est une bonté parmanable qui est amour parmanable, qui tend par nature de charité a donner et espandre toute sa bonté; laquelle bonté parmanable engendre bonté agreable; de laquelle bonté parmanable et de laquelle bonté agreable est l'amour amiable de l'amant en l'aymee . . ."

58. Chapter 22, lines 19–20, CCCM, 84: "en elle saintiffié son non et la Trinité divine y a sa maison." Latin has "nomen."

59. Other Beguines espoused image doctrines focusing on salvation and the loving response of the soul to God. This is in marked contrast to Porete's notion of essential passivity.

60. Chapter 50, lines 3–6, CCCM, 148: "Ceste Ame est emprainte en Dieu, et a sa vraye emprainture detenue par l'union d'amour; et a la maniere que la cire prent la forme du seel, en telle maniere a ceste Ame prinse l'emprainte de cest vray exemplaire."

61. Chapter 11, lines 102–104, CCCM, 44: "que Dieu ayme mieulx le plus de ceste Ame en luy, que moins d'elle mesmes."

62. Chapter 35, lines 27–35, CCCM, 114 and 116: "Raison, dit l'Ame, se je suis amee sans fin des trois personnes de la Trinité, j'ay aussi esté amee d'elles sans commencement. Car aussi bien comme de sa bonté il me aymera sans fin, aussi pareillement ay je esté ou savoir de sa sapience que je servie cree<e> de l'oeuvre de sa divine puissance. Ainsy donc, puisque des lors que Dieu est, qui est sans commancement, j'ay esté ou savoir divin, et que je seroie sans fin, doncques des lors ama il, dit l'Ame, de sa bonté l'oeuvre qu'il feroit en moy de sa divine puissance."

63. For a full discussion of trinitarian parallels in human faculties of knowledge, see Ellen Babinsky, "A Beguine in the Court of the King: The Relation of Love and Knowledge in The Mirror of Simple Souls by Marguerite Porete," unpublished dissertation, University of Chicago, June 1991, 198–220.

64. Chapter 115, lines 10–19, CCCM, 308: "Laquelle divine amour d'unité engendre . . . substance permable, fruiction aggreable, conjunction amiable. De laquelle substance permable la memoire a la puissance du Pere. De laquelle fruiction aggreable l'entendement a la sapience du Filz. De laquelle conjunction amiable la voulenté a la bonté du Saint Esperit. Laquelle bonté du Saint Esperit le conjoingt en l'amour du Pere et du Filz. Laquelle conjunction mect Ame en estres sans estres, qui est Estres. Lequel Estre est le Saint Esperit mesmes, qui est amour du Pere et du Filz."

65. This Augustinian definition is found in *De Trin.* 10.11.7.

66. Chapter 12, lines 49–50, CCCM, 52: "qu'il est ung estre entre les estres, le plus noble de tous les estres . . ."

67. See, for example, chapter 86.

68. Chapter 87, lines 7–10, CCCM, 246: "mais je suis, dit ceste Ame, et suis et seray tousjours sans faillir, car Amour n'a commencement ne fin ne comprennement, et je ne suis, fors que Amour. Comment donc l'auroie je? Ce ne pourroit estre."

69. Chapter 70, lines 5–11, CCCM, 196: "Je suis, dit ceste <Ame>, de la grace Dieu ce que je suis. Donc suis je tant seulement et nulle autre chose, ce que Dieu est en moy; et Dieu est aussi ce mesmes qu'il est en moy; car nient est nient. Ains est, ce qui est; donc ne suis je, se je suis, sinon ce que Dieu est; et nul n'est fors Dieu; et pource ne trouve je fors Dieu, quelque part que je m'enbate; car il n'est fors que luy . . ."

70. Chapter 70, line 16, CCCM, 198: "se mucent par faulte d'innocence, par le peché de Adam."

71. Chapter 107, lines 3–7, CCCM, 290: "que elle se voie tousjours (se ainsi est qu'elle voie nulle chose) ou elle estoit quant Dieu fist de nient tout, et si soit certaine que elle n'est aultre chose que ce—quant est d'elle—, ne ne sera sans fin, pouse qu'elle n'eust oncques meffait a la bonté divine."

72. Chapter 107, lines 8–11, CCCM, 290 and 292: "qu'elle voie qu'elle a fait de sa franche voulenté, que Dieu luy avoit donnee; si verra, que elle a a Dieu mesmes sa voulenté tollue, en ung seul moment de consentement de peché."

73. For an extended discussion of the role of the body in Porete's thought, see Hollywood, *The Soul as Virgin Wife: Mechtild of Magdeburg, Marguerite Porete, and Meister Eckhart*, as well as her "Suffering Transformed: Marguerite Porete, Meister Eckhart, and the Problems of Women's Spirituality," in *Meister Eckhart and the Beguine Mystics*, ed. Bernard McGinn (New York: Continuum, 1997), 87–113. More generally on medieval bodies and spirituality (and from a different perspective), see Caroline Walker Bynum, *Fragmentation and Redemption: Essays on Gender and the Human Body in Medieval Religion* (New York: Zone, 1991).

74. See Chapter 109. This perhaps reflects an Origenist notion of intelligible souls falling into corporeal bodies as a manner of punishment.

75. See, for instance, chapter 102.

76. The healing of body and soul is described as freedom from encumbrances. See, for instance, chapter 78.

77. Chapter 69, lines 19–20, CCCM, 194: "mais je l'ay, pour le myen de luy atteindre; le mien est, que je soie en mon nient plantee."

78. See chapter 110.

79. Chapter 138, lines 4–6, CCCM, 400 and 402: "et a fait de deux ung. Mais quant est cest ung? Cest ung est, quant l'Ame est remise en celle simple Deité . . ."

80. Chapter 102, lines 6–12, CCCM, 280: "Hee, Dieu! quelle pitié, quant mauvaistié a victoire sur bonté! Et ainsi est du corps et de l'esperit. L'esperit est de Dieu creez, et le corps est de Dieu formez. Or sont ces deux natures, adjoinctes ensemble par nature et par droiture en corrupcion, es fons de baptesme sans correpcion. Et pource sont bonnes ces deux natures de la divine droiture qui a fait ces deux natures." It is interesting to note that Porete fails to mention the division of humanity into sexes. The estrangement here is not male from female but body from soul.

81. Chapter 102, lines 12–15, CCCM, 280: "et quant deffaulte vainct ceste complexion et ceste creacion, qui sont faittes de la bonté divine, nulle pitié ne ressemble ceste cy, tant soit petite la deffaulte."

82. Chapter 126, lines 21–25, CCCM, 364. "se il eust trouvé en vous autant de vuide, . . . il n'eust ja de vous fait sa mere. Dame, il ne povoit estre que vous le fussez, et si ne povoit estre que vous ne le fussiés." The ellipsis is a colloquial Old French remark that is not easily translated.

83. Chapter 128, lines 14–16, CCCM, 370.

84. Chapter 128, lines 20–22, CCCM, 370: "Il n'en peust aultre chose estre: puisque l'Ame estoit joincte a nature divine, le corps, qui estoit mortel, ne luy eust peu faire nul empeschement."

85. See, for instance, chapter 97, chapter title and lines 5–6, CCCM, 268: "Comment paradis n'est aultre chose que Dieu veoir" and "aultre chose n'est paradis, que Dieu tant seulement veoir."

86. See Chapters 73 and 97.

87. Chapter 97, lines 7–13, CCCM, 268: "fut le larron en paradis, tantost que l'ame fut partie de son corps, pouse que Jhesucrist, le Filz de Dieu, ne remontast ou ciel jusques a l'Ascencion, et le larron fut en paradis le propre jour du Bon Vendredi. Et comment peut ce estre? Certes estre l'esconvient, puisque Jhesucrist luy avoit promis. Et est vray, qu'il fut en paradis le propre jour: pource que il vit Dieu, il fut et eut paradis, car aultre chose n'est paradis, que Dieu veoir."

88. This is reminiscent of Eriugena's doctrine of general and special returns.

89. Chapter 14, lines 18–20, CCCM, 62: "mais l'umanité est en paradis glorifiee, joincte a la personne du Filz, et ou Sacrement de l'Autel tant seulement."

90. Chapter 37, lines 3–7, CCCM, 118: "Sire, dit l'Ame, mes pechez ne peut nul cognoistre en ce monde, en si laide figure ne hideuse comme ilz sont, fors vous. Mais, sire, en paradis tous ceulx qui y seront en auront cognoissance, non mye a ma confusion, mais a ma tres grant gloire."

91. This is also reminiscent of Eriugena's doctrine that not all will eat of the Tree of Life.

92. Chapter 79, line 33, CCCM, 224: "par lequel l'ay derechef vie."

93. Chapter 109, lines 17–20, CCCM, 296: "nient . . . des avant que vous m'eussez nient forfait de ce que je vous donnay. Or estes vous une aultre, car vous estes moins que nient, par tant de foiz, dit Verité, comme vous avez aultre chose voulu que ma voulenté."

94. Chapter 131, lines 122–125, CCCM, 386 and 388: "Se j'avoye ce mesmes que vous avez, avec la creacion que vous m'avez donnee; et ainsi, sire, que je seroie egal a vous, excepté en ce point, que je pourroye ma voulenté changer pour aultruy que pour moy,—laquelle chose vous ne faites mie."

95. Chapter 103, lines 11–13 and 15–18, CCCM, 282: "car il convient que Dieu ne soit pas Dieu, se vertuz m'est tollue malgré moy! . . . Et se je le vouloie, pourquoy ne le souffreroit il? Se il ne le souffroit, son povoir me touldroit franchise. Mais sa bonté ne le pourroit souffrir, que son povoir me deffranchist de riens . . ."

96. Chapter 72, lines 10–19, CCCM, 200: "Quant la divine Trinité cra les anges de la courtoisie de sa divine bonté, ceulx qui mauvais furent, par leur perverse election

s'accorderent au mauvais vouloir de Lucifer, qui voult avoir par nature de luy ce qu'il ne pot avoir fors par grace divine. Et tantost qu'ilz vouldrent ce de leur forfaicte voulenté, ilz perdirent l'estre de bonté. Or sont ilz en enfer sans estre, et sans jamais recouvrer misericorde de veoir Dieu. Et ceste haulte vision leur fist perdre leur voulenté, qu'ilz eussent eue pour donner leur voulenté, laquelle ilz retindrent. Or regardez a quel chef ilz en vindrent!"

97. Chapter 109, line 56, CCCM, 298: "c'est faulte de cognoissance . . ."

98. Chapter 94, lines 31–33, CCCM, 264: "Tous ce mucent encore donc par le peché de Adam, fors ceulx qui sont adnientiz: ceulx cy n'ont que mucer." Porete would include the Virgin Mary and Jesus Christ among those who do not hide.

99. See, for example, chapters 13 and 16.

100. Chapter 105, lines 4–11, CCCM, 286: "C'est a entendre, quant la voulenté du juste est toute donnee, sans aultre empeschement, a contempler la divine bonté, que, par la nourriture du peché de Adam, le corps est foible et endui a deffaultes; et pource s'encline souvent a entendre maindre chose que de la bonté de Dieu; et ce appelle l'Escripture cheue, car aussi est ce; mais la voulenté du juste se garde de consentir a la deffaulte, qui de telle inclinacion pourroit naistre."

101. See chapter 89, lines 6–7.

102. Chapter 117, lines 77–84, CCCM, 316: "car Dieu lesse aucunes foiz aucun mal estre fait, pour plus grant bien qui en doit après naistre. Car tous ceulx qui sont plantez du Pere, et venuz en ce monde, sont descenduz de parfait en imparfait, pour actaindre a plus parfait. Et la est ouverte la plaie, pour guerir ceulx qui estoient navrez sans leur sceu. Telz gens se sont humiliez d'eulx mesmes. Ilz ont porté la croix de Jhesucrist, par l'oeuvre de bonté, *ou ilz portent la leur mesmes.*" Emphasis mine.

103. Chapter 62, lines 17–19, CCCM, 180: "telz gens sont petis en terre et tres petis en ciel, et mal courtoisement se sauvent." By this Porete probably means that they are saved but not according to the rules of behavior established for attaining salvation correctly; that is, through abandoning the will entirely to the beloved, God.

104. Chapter 62, lines 33–36, CCCM, 182: "Ilz ont oblié que il ne souffisit pas a Jhesucrist faire pour eulx, se il n'eust fait tout ce que l'umanité en peut porter, jusques a la mort."

105. Chapter 63, lines 20–22, CCCM, 184: "ceulx n'oblieront jamais les dons de vostre souffrance, ainçoys est tousjours a eulx mirouer et exemplaire."

106. Chapter 77, lines 50–60, CCCM, 216: "Je vous envoyay les Thrones pour vous reprendre et aorner, les Cherubins pour vous enluminer, et les Seraphins pour vous embraser. Par tous les messages je vous demandoye, dit Amour, (et ilz le vous faisoient savoir) ma voulenté, et les estres ou je vous demandoye, et vous n'en faisoiez tousjours compte. Et je vi, ce dit Amour, je vous laissay en vostre mainburnie, en vous sauvant; et se a moy obeÿ eussiez, vous feussiez ung aultre, a tesmoing de vous mesmes; mais vous vous sauverez bien par vous, combien que ce soit en vie encombree de vostre esperit mesmes, qui jamais ne sera sans aucun encombrier de luy."

107. Chapter 123, lines 14–16, CCCM, 348: "qu'ilz l'amoient trop tendrement selon la nature humaine, et foiblement selon sa divine nature."

108. Chapter 125, lines 14–15, CCCM, 362: "de Jhesucrist detenir en sa personne humaine . . ."

109. Chapter 123, lines 23–25, CCCM, 350: "mais elle empesche les dons du Saint Esperit, qui ne pevent souffrir, fors divine amour, pure, sans mesleure de nature."

110. Chapter 134, lines 15–17 and 19–20, CCCM, 394: "Elle a passé la poincte du glaive, en occiant les plaisances du corps, et en tuant les vouloirs de l'esperit . . . Le plus l'a delivree des debtes qu'elle devoit a Jhesucrist, et pource . . ." and lines 17–18, 395: "et ideo sibi nichil debet, quomodocumque fuerit obligata." This reference to death to the spirit indicates that the soul has surpassed the fourth stage, as described in the previous chapter.

111. Chapter 80, lines 12–18, CCCM, 226: "Car ainsi comme Dieu est incomprehensible au regart de sa puissance, aussi pareillement est ceste Ame endebtee de son nient incomprehensibele d'une heure du temps, sans plus, que elle a eu voulenté contre luy. A celluy doit elle sans descompt la debte que sa voulenté vault, et tant de foiz comme elle a eu voulenté d'embler a Dieu sa voulenté."

112. Chapter 109, lines 45–50, CCCM, 298: "Il n'eut aultre regart, en ce faisant, que la voulenté de Dieu son Pere tant seulement. Et le filz de Dieu est exemple de nous, et pource le devons nous en ce regart ensuir, car nous devons vouloir en toutes choses tant seulement la divine voulenté; et ainsi serions nous filz de Dieu le Pere, a l'exemple de Jhesucrist son filz."

113. On the influence of this notion on Jan van Ruusbroec, see Edmund Colledge and J. C. Marler, "Poverty of the Will: Ruusbroec, Eckhart and the *Mirror of Simple Souls*," in *Jan van Ruusbroec, The Sources, Content and Sequels of his Mysticism*, ed. P. Mommaers and N. de Paepe (Leuven: University Press, 1984), 14–47.

114. Chapter 101, lines 36–39, CCCM, 278: "et paix de paix, et de telle paix sourprinse, que la corrupcion de vostre complexion n'y pourroit jamais faire cause de correction, se vous demourez en la paix sourprinse." Here I depart from Babinsky, who translates "sourprinse" as "surpassing".

115. See chapters 9, 16, and 41.

116. Chapter 135, lines 5–8, CCCM, 397: "unus occursus illius ultra permanentis antiquae nouae bonitatis plus ualet quam aliquid, quod creatura facere posset in centum milibus annis, nec etiam tota sancta ecclesia." This passage is extant only in Latin and Middle English.

117. Chapter 80, lines 28–29.

118. Chapter 124, lines 82–84, CCCM, 356: "Si elle fut en Jhesucrist, ce a esté pour le coulpe d'umain lignage, et si elle est en nous, c'est par nostre coulpe vraiement . . ."

119. Chapter 127, lines 4–5 and 12–13, CCCM, 366 and 368: "O vray Dieu, qui est celluy qui pourroit souffisanment cecy penser?" and "qui est celluy qui eust osé demander tel oultrage?" "Oultrage" can also be translated "outrage."

120. Chapter 128.

121. Chapter 111, lines 29–30, CCCM, 304: "pour paier le forfait que nous avons forfait de nostre forfaicte voulenté."

122. Chapter 126, lines 39–41 and 45–51, CCCM, 366: "Pource que autant de son benoist sang, comme l'en pourroit tenir sur la pointe d'une aguille, eust esté souffisante pour rachater cent mille mondes, se tant en estoit; . . . Pource, car je tiens que, se toutes les mesaises et de mort et d'aultres tourmens, quelx qu'ilz aient esté, ou soient,

ou seront, depuis le temps de Adam jusques au temps de l'Antecrist, et fussent toutes mesaises dessusdictes ensemble en une, vrayement encore ne seroit ce que ung point de mesaise, au regard de la mesaise que Jhesucrist eust eue . . ."

123. See chapters 118 and 73.

124. Chapter 19, lines 24–26, CCCM, 76: "Icelluy seul Dieu, dit Amour, qui les a creees et rachetees, et par aventure maintes foiz recree,e.s, pour l'amour duquel seulement elles sont exillees, adnienties et obliees."

Chapter Four

NOBILITY AND ANNIHILATION

1. Chapter 117, lines 4–9, CCCM, 310: "Dieu n'a, dit il, ou mectre sa bonté, se il ne la mect en moy, ne plus n'a de haberge qui soit pour luy convenable, ne ne peut avoir lieu ou il se puisse tout mectre, sinon en moy; et parmy ce suis exemple de salut. *Mais encore, qui plus est, le salut mesmes de toute creature, et la gloire de Dieu* . . ." My emphasis.

2. See chapter 73, lines 41–42, CCCM, 206: "vaissel de telle eleccion"; chapter 13, line 12, CCCM, 54: "precieusement esleuz et appellez"; and chapter 121, line 66, which introduces the character "L'Ame Esleue".

3. Chapter 133, lines 22–23, CCCM, 392: "pou de gens se disposent pour recevoir telle semence."

4. Chapter 84, line 44, CCCM, 240: "n'ay je de quoy ne pour quoy."

5. Meister Eckhart uses this expression throughout Sermon 52. See *Meister Eckhart: The Essential Sermons, Commentaries, Treatises, and Defense*, ed. Edmund Colledge and Bernard McGinn (New York: Paulist, 1981), 199–203. On the parallels between this sermon and Porete's text, see especially Edmund Colledge and J.C. Marler, "Poverty of the Will".

6. Chapter 121, lines 32–33, CCCM, 338: "Et ne scevent la grant noblece / d'estre a nient deviser."

7. Chapter 91, lines 23–24, CCCM, 258: "Et ycy point, car c'est le plus noble estre . . ." Peter Dembowski's "Vocabulary of Old French Courtly Lyrics" reminds the reader that these three attributes could be taken as synonyms.

8. Chapter 58, lines 8–10 and 12–15, CCCM, 168: "La ne fault elle mie, et si est souvent ou siziesme ravie, mais pou ce luy dure. Car ,c'est. une ouverture a maniere de esclar et de hastive closure, ou l'en ne peut longuement demourer. . . . L'ouverture ravissable de l'espandement de celle ouverture fait l'Ame, après sa closure, de la paix de son o,uevre. si franche et si noble et si descombree de toutes choses (tant comme la paix dure, qui est donnee en ceste ouverture) . . ."

9. Chapter 118, lines 171–173, CCCM, 330: "et pource est elle toute en repos, et de franc estre mise en possession, qui la repouse par excellente noblesse de toutes choses."

10. On this distinction, see especially Bernard McGinn, "Love, Knowledge, and *Unio Mystica* in the Western Christian Tradition," in Moshe Idel and Bernard McGinn, eds., *Mystical Union and Monotheistic Faith: An Ecumenical Dialogue* (New York: MacMillan, 1989), 59–86.

11. McGinn, *Flowering*, 440, fn. 284.

12. See chapter 51.

13. Meister Eckhart posits a similar notion in "The Book of Benedictus: Of the Nobleman," in *Meister Eckhart. The Essential Sermons, Commentaries, Treatises, and Defense*, 247: "Who then is nobler than he who on one side is born of the highest and best among created things, and on the other side from the inmost ground of the divine nature and its desert? 'I,' says the Lord through the prophet Hosea, 'will lead the noble soul out into the desert [einode] and there I will speak to her heart, one with One, one from One, one in One, and in One, one everlasting. Amen.' "

14. Chapter 66, lines 15–17, CCCM, 188: "mais ceste leçon n'est mie mise en escript de main d'omme, mais c'est du Saint Esperit, qui escript ceste leçon merveilleusement, et l'Ame est parchemin precieusement."

15. Chapter 42, lines 9–12 and 15–19, CCCM, 130: "et luy donnent trouver le tresor mucié et caché qui est enclos en la Trinité pardurablement. *Non mye, dit le Saint Esperit, par nature divine, car ce ne peut estre, mais par la force d'amour, car ce convient il estre.* . . . Voire, dit le Saint Esperit, encore tout ce que j'ay du Pere et du Filz. Et puisque elle a tout ce que j'ay, dit le Saint Esperit, et le Pere et le Filz n'ont rien que je n'aye en moy, dit Amour, donc a ceste Ame en elle, dit le Saint Esperit, le tresor de la Trinité, mucié et enclos dedans elle."

16. Chapter 118, lines 95–96, CCCM, 324: "et elle n'est mie, si n'est dont toute chose est."

17. Chapter 130, lines 32–34, CCCM, 374: "Sire, vous estes une bonté, par bonté espandue, et tout en vous. Et je suis une mauvaistié, par mauvestié espandue, et tout en moy."

18. Chapter 130, lines 35–38, CCCM, 374: "Sire, vous estes, et pour ce est toute chose parfaicte par vous, et nulle chose est faicte sans vous. Et je ne suis mie; et pour ce est toute chose faicte sans moy; et nulle chose est faicte par moy."

19. Chapter 130, lines 43–45, CCCM, 374: "ung seul Dieu en trois personnes. . . . Et je suis une seule ennemie, en trois meschancetez . . ."

20. See chapter 130.

21. Chapter 131, lines 132–135, CCCM, 388: "Mon cueur cuidoit jadis tousdis vivre d'amour par desirer de bonne voulenté. Or maintenant sont ces deux choses en moy finees, qui m'ont fait hors de mon enffance yssir."

22. Chapter 117, lines 9–13, 19–21, and 26–28, CCCM, 310 and 312: "et vous diray comment, pourquoy, et en quoy. Pource que je suis la somme du tous maulx. Car je contiens de ma propre nature ce que mauvastié est, donc suis je toute mauvaistié. Et celluy qui est la somme de tous biens, contient en luy, de sa propre nature, toute bonté; donc est il toute bonté. . . . par quoy il m'esconvient avoir toute sa bonté, ains que ma mauvaistié puisse estre estanchee; ne de moins ne se peut ma pouvreté passer. . . . Et par ce moyen ay je de sa pure bonté, en moy, par bonté, toute sa bonté divine, et ay eu sans commencement, et auray sans fin . . ." My emphasis.

23. Chapter 84, lines 44–47, CCCM, 240: "a Dieu en est de ceste oeuvre, qui fait en moy ses oeuvres. Je ne luy doy point de oeuvre, puisque luy mesmes oeuvre en moy; et se je y mectoye le mien, je defferoye son oeuvre."

24. Chapter 100, lines 22–24, CCCM, 276: "Il n'a nient plus a faire de luy ne d'aultruy ne de Dieu mesmes, nient plus que se il ne fust mie; si que il est."

25. See chapter 139.

26. Chapter 86, lines 7–11, CCCM, 242: "car ce sont gens a piez sans voie, et a mains sans oeuvre, et a bouche sans parole, et a yeulx sans clarté, et a oreilles sans oïr, et a raison sans raison, et a corps sans vie, et a cueur sans entendement, de tant comme touche cest estre."

27. See chapter 110.

28. Chapter 41, lines 6–10, CCCM, 128: "que elle est morte a tous sentemens de dedans et dehors, en tant que telle Ame ne fait plus nulles oeuvres, ne pour Dieu ne pour elle, et si a tous ses sens si perduz en cest usaige, que elle ne scet querir Dieu ne trouver, ne elle mesmes conduire."

29. Chapter 114, lines 8–16, CCCM, 306: "est 'sans' elle, quant elle n'a nul sentement de nature, ne oeuvre, ne nulle oeuvre de dedans, ne honte ne honnour, ne de rien qui adviengne nulle crainte, ne affection nulle en la divine bonté; ne ne sçait plus nul habergement de voulenté, aincois est en toutes heures sans voulenté. Adonc est elle adnientie, `sans' elle, quelque chose que ce soit que Dieu souffre d'elle. Adonc fait elle tout sans elle, et si lesse tout sans elle. Ce n'est pas merveille: elle n'est més `pour' elle, car elle vit de substance divine."

30. Chapter 91, lines 16–18, CCCM, 258: "Il sera de luy en telle bonté ce qu'il savoit de luy ains que elle ne fust mie, quant il luy donna sa bonté, dont il la fist dame."

31. Chapter 108, lines 45–46, CCCM, 294: "Et Dieu me donna voulenté pour faire sa voulenté, pour gaigner de luy luy mesmes."

32. Chapter 92, lines 21–22, CCCM, 260: "et quant tel nient est, adonc vit Dieu luy mesmes en telle creature, sans empeschement de sa creature." This mutuality is found also in Hadewijch. On this see McGinn, "The Abyss of Love."

33. Chapter 91, lines 10–13, CCCM, 256 and 258: "Sa voulenté est nostre, car elle est cheue de grace en parfection de l'oeuvre des Vertuz, et des Vertuz en Amour, et d'Amour en Nient, et de Nient en Clarifiement de Dieu, qui se voit des yeulx de sa majesté . . ."

34. See chapter 100, lines 10–12 and 28–29, CCCM, 274 and 275: "Il est tres bien nez, qui est de tel lignage. Ce sont gens royaulx. Ilz ont les cueurs excellentement nobles . . . l'aveugle soustient a ceste cy ses piez; la clere est la plus noble et la plus gentile . . ."

35. Chapter 114, lines 3–4, CCCM, 306: "Je demande aux aveugles, ou aux clariffiez qui mieulx voient que ne font ceulx de devant . . ." On this see Meister Eckhart's Sermon 12: "the eye in which I see God is the same eye in which God sees me. My eye and God's eye are one eye and one seeing, on knowing, and one loving." See *Meister Eckhart. The Essential Sermons, Commentaries, Treatises, and Defense.*

36. Chapter 30, lines 42–45 and 57–60, CCCM, 100: "Hee, tres doulce Amour, dit ceste Ame Esbahye, pour Dieu! dictes moy pourquoy estoit il si soigneux de moy creer ne racheter ne recreer, pour si pou me donner, luy qui a tant a donner? . . . Hee, doulce Ame, dit Amour, vous savez plus que vous ne dictes. Et se vous luy avez tout donné, c'est le mieulx qui vous puisse avenir; et encore ne luy donnez vous chose qui sienne ne soit, avant que vous la luy donnez."

37. Chapter 37, lines 17–18, CCCM, 120: "car pour aultre chose n'est creee l'Ame, que pour avoir en elle sans fin l'estre de pure charité."

38. Chapter 113, lines 14–17, CCCM, 307: "Et ideo sumus nichil, quia nichil a nobis habemus. Videatis hoc totum nudum nichil celando aut uelando, et tunc habebit ille qui est in nobis suum uerum esse." This passage survives only in Latin.

39. See chapter 52.

40. See the description of how abandoning the will removes the soul from a state of "warfare and deficiency" in chapter 118, line 123, CCCM, 326: "l'Ame n'ayt ou guerre ou deffaillance."

41. Chapter 95, lines 3–11, CCCM, 264 and 266: "Il a moult long chemin du pays des Vertuz, que les Marriz tiennent, a celluy des Obliz et des Nuz adnientiz, ou des Clarifiez, qui sont ou plus hault estre, la ou Dieu est relignqui de luy en luy mesmes. Adonc n'est il cogneu, ne amé, ne loé de telles creatures, fors seulement de ce, que on ne le peut cognoistre, ne amer, ne louer. C'est la somme de toute leur amour, et le darnier cours de leur voie: le darnier se accorde au premier, car le moyen ne se discorde mie. C'est droit, puisque elle a <fini> le cours, que elle se repose en celluy . . ."

42. Chapter 11, lines 45–48, CCCM, 40: "n'a confort, ne affection, ne esperance en creature que Dieu ait creee, ne en ciel ne en terre, si non seulement en la bonté Dieu. Telle Ame ne mendie, ne ne demande rien a creature."

43. Chapter 89, lines 7–9 and 12–13, CCCM, 252: "Or elle n'a garde de pecher, se elle lesse sa voulenté la ou elle est plantee, c'est en celluy qui la luy avoit donnee de sa bonté franchement. . . . Et jusques ad ce n'eut elle paix plantureuse ne assiduelle, qu'elle fut de son vouloir purement desnuee."

44. See chapter 73.

45. Chapter 48, lines 29–30, CCCM, 146: "sans avoir crainte des choses doubtables, ne desirer nulles des choses tres delectables."

46. Chapter 81, lines 15–19, CCCM, 230: "noe et onde et flote et suronde de divine paix, sans soy mouvoir de son dedans et sans son oeuvre de par dehors. Ces deux choses luy osteroient ceste paix, se elles s'i povoient embatre, mais elles ne pevent; car elle est en l'estre de souveraineté, par quoy ilz ne la pevent grever ne de rien destourber." Porete also refers to "exterior work" in the opening exemplum of the maiden who loves the faroff Alexander through works and an image of her beloved.

47. Chapter 85, lines 16–17, CCCM, 242: "et la pouldre d'elle gittee en haulte mer par nient de voulenté."

48. Chapter 28, lines 4–6, CCCM, 96: "et si nage et flue en joye, sans sentir nulle joye, car elle demoure en Joye, et Joye demoure en elle . . ."

49. Chapter 76, lines 19–21, CCCM, 212: "que luy ne les aultres n'eurent de ce honte, ne honnour, ne voulenté d'eulx mucer ne cacher."

50. Chapter 76, lines 11–12, CCCM, 210: "et pource n'avoit de qui il luy chaillist, sinon de luy." Lk. 10:38–42 and 8:2.

51. See chapter 76. Mt. 26:69–75; Mk. 14:66–72; Lk. 22:54–62; Jn. 18:15–18 and 25–57; Acts 5:15.

52. See chapter 76. Mk. 14:51–52.

53. Chapter 49, lines 5–7, CCCM, 146: "Il ne lui fault ne enfer, ne paradis, ne chose creee. Elle ne veult ne ne desveult chose qui soit ycy nommee."

54. See, for instance, chapter 133, lines 32–33.

55. Chapter 44, lines 18–19, CCCM, 136: "que le monde ne la char ne les enne-mis ne la pevent grever, car ilz ne la pevent en leurs oeuvres trouver."

56. Chapter 5, lines 44–48, CCCM, 22: "car pouse qu'elle soit ou monde, et qu'il feust possible que le monde, la char et le deable et les quatre elemens et les oyseaux de l'air et les bestes mues la tourmentassent, despeçassent ou devorassent, si ne peut elle rien perdre, se Dieu luy demoure."

57. Chapter 44, lines 15–16, CCCM, 136: "Elle a prins fin au monde, ce dit Amour, et le monde a prins congié et fin en elle"; and chapter 81, lines 6–7, CCCM, 230: "et toute chose creee luy est si loing, qu'elle ne le peut sentir . . ."

58. Chapter 16, lines 49–52, CCCM, 68: "Mais les pensees de telles Ames sont si divines, que elles ne se arrestent mie tant es choses passees ne cree,e.s, qu'elles conçoivent mesaise dedans elle, puisque Dieu est bon sans comprennement."

59. Another favored metaphor of rivers flowing into the sea will be explored at length in the following chapter. Porete also uses intoxication in a negative sense in showing how it dazzles and captivates the soul in the fourth stage and disables her from moving onward. On these and similar metaphors, see Jean Pépin, " 'Stilla aquae mod-ica multo infuso vino, ferrum ignitum, luce perfuses aer': L'origin de trois comparaisons familières à la théologie mystique médiévale," *Divinitas* 11 (1967): 331–375.

60. Chapter 1, lines 49–51, CCCM, 14: "Ils sont sept estres de noble estre, desquieulx creature reçoit estre, se elle se dispouse a tous estres, ains qu'elle viengne a parfait estre . . ."

61. Chapter 124, lines 88–93, CCCM, 356 and 358: "il esconvient a l'enfant avoir en luy et faire oeuvres d'enfant, ains qu'il soit homme parfait; ainsi pareille-ment convient homme sotoier et foloier par oeuvres humaines de luy, avant qu'il ait le vray noyau de l'estre de franchise, lequel l'ame oeuvre de divin usage, sans son oeuvre."

62. Chapter 57, lines 46–48, CCCM, 166: "Car tout estre, quel qu'il soit, n'est que ung jeu de pelote et jeu d'enfant envers le souverain estre de nient vouloir . . ."

63. Chapter 123, lines 4–5, CCCM, 348: "et que je vivoie de lait et de papin . . ."

64. Chapter 188, lines 163–164, CCCM, 328: "Et la pert l'Ame orgueil et jeunesse, car l'esperit est veillart devenu, qui ne la laisse plus estre deduisant ne jolye . . ."

65. Chapter 94, lines 23–25, CCCM, 264: "Et cest estre, dont nous parlons, dont Amour nous donne de sa bonté forme, ramaine en l'ame le premier jour a celluy d'uy." Cf. chapter 99, lines 3–4.

66. Chapter 117, line 69, CCCM, 316: "Car le plus fort mue en luy le plus foible."

67. See, for example, chapter 118, *passim.*

68. Chapter 52, lines 15–17, CCCM, 152: "comme le fer est vestu du feu, et a la semblance perdue de luy, pource que le feu est le plus fort qui l'a mue,e. en luy." See a similar metaphor in Richard of St. Victor's *De Trinitate* 6.14, in which he likens the transformative action of the Holy Spirit upon the human spirit to the transformation of iron by fire.

69. Chapter 52, lines 17–19, CCCM, 152: "ceste Ame vestue de ce plus, et nour-rie et muee en ce plus, pour l'amour de ce plus, sans faire compte du moins . . ."

70. Chapter 25, lines 11–14, CCCM, 90 and 92: "si arse en la fournaise du feu d'amour, qu'elle est devenue proprement feu, par quoy elle ne sent point de feu, car en elle mesmes elle est feu, par la vertu d'Amour qui l'a muee ou feu d'amour."

71. Chapter 25, lines 23–24, CCCM, 92: "voit si cler en toutes choses, que il prise les choses selon ce que on les doit priser." See also chapter 64, lines 12–13.

72. See, for example, chapter 83, line 7–9.

73. See chapters 64 and 74.

74. Chapter 32, lines 30–33, CCCM, 108: "se luy mesmes ne le me donnoit proprement de luy, je y fauldroye avant a tousjoursmés sans fin, que que je le prensisse ne ne voulsisse prendre d'aultre que de luy . . ."

75. Chapter 5, lines 23–25, CCCM, 20: "comment il y a grant difference entre don d'amy par moyen a amie et don qui est sans moyen d'amy a amye!"

76. Chapter 5, lines 18–21.

77. Chapter 93, lines 24–25, CCCM, 262: "elle, sans nul entredeux en l'ame d'elle, en ung corps mortel de la Trinité glorieuse vie."

78. Chapter 23, lines 43–49, CCCM, 88: "En ce tonneau de divine boisson a sans faille pluseurs broches. Ce sçait l'umanité qui est joincte a la personne du Filz de Dieu, qui boit a la plus noble, aprés la Trinité; et la Vierge Marie boit a celle d'aprés et est de la plus haulte ceste noble dame yvre. Et aprés elle, boyvent les ardans Seraphins, sur les ales desquelx ces Franches Ames volent."

79. Chapter 23, lines 29–32, CCCM, 86: "le plus la fait yvre, non mye pour chose qu'elle ait beu de ce plus, ainsi comme dit est; mais si a, puisque son amy en a beu, car entre luy et elle par muance d'amour n'a nulle difference, quelque chose qu'il soit des natures."

80. Chapter 121, line 47, CCCM, 338: "Que le floret sans plus vous fist yvre . . ."

81. Porete refers to specifically to lineage in chapters 52, 58, 63, 74, 82, 89, 98, 114, 118, and 121.

82. Bloch, *Etymologies and Genealogies*, 81.

83. Chapter 117, lines 33–35, CCCM, 312 and 314: "l'umain lignage . . . de Jhesucrist son Filz; lequel Filz est la louenge du Pere parmanablement, et le rachat d'umaine creature."

84. See, for instance, chapters 82 and 91.

85. Chapter 77, lines 74–76, CCCM, 218: "Car j'ay souvent soing, dit elle, vueille ou non, de ces deux natures, que les frans n'ont mie, *ne ne pevent avoir.*" My emphasis.

86. Chapter 63, lines 12–15, CCCM, 184: "ilz sont hors mis de la court de voz secrez, ainsi comme seroit ung villain de la court d'ung gentil homme en jugement de pers, ou il n'en peut nul avoir, se il n'est de lignage."

87. Chapter 85, lines 6–10, CCCM, 240 and 242: "Ceste Ame a son lot de franchise affinee, checun costé en a sa plaine pinte. Elle ne respont a nully, se elle ne veult, se il n'est de son lignage; car ung gentilhomme ne daigneroit respondre a ung vilain, se il l'appelloit ou requeroit de champ de bataille."

88. Chapter 79, lines 28–30, CCCM, 224: "Et non pour tant, dit Amour, pitié et courtoisie n'est mie despartie de telle Ame, quant il est temps et lieu." The Latin (lines

26–28, 225) reads: "Et nichilominus, dicit Amor, pietas et curialitas non est extra eam, quando tempus et locus id requirit." My translation.

89. See chapter 84.

90. Chapter 60, lines 17–19, CCCM, 174: "quant il advient que blanc et noir et ensemble, l'en voit mieulx ces deux coulours l'une pour l'aultre, que checun par soy."

91. See chapter 88, lines 5–7.

92. Chapter 88, lines 31–52, CCCM, 250: "Ceste Humilité, qui est tante et mere / est fille de Divine Majesté, et si naist de Divinité. / Deité en est mere et ayeule de ses branches, / dont les gittons font si grant fructifiance. / Nous nous en tairons, car le parler les gaste. / Ceste, c'est assavoir Humilité, / a donné le stoc et le fruit de ces gictons, / pource y est pres / la paix de ce Loingprés, / qui de oeuvre le descombre / et le parler le tourne, / penser y fait umbre, / ce Loingprés le descombre, / nulle rien ne l'encombre. / Ceste est quicte de tous services, / car elle vit de franchise. / Qui sert, il n'est mie franc, / qui sent, il n'est mie mort, / qui desire, il veult, / qui veult, il mendie, / qui mendie, il a deffaillance / de divine souffisance."

93. Chapter 117, lines 79–81, CCCM, 316: "Car tous ceulx qui sont plantez du Pere, et venuz en ce monde, sont descenduz de parfait en imparfait, pour actaindre a plus parfait."

94. Chapter 118, lines 20 and 21, CCCM, 318: "cueur gentil" and "noble courage."

95. Chapter 118, line 69, CCCM, 322: "l'Ame est si dangereuse, noble, et delicieuse."

96. Chapter 118, lines 171–73, CCCM, p. 330.

97. Chapter 118, lines 202–203, CCCM, 332: "par sa haulte noblesse a ceste debte payee."

98. Chapter 59, lines 15–17, CCCM, p. 172.

99. Chapter 60, line 34–35, CCCM, 176: "ceste concordance est finement noble."

100. Chapter 82, lines 3–5, and chapter 79 for a mention of "nobility of intellect," extant in the Latin only.

101. Chapter 82, lines 7–9, 13–15, 19–21, 30–31 and 37–38, CCCM, 232 and 234: "Le premier costé, dont ceste Ame est franche, c'est que elle n'ait point de reprennement en elle, pourtant se elle ne fait ou oeuvre les oeuvres des Vertuz. . . . Le second costé est, que elle n'ait point de voulenté, nient plus que ont les mors des sepulcres, si non tant seulement la divine voulenté. . . . Le tiers costé est, qu'elle croit et tient que il ne fut oncques, ne n'est, ne jamais ne sera pire d'elle, ne mieulx amee de celluy qui l'ayme selon ce que'elle est. . . . Il est de luy en luy pour elle ces mesmes . . . elle pert son nom, car elle monte en souveraineté."

102. Chapter 59, lines 23–24, CCCM, 172: "qui pouroit comprendre le prouffit d'ung mouvement de tel adnientissement."

103. Chapter 48, lines 9–10, CCCM, 144: "Pour telle gent, dit Amour, refusa Dieu son royaulme"; and line 6: "est il serf a luy mesmes."

104. Chapter 87, lines 15–18, CCCM, 248: "Car tant comme je vous ay eue, dame Raison, je n'ay peu tenir franchement mon heritage, et ce qui estoit et est mien; mais maintenant je le puis tenir franchement, puisque je vous ay d'amour a mort navree."

105. Chapter 111, lines 31–36, CCCM, 304: "Or ne puis je estre . . . ce que je doy estre, jusques ad ce que je ressoie la ou je fus, en ce point que je fus, ains que je yssisse de luy aussi nue comme Il est, qui est; aussi nue comme j'estoie, quant j'estoie qui n'estoie mie. Et ce me convient avoir, se je vueil le mien ravoir, aultrement ne l'auroie je mie."

106. Chapter 86, lines 20–25, CCCM, 244: "Se ung roy donnoit a ung de ses servans, qui loyaulment l'a servi, ung grant don, duquel don le servant soit a tousjourmés riche, sans jamais service faire, pourquoy se esmerveilleroit ung sages homs de ce? Sans faille il ne s'en devroit point esmerveiller, car en ce blasmeroit le roy et son don et l'enfranchi de ce don."

107. Chapter 96, lines 5–8, CCCM, 266: "He, pour Dieu! ne laissons nulles choses de nous ne d'autruy jamais entrer dedans nous, pourquoy il conviengne Dieu de sa bonté hors mectre!"

108. Chapter 120, lines 3–7, CCCM, 336: "O esmeraude et precieuse gemme, / Vray dyamant, royne et emperetriz, / Vous donnez tout de vostre fine noblesse, / Sans demander a Amour ses richesses, / Fors le vouloir de son divin plaisir."

109. Chapter 79, lines 20–22, CCCM, 222: "qu'ilz n'eussent point de oeuvre par deliberacion hors du vouloir de l'esperit, il actaindroit aprés ce, comme hoir droicturier, au plus pres de cest estre, dont nous parlons."

110. See chapter 51.

111. See chapter 81 and Mal. 2:15.

112. Chapter 50, lines 22–25, CCCM, 150: "dit la personne de Dieu le Pere, pource que ytelle doit estre mon ainsnee fille, qui est heritiere de mon royaulme, qui scet les secrez du Filz par l'amour du Saint Esperit, qui de luy a ceste Ame cy dounee."

113. Chapter 32, lines 7–9, CCCM, 106: "puisque mon amy a assez en luy de sa droicte noblesse sans commancement, et aura sans fin. Et que me fauldroit il donc?"

114. Chapter 89, lines 4–13, CCCM, 252: "en laquelle Trinité ceste Ame plante si nuement sa voulenté, que elle ne peut pecher, se elle ne se desplante. Elle n'a de quoy pecher, car sans voulenté nul ne peut pecher. Or elle n'a garde de pecher, se elle lesse sa voulenté la ou elle est plantee, c'est en celluy qui la luy avoit donnee de sa bonté franchement; et pource la vouloit ravoir, par son preu, de s'amye nuement et franchement, sans nul pourquoy pour elle, pour deux choses: pource que il le veult, et que il le vault. Et jusques ad ce n'eut elle paix plantureuse ne assiduelle, qu'elle fut de son vouloir purement desnuee."

115. Chapter 85, lines 3–7, CCCM, 240: "Ceste Ame, dit Amour, est franche, mais plus franche, mais tres franche, mais surmontamment franche, et de plante et de stocs et de toutes ses branches, et de tous les fruiz de ses branches. Ceste Ame a son lot de franchise affinee, checun costé en a sa plaine pinte."

116. Chapter 86, lines 38–44, CCCM, 244: "Mon amy est grant, qui grant don me donne, et si est tout nouveau, et nouveau don me donne, et si est tout nouveau, et nouveau don me donne, et si est plain et assovy d'abondance de tous biens de luy mesmes; et je suis plaine et assovye, et habondamment remplie d'abondances de delices de l'espandue bonté divine, sans le querir par paine ne par halage en ses assovyemens, que ce livre devise." Here "Nobility of the Unity of the Soul" speaks.

117. Chapter 53, lines 4–6, CCCM, 154 and 156: "tres noble pierre en la largeur du plain de verité, et seule seurmontaine, fors ceulx de vostre domaine." On these

themes see Bernard J. McGinn, "Ocean and Desert as Symbols of Mystical Absorption in the Christian Tradition," *Journal of Religion* 74 (1994): 155–181.

118. Chapter 71, lines 10–11, CCCM, 198: "qui luy donne en tous lieux magistrale franchise."

119. Chapter 47, lines 17–21, CCCM, 142 and 44: "Ceste Ame a en tous lieux sa paix, car elle porte paix tousdis avec elle, si que pour telle paix luy sont tous lieux convenables, et toutes choses aussi. Si que telle Ame se siet sans soy mouvoir ou siege de paix ou livre de vie, en tesmoignage de bonne conscience et en franchise de parfaicte charité."

120. Chapter 75, lines 30–32, CCCM, 208 and 210: "que nul ne peut veoir les choses divines, tant comme il se melle ou entremect des choses temporelles, c'est assavoir de maindre chose que de Dieu."

121. It is interesting to note that, unlike many mystical authors before and after her, Porete does not employ "ascent" language to describe the soul's movement toward annihilation. Ascending requires will: the will-less soul, no longer the willful soul of the fall, is "taken up" by God.

122. See chapter 77.

123. See chapters 57 and 68.

124. Chapter 81, lines 13–14, CCCM, 230: "Ceste Ame, dit Amour, est emprisonnee et detenue du pays d'entiere paix . . ."

125. Chapter 74, lines 7–9, CCCM, 206: "mais son droit nom est parfaictement noble. Elle a nom `pure', `celestielle', et `espouse de paix'."

126. See, for instance, chapters 10 and 28.

127. Chapter 82, lines 40–46, CCCM, 234 and 236: "Ainsi comme feroit une eaue qui vient de la mer, qui a aucun nom, comme l'en pourroit dire Aise, ou Sene, ou une aultre riviere; et quant celle eaue ou riviere rentre en mer, *elle pert son cours et le nom d'elle*, dont elle couroit en plusieurs pays en faisant son oeuvre. Or est elle en mer, la ou elle se repouse, et ainsi a perdu tel labour." Emphasis mine.

128. On similar metaphors, see Robert E. Lerner, "The Image of Mixed Liquids in Late Medieval Thought," *Church History* 40 (1971): 397–411, as well as Jean Pepin's " 'Stilla aquae.' "

129. Chapter 83, lines 3–6, CCCM, 236: "Or est telle Ame sans nom, et pource a le nom de la muance ou Amour l'a muee. Ainsi comme ont les eaues, dont nous avons parlé, qui ont nom de mer, car c'est toute mer, si tost commes elles son en la mer rentrees."

130. Chapter 82, lines 49–50, CCCM, 236: "fors le nom de celluy en quoy elle est parfaictement muee."

131. Chapter 17, lines 51–52, CCCM, p. 72.

132. Chapter 40, lines 13–17, CCCM, 126: "que il se voit dessoubz toutes creatures, en mer de peché. Et pource que les ennemis sont sers de peché, et ceste Ame a pieça veu que elle est dessoubz eulx, serve a peché (sans nulle comparayson d'elle envers eulx, tant comme est d'elle et de ses oeuvres), . . ."

133. Chapter 85, lines 17–19, CCCM, 242: "Ceste est gentilement noble en prosperité, et haultement noble en adversité, et excellentement noble en tous lieux, quelx qu'ilz soient." My translation.

134. See chapter 19.

135. Chapter 22, lines 13–17, CCCM, 82 and 84: "Ceste Ame ne s'effroie pour tribulacion, ne ne arreste pour consolacion, ne ne desseure pour temptacion, ne ne amenuyse pour nulle substraction. Elle est commune a tous par largesse de pure charité, et si ne demande nient de nully par la noblesse de la courtoisie de pure bonté, dont Dieu l'a remplie."

136. Chapter 124, lines 102–103, CCCM, 358: "car il ne se peut avec ce haberger, il est trop grant pour haberger avec luy hoste estrange."

137. Chapter 99, lines 3–7, CCCM, 274: "Celles gens, qui en l'estre sont, sont de toutes choses en souveraineté. Car leur esperit est en la plus haulte noblesse des ordres des anges creees et ordonnees. Or ont telz gens de tous les ordres pour l'esperit la plus haulte mancion, et de nature la plus gentile complexion; . . ."

138. Chapter 84, lines 10–11, CCCM, 238: "gentile de toutes ses branches qui d'elle sont descendues (nul vilain n'y est prins par mariage, et pource ainsi est tres noble) . . ." My translation.

139. Chapter 139, lines 24–28, CCCM, 404: "Et pource vous dis je, pour conclusion, se Dieu vous a donnee haulte creacion et excellente lumiere et singuliere amour, comprolissez et multipliez sans deffaillance ceste creacion; car ses deux yeulx vous regardent tousdis; et se bien ce considerez et regardez, ce regart fait estre l'Ame simple."

140. See such a claim in Kathleen Garay, " 'She Swims and Floats in Joy': Marguerite Porete, an 'Heretical' Mystic of the Later Middle Ages," *Canadian Woman Studies/Les Cahiers de la femme* 17 (Winter 1997): 21.

141. See Colledge, "Liberty of the Spirit," 114.

142. Newman, *From Virile Woman*, 137 and 138.

143. Newman, *From Virile Woman*, 142.

144. Ibid.

145. Garay, 21.

146. Chapter 55, lines 3–6, CCCM, 158: "ceulx qui vivent comme dit ce livre (ce sont ceulx qui on ataint l'estre de telle vie), l'entendent brefment, sans ce qu'il conviengne ja declarer les gloses."

147. Chapter 98, lines 16–22, CCCM, 272: "vous recognoistrez en ce livre vostre usage. Et celles qui ne le sont ne furent ne ne seront, ne sentiront cel estre, ne ne cognoistront. Ilz ne le pevent faire, ne ne feront. Ilz ne sont point, ce sachez, du lignage dont nous parlons, neant plus que les anges du premier ordre ne sont mie Seraphins, ne ne pevent estre, car Dieu ne leur donne point des Seraphins l'estre." See also chapter 84, lines 23–24.

148. Chapter 98, lines 24–27, CCCM, 272 and 274: "par force du lignage dont ilz sont et seront. . . . Et telles gens, dont nous parlons, qui le sont et seront, ce sachez, recognoistront, si trestost comme ilz orront, le lignage dont ilz sont."

149. Chapter 122, lines 94–104, CCCM, 344: "Amis, que diront beguines, /et gens de religion,/Quant ilz orront l'excellence/de vostre divine chançon?/ Beguines dient que je erre,/prestres, clers, et prescheurs,/Augustins, et carmes,/et les freres mineurs,/Pource que j'escri de l'estre/de l'affinee Amour./Non fais sauve leur Raison . . ."

150. Chapter 59, lines 29–32, CCCM, 172: "non mie, dit elle, pour ceulx qui le sont, mais pour ceulx qui ne le sont, qui encore le seront, mais tousjours mendieront, tant comme ilz seront eulx mesmes."

151. See chapters 1, 9, 17, 52, 62–63, 68, 75–76, 84–86, 96, 98, 111, 121–122, 132–133 and 139.

152. See Keen, *Chivalry*, 160.

153. Chapter 139, lines 22–23, CCCM, 404: "le coron ou la parfection de franchise."

APPENDIX

1. Verdeyen, "Le Procès", 78: Processus siquidem talis est. Tempore quo Margarita dicta Porete suspecta de heresi fuit, in rebellione et inobedientia nolens respondere nec iurare coram inquisitore de hiis que ad inquisitionis sibi commisse officium pertinent, ipse inquisitor contra eam nichilominus inquisivit et ex depositione plurium testium invenit, quod dicta Margarita librum quemdam composuerat continentem hereses et errores, qui de mandato reverendi patris domini Guidonis, condam Cameracensis episcopi, publice et sollempniter tamquam talis fuit condempnatus et combustus. Et per litteram predicti episcopi fuit ordinatum quod, si talia sicut ea que continebantur in libro, de cetero attemptaret verbo vel scripto, eam condempnabat et relinquebat iustitiandam iustitie seculari. Invenit etiam idem inquisitor quod ipsa recognivit in iudicio semel coram inquisitore Lotharingie et semel coram reverendo patre domino Philippo, tunc Cameracensi episcopo, se post condempnationem predictam habuisse librum dictum et alios. Invenit etiam inquisitor quod dicta Margarita dictum librum in suo consimili eosdem continentem errores post ipsius libri condempnationem reverendo patri domino Johanni, Dei gratia Cathalaunensi episcopo, communicavit ac necdum dicto domino sed et pluribus aliis personis simplicibus, begardis et aliis, tamquam bonum." Also in Fredericq, *Corpus inquisitionis neerlandicae*, 1:156–157.

2. Fredericq, *Corpus documentorum*, 2:63–64: "primus talis est: 'Quod anima adnichilata dat licentiam virtutibus nec est amplius in earum servitute, quia non habet eas quoad usum, sed virtutes obediunt ad nutum.' Item decimus quitus articulus est: 'Quod talis anima non curat de consolacionibus Dei nec de donis ejus, nec debet curare nec potest, qui tota intenta est circa Deum, et sic impediretur ejus intentio circa Deum'."

3. From *Decrees of the Ecumenical Councils*, edited by Norman P. Tanner. Volume 1: Nicaea 1 to Lateran 1 (Washington, D. C.: Georgetown University Press, 1990), 383–84 "Primo videlicet quod homo in vita praesenti tantum et talem perfectionis gradum potest aquirere, quod reddetur penitus impeccabilis et amplius in gratia proficere non valebit: nam, ut dicunt, si quis semper posset proficere, posset aliquis Christo perfectior inveniri. Secundo, quod ieiunare non oportet hominem nec orare, postquam gradum perfectionis huiusmodi fuerit assecutus; quia tunc sensualitas est ita perfecte spiritui et rationi subjecta, quod homo potest libere corpori concedere quicquid placet. Tertio, quod illi, qui sunt in praedicto gradu perfectionis et spiritu libertatis, non sunt humanae subjecti oboedientiae, nec ad aliqua praecepta Ecclesiae obligantur; quia, ut asserunt, ubi spiritus Domini, ibi libertas. Quarto, quod homo potest ita finalem beati-

tudinem secundum omnem gradum perfectionis in praesenti assequi, sicut eam in vita obtinebit beata. Quinto, quod quaelibet intellectualis natura in se ipsa naturaliter est beata, quodque anima non indiget lumine gloriae, ipsam elevante ad Deum videndum et eo beate fruendum. Sexto, quod se in actibus exercere virtutum est hominis imperfecti, et perfecta anima licentiat a se virtutes. Septimo, quod mulieris osculum, cum ad hoc natura non inclinet, est mortale peccatum; actus autem carnalis, cum ad hoc natura inclinet, peccatum non est, maxime cum tentatur exercens. Octavo, quod in elevatione corporis Iesu Christi non debent assurgere nec eidem reverentiam exhibere, asserentes, quod esset imperfectionis eisdem, si a puritate et altitudine suae contemplationis tantum descenderent, quod circa ministerium seu sacramentum eucharistiae aut circa passionem humanitatis Christi aliqua cogitarent. . . . nos, sacro approbante concilio, sectam ipsam cum praemissis erroribus damnamus et reprobamus omnino, inhibentes districtius, ne quis ipsos de cetero teneat, approbet vel defendet." This text is also printed in Fredericq, *Corpus documentorum inquisitionis haereticae pravitatis neerlandicae*, 2 vols. (Ghent: n.p., 1889–1906), 1:168–169, as well as in *Enchiridion Symbolorum: Definitionum et declarationum de rebus fidei et morum*, ed. Heinrich Denzinger (Freiburg: Herder, 1965), 282.

BIBLIOGRAPHY

EDITIONS OF THE MIRROR OF SIMPLE SOULS

Doiron, Marilyn, ed. *The Mirror of Simple Souls: A Middle English Translation.* In *Archivio Italiano per la Storia della Pietà* 5 (1968): 242–355.

Guarnieri, Romana, ed. *Archivio Italiano per la Storia della Pietà* 4 (1965): 513–635.

———, and Paul Verdeyen, eds. *Corpus Christianorum: Continuatio Mediaevalis* 9. Turnhout: Brepols, 1986.

FULL MODERN TRANSLATIONS

Babinsky, Ellen, translator. *Marguerite Porete. The Mirror of Simple Souls.* New York: Paulist Press, 1993.

Crawford, Charles, editor. *A Mirror for Simple Souls* (by "An Anonymous Thirteenth Century French Mystic"). New York: Crossroad, 1981.

Feroldi, Donato, translator. *Marguerite Porete. Lo Specchio delle anime semplici.* Palerme: Sellerio, 1995.

Fozzer, Giovanna, translator. *Marguerite Porete. Lo Specchio delle anime semplici.* Milan: San Paolo, 1994.

Gari, Blanca and Alicia Padros-Wolf, translators. *Marguerite Porete. El Espejo de las almas simples.* Barcelone: Icaria, 1995.

Kirchberger, Clare, translator. *The Mirror of Simple Souls.* London: Downside, 1927.

Longchamp, Max Huot de, translator. *Marguerite Porete. Le Miroir des simples âmes anéanties et qui seulement demeurent en vouloir et désir d'amour.* Paris: Albin Michel Editions, 1984.

Louis-Combet, Claude, translator. *Marguerite Porete. Le Miroir des simples âmes anéanties et qui seulement demeurent en vouloir et désir d'amour.* Grenoble: Jérôme Millon, 1991.

ENGLISH TRANSLATIONS OF SELECTIONS

Brunn, Emilie Zum, and Georgette Epiney-Burgard. *Women Mystics in Medieval Europe.* Translated by Sheila Hughes. New York: Paragon House, 1989, 143–175.

Dronke, Peter. *Women Writers of the Middle Ages: A Critical Study of Texts from Perpetua (d. 203) to Marguerite Porete (d. 1310)*. New York: Cambridge University Press, 1985, 275–278.

Petroff, Elizabeth A., ed. *Medieval Women's Visionary Literature*. Translated by Dom Eric Levine. New York: Oxford University Press, 1986, 294–298.

Wilson, Katherine M., ed. *Medieval Women Writers*. Translated by Gwendolyn Bryant. Athens, Ga: University of Georgia Press, 1986, 204–226.

OTHER PRIMARY SOURCES

Andreas Capellanus. *The Art of Courtly Love*. Translated by John J. Parry. New York: Columbia University Press, 1960.

Bernard of Clairvaux. *The Letters of St. Bernard of Clairvaux*. Translated by Bruno Scott James. Kalamazoo: Cistercian Publications, 1998.

———. *Selected Works*. Translated by G. R. Evans. New York: Paulist Press, 1987.

Christ, Karl, ed. "*La regle des fins amans*. Eine Beginenregal aus dem Ende des XIII Jahrhunderts." *Festschrift für K. Voretzsch*. Halle: n.p., 1927, 192–206.

Dante Alighieri. *Il Convivio*. Translated by Richard H. Lansing. New York: Garland, 1990.

Decrees of the Ecumenical Councils. Edited by Norman P. Tanner. Volume 1: Nicaea 1 to Lateran 1. Washington, D. C.: Georgetown University Press, 1990.

Fredericq, Paul, ed.. *Corpus documentorum inquisitionis haereticae pravitatis neerlandicae*. 2 volumes. Ghent: The Hague, 1889–1906.

Hadewijch. *The Complete Works*. Translated by Mother Columba Hart. New York: Paulist Press, 1980.

Hildegard of Bingen. *The Letters of Hildegard of Bingen*, Volume 1. Translated by Joseph L. Baird and Radd K. Erman. Oxford: Oxford University Press, 1994.

Hildegard of Bingen. *Scivias, Corpus Christianorum: Continuatio Medievalis* 43 and 43A (Turnholt: Brepols, 1978)

Hildegard of Bingen. *Scivias*. Translated by Mother Columba Hart and Jane Bishop. New York: Paulist Press, 1990.

Hrotsvit of Gandersheim. *Hrotsvit of Gandersheim: A Florilegium of Her Works*. Translated by Katharina M. Wilson. Rochester: Boydell and Brewer, 1998.

Langlois, Ernest, ed. *Le Roman de la Rose, par Guillaume de Lorris et Jean de Meun, publié d'après les manuscrits*, 5 vols. Paris: Librairie Ancienne Honoré Champion.

Lea, H. C. *History of the Inquisition of the Middle Ages*. Volume II. New York: Harper Brothers, 1901.

Meister Eckhart. The Essential Sermons, Commentaries, Treatises, and Defense. Edited by Edmund Colledge and Bernard McGinn. New York: Paulist Press, 1981.

Verdeyen, Paul. "Le Procès d'inquisition contre Marguerite Porete et Guiard de Cressonessart (1309–1310)," *Revue d'histoire ecclésiastique* 81 (1986): 47–94.

Viard, J., ed. *Les grandes chroniques de France*, Vol. VIII. Paris: n.p., 1934.

SECONDARY SOURCES

Arden, Heather. *The Romance of the Rose*. Boston: Twayne Publishers, 1987.

———. *The Romance of the Rose: An Annotated Bibliography*. New York: Garland, 1993.

Babinsky, Ellen L. "A Beguine in the Court of the King: The Relation of Love and Knowledge in *The Mirror of Simple Souls* by Marguerite Porete." University of Chicago Dissertation. June 1991.

Bachrach, Bernard S. "Some Observations on *The Medieval Nobility*: A Review Essay," *Medieval Prosopography* 1 (1980): 15–33.

Baker, Derek, ed., *Medieval Women*. Oxford: Basil Blackwell, 1978.

Baldwin, John W. *Masters, Princes, and Merchants: The Social Views of Peter the Chanter*. 2 volumes. Princeton: Princeton University Press, 1970.

Bambeck, Manfred. "Marguerite Porete Le Mirouer des simples âmes und der französische Wortschatz," *Romanische Forschungen* 97 (1985): 226–230.

Barbero, Alessandro. *L'aristocrazia nella società francese del medioevo. Analisi delle fonti letterarie (secoli X–XIII)*. Bologna, n.p., 1987.

———. "Noblesse et chevalerie en France au Moyen Age: une réflexion," *Moyen Age* 97 (1991): 431–437.

Barthélemy, Dominique. "L'état contre le „lignage..: une thème a développer dans l'histoire des pouvoirs en France aux Xie, XIIe, et XIIIe siècles," *Medievales* 10 (1986): 37–50.

———. "Qu'est-ce que le servage, en France, au Xie siècle?" *Revue historique* 582 (1992): 233–284.

Benton, John F. "Clio and Venus: A Historical View of Medieval Love." In *Culture, Power, and Personality in Medieval France*, edited by Thomas N. Bisson, 99–121. London: Hambledon Press, 1991.

Benz, Ernst. "Über den Adel in der deutschen Mystik," *Deutsche Vierteljahrsschrift für Literaturwissenschaft und Geistesgeschichte* 14, No. 4. Edited by Paul Kluckhorn and Erich Rothacker. Halle: Niemeyer, 1936: 505–535.

Bérion, N. "La prédication au béguinage de Paris pendant l'année liturgique 1272–3," *Recherches Augustiniennes* 13 (1978): 105–229.

Bertho, Marie. *Le Miroir des âmes simples et anéanties de Marguerite Porète. Une vie blessée d'amour*. Paris: Larousse, 1993.

Bisson, Thomas N. *Cultures of Power: Lordship, Status, and Process in Twelfth-Century Europe*. Philadelphia: University of Pennsylvania Press, 1995.

———. "Nobility and Family in Medieval France: A Review Essay," *French Historical Studies* 16, No. 3 (Spring 1990): 597–613.

Bloch, Marc. *La Société féodale*, 2 vols. Paris, 1939–1940. Translated by L. A. Manyon as *Feudal Society*. Chicago: University of Chicago Press, 1961.

Bloch, R. Howard. *Etymologies and Genealogies: A Literary Anthropology of the French Middle Ages*. Chicago: University of Chicago Press, 1983.

Bolton, Brenda. "*Mulieres Sanctae*." In *Women in Medieval Society*, edited by Susan Mosher Stuard, 141–158. Philadelphia: University of Pennsylvania Press, 1976.

————. "*Paupertas Christi*: Old Wealth and New Poverty in the Twelfth Century." In *Renaissance and Renewal in Christian History*, edited by Derek Baker, 95–104. Volume 14 of *Studies in Church History*. Oxford: Blackwell, 1977.

————. "Some Thirteenth-Century Women in the Low Countries: A Special Case?" *Nederlands Archief voor Kerkgeschiedenis* 61, No. 1 (1981): 7–29.

————. "*Vitae Matrum*: A Further Aspect of the *Frauenfrage*." In *Medieval Women*, edited by Derek Baker, 253–273. Oxford: Blackwell, 1978.

Bonenfant, P., and G. Despy. "La Noblesse en Brabant au XIIe et XIIIe siècles," *Le Moyen Age* 64 (1958): 27–66.

Borreson, Kari Elisabeth. *The Image of God and Gender Models in Judaeo-Christian Tradition*. Atlantic Highlands, N. J.: Humanities Press, 1991.

Bothe, Catherine Müller. "Writing as Mirror in the Work of Marguerite Porete," *Mystics Quarterly* 20, No. 3 (1994): 105–112.

Bouchard, Constance B. "Community: Society and the Church in Medieval France," *French Historical Studies* 17, No. 4 (Fall 1992): 1035–1047.

————. "The Origins of the French Nobility," *American Historical Review* 1, No. 3 (1981): 501–532.

————. '*Strong of Body, Brave and Noble*': *Chivalry and Society in Medieval France*. Ithaca: Cornell University Press, 1998.

————. *Sword, Miter, and Cloister: Nobility and the Church in Burgundy, 980–1198*. Ithaca: Cornell University Press, 1987.

Bradley, Rita Mary. "Backgrounds of the Title 'Speculum' in Medieval Literature," *Speculum* 29 (1954): 100–115.

Breuer, Wilhelm. "Mystik als alternative Lebensform. Das 37. Strophische Gedicht der Suster Hadewijch," *Zeitschrift für deutsche Philologie* 103 (1984): 103–115.

Broughton, Bradford B. *Dictionary of Medieval Knighthood and Chivalry: Concepts and Terms*. New York: Greenwood Press, 1986.

Brown, Elizabeth A. R. "The Tyranny of a Construct: Feudalism and Historians of Medieval Europe," *American Historical Review* 79 (1974): 1063–1088.

Brown, Peter. *The Cult of the Saints: Its Rise and Function in Latin Christianity*. Chicago: University of Chicago Press, 1981.

Bullough, D. A. "Early Medieval Social Groupings: The Terminology of Kinship," *Past and Present* 45 (1969): 3–18.

Bumke, Joachim. *The Concept of Knighthood in the Middle Ages*. New York: AMS Press, 1982.

————. *Courtly Culture: Literature and Society in the High Middle Ages*. Translated by Thomas Dunlap. Berkeley: University of California Press, 1991.

Bynum, Caroline Walker. *Fragmentation and Redemption: Essays on Gender and the Human Body in Medieval Religion*. New York: Zone Books, 1991.

————. *Holy Feast and Holy Fast: The Religious Significance of Food to Medieval Women*. Berkeley: University of California Press, 1987.

Carlson, Thomas A. "The Poverty and Poetry of Indiscretion: Negative Theology and Negative Anthropology in Contemporary and Historical Perspectives," *Christianity and Literature* 47, No. 2 (Winter 1998): 167–193.

Carozzi, Claude. "Les fondements de la tripartition sociale chez Adalbéron de Laon," *Annales: Économies, sociétés, civilisations* 33 (1978): 683–702.

Chenu, M.-D. *Nature, Man, and Society in the Twelfth Century: Essays on New Theological Perspectives in the Latin West*. Edited by Jerome Taylor and Lester K. Little. Chicago: University of Chicago Press, 1968.

Cherchi, Paolo. *Andreas and the Ambiguity of Courtly Love*. Toronto: University of Toronto Press, 1994.

Cheyette, Fredric L. *Lordship and Community in Medieval Europe*. New York: Holt, Rinehart, and Winston, 1968.

Cohn, Norman. *The Pursuit of the Millenium*. New York: Oxford University Press, 1970.

Colledge, Edmund. "Liberty of Spirit: 'The Mirror of Simple Souls'." In *Theology of Renewal*, edited by L. K. Shook, volume 2, 100–117. Dorval, Quebec: Palm, 1968.

———, and Romana Guarnieri. "The Glosses by 'M.N.' and Richard Methley to 'The Mirror of Simple Souls,'" *Archivio Italiano per la Storia della Pietà* 5 (1968): 357–382.

———, and J. C. Marler. "Poverty of the Will: Ruusbroec, Eckhart, and the *Mirror of Simple Souls*." In *Jan van Ruusbroec, The Sources, Content, and Sequels of his Mysticism*, edited by P. Mommaers and N. de Paepe, 14–47. Leuven: University Press, 1984.

Constable, Giles. "The Orders of Society." In *Three Studies in Medieval Religious and Social Thought*, 249–360. Cambridge: Cambridge University Press, 1995.

———. *The Reformation of the Twelfth Century*. Cambridge: Cambridge University Press, 1996.

Copleston, Frederick C. *A History of Philosophy*. Volume 1. New York: Doubleday, 1993.

Corduan, Winfried. "The Gospel According to Margaret," *Journal of the Evangelical Theological Society* 35, No. 4 (December 1992): 515–530.

Cottrell, Robert D. "Marguerite Porete's Le Mirouer des simples ames and the Problematics of the Written Word," *Medieval Perspectives* 1.1 (1986): 151–158.

Degler-Spengler, Brigitte. "Die religiöse Frauenbewegung des Mittelalters: Konversen –Nonnen - Beginen," *Rottenburger Jahrbuch für Kirchengeschichte* 3 (1984): 75-88.

Delmaire, Bernard. "Les Béguines dans le Nord de France au premier siècle de leur histoire (vers 1230-vers 1350)." In *Les religieuses en France au XIIIe siècle*, edited by Michael Parisse, 120–162. Nancy: Presses Universitaires de Nancy, 1985.

Dembowski, Peter F. "Vocabulary of Old French Courtly Lyrics: Difficulties and Hidden Difficulties," *Critical Inquiry* 2 (1975/6): 763–779.

Denomy, Alex J. *The Heresy of Courtly Love*. Gloucester, Mass.: Peter Smith, 1965.

Despy, G. "La Noblesse en Brabant au XIIe et XIIIe siècles," *Le Moyen Age* 64 (1958): 27–66.

Devlin, Dennis. "Feminine Lay Piety in the High Middle Ages: The Beguines." In *Medieval Religious Women*, edited by John A. Nichols and Lillian Thomas Shank, 183–196. Volume 1 of *Distant Echoes*. Cistercian Studies Series 71. Kalamazoo, Mich.: Cistercian Publications, 1984.

Dietrich, Julia. "The Visionary Rhetoric of Hildegard of Bingen." In *Listening to Their Voices: The Rhetorical Activities of Historical Women*, edited by Molly Meijer Wertheimer, 199–214. Columbia, S. C.: University of South Carolina Press, 1997.

Dinzelbacher, Peter. "Europäische Frauenmystik des Mittelalters: Ein Überblick." In *Frauenmystik im Mittelalter*, 11–23. Stuttgart: Schwabenverlag, 1985.

Di Salvo, Antonio. "Ramon Lull and the Language of Chivalry," *Mystics Quarterly* 14 (December 1998): 197–206.

Duby, Georges. *The Chivalrous Society*. Translated by Cynthia Postan. Berkeley: University of California Press, 1977.

———. "The Diffusion of Cultural Patterns in Feudal Society," *Past and Present* 39 (1968): 3–10.

———. *La société aux Xie et XIIe siècles dans la région mâconnais*. Paris, 1971.

———. *The Three Orders: Feudal Society Imagined*. Translated by Arthur Goldhammer. Chicago: University of Chicago, 1980.

Dumeige, Gervais. "Dissemblance." *Dictionnaire de spiritualité, ascetique et mystique, doctrine et histoire*. 3:1330–1346. Paris: Beauchesne, 1957.

Evergates, Theodore, "Nobles and Knights in Twelfth-Century France." In *Cultures of Power: Lordship, Status, and Process in Twelfth-Century Europe*, edited by Thomas N. Bisson, 11–35. Philadelphia: University of Pennsylvania Press, 1995.

Flanagan, Sabina. " 'For God Distinguishes the People of Earth as in Heaven': Hildegard of Bingen's Social Ideas," *The Journal of Religious History* 22, No. 1 (February 1998): 14–34.

———. *Hildegard of Bingen, 1098–1179: A Visionary Life*. New York: Routledge, 1989.

Flori, Jean. *L'essor de la chevalerie, Xie-XIIe siècles*. Travaux d'histoire éthico-politique XLVI. Paris, 1986.

———. "Chevalerie, noblesse, et lutte de classes au Moyen Age," *Le Moyen Age* 94 (1988): 257–279.

Fossier, Robert. *Enfance de l'Europe*, 2 vols. Paris, 1982.

Fozzer, Giovanna. " 'Parfaicte franchise n'a nul pourquoi.' Notizia sullo 'Specchio delle Anime Semplici' di Margherita Porete," *Revista di Ascetica e Mistica* (1991): 375–395.

Freed, John B. "Urban Development and the *Cura Monialium* in the Thirteenth Century," *Viator* 3 (1972): 311–327.

Galloway, Penelope. " 'Discreet and Devout Maidens': Women's Involvement in Beguine Communities in Northern France, 1200–1500." In *Medieval Women in Their Communities*, edited by Diane Watt, 92–115. Toronto: University of Toronto Press, 1997.

Garay, Kathleen. " 'She Swims and Floats in Joy': Marguerite Porete, an 'Heretical' Mystic of the Later Middle Ages," *Canadian Woman Studies/Les Cahiers de la femme* 17, No. 1 (Winter 1997): 18–21.

Gardner, Elizabeth J. "The English Nobility and Monastic Education, c. 1100–1500." In *The Cloister and the World*, edited by John Blair and Brian Golding. Oxford: Clarendon, 1996.

Genicot, Léopold. "La noblesse au moyen âge dans l'ancienne 'Francie'," *Annales* 17 (1962): 1–8.

———. "La noblesse médiévale: Encore!" *Revue d'histoire ecclésiastique* 88 (1993): 173–201.

———. "La noblesse médiévale: Pans de lumière et zones obscures," *Tijdschrift voor Geschiedenis* 93 (1980): 341–356.

———. "Recent research on the Medieval Nobility." In *The Medieval Nobility*, edited and translated by Timothy Reuter, 17–36. Volume 14 of *Europe in the Middle Ages, Selected Studies*. New York: North-Holland Publishing, 1979. First published as "Les recherches relatives à la noblesse médiévale," *Bulletin de l'Académie Royale de Belgique*, classe de lettres, 5e série (1975): 45–68.

Gersh, Stephen. *Middle Platonism and Neoplatonism: The Latin Tradition*. 2 volumes. Notre Dame: University of Notre Dame Press, 1986.

Gilson, Etienne. *The Mystical Theology of St. Bernard*. London: Sheed and Ward, 1940.

———. "*Regio Dissimilitudinis* de Platon á Saint Bernard de Clairvaux," *Mediaeval Studies* 9 (1947): 108–130

Gnädinger, Louise. "Die Lehre der Margareta Porete von der Selbst- und Gotteserkenntnis. Eine Annäherung." In *Denkmodelle von Frauen im Mittelalter*, edited by Béatrice Acklin-Zimmermann, 125–148. Fribourg, Switzerland: Universitätsverlag, 1994.

———. "Margareta Porete, eine Begine." In *Der Spiegel der Einfachen Seelen*, 215–239. Zürich: Artemis, 1987.

Gössmann, Elisabeth. " 'Ein Wissen, das Frauen nicht zukommt'. Die Geschichte der 1310 hingerichteten Mystikerin Marguerite Porete," *Orientierung* 52, No. 4 (February 28, 1988): 40–43.

Grabes, Herbert. *The Mutable Glass: Mirror Imagery in Titles and Texts of the Middle Ages and English Renaissance*. Translated by Gordon Collier. Cambridge: Cambridge University Press, 1982.

Greven, Joseph. *Anfänge der Beginen*. Münster: Aschendorff, 1912.

Grundmann, Herbert. *Religiöse Bewegungen im Mittelalter: Untersuchungen über die geschichtlichen Zusammenhangen swischen der Ketzerei, den Bettelorden, und der religiösen Freauenbewegung im 12. und 13. Jahrhundert und die geschichtlichen Grundlagen der deutschen Mystik*. Berlin: n.p., 1935; Hildesheim: Georg Olms, 1961. Translated by Steven Rowan as *Religious Movements in the Middle Ages*. Notre Dame: University of Notre Dame Press, 1995.

Guarnieri, Romana. "Frères du Libre Esprit." In *Dictionnaire de Spiritualité* 5:1241–1268. Paris: Beauchesne, 1964.

Guest, Tanis M. *Some Aspects of Hadewijch's Poetic Form in the "Strofische Gedichten."* The Hague: Martinus Nijhoff, 1975.

Guilhiermoz, Paul. *Essai sur l'origine de la noblesse en France*. Paris: n.p., 1902.

Haas, Alois H. "Marguerite Porete." In *Geistliches Mittelalter*, edited by Alois M. Haas, 407–409. Fribourg, Switzerland: Universitätsverlag, 1984.

Heid, Ulrich. "Studien zu Marguerite Porète und ihrem Miroir des simple âmes." In *Religiöse Frauenbewegung und mystische Frömmigkeit im Mittelalter*, edited by Peter Dinzelbacher and Dieter R. Bauer. *Archiv für Kulturgeschichte* 28, 185–214. Vienna: Böhlau, 1988.

Heinzelmann, Martin. "La noblesse du haut moyen âge (VIIIe–Xie siècles)," *Le Moyen Âge* 83 (1977): 131–44.

Herlihy, David. *The Social History of Italy and Western Europe, 700–1500*. London: Variorum, 1978.

Hess, W. "Imago Dei (Gen. 1.26)," *Benediktinische Monatsschrift* 29 (1953): 371–386.

Hollywood, Amy Marie. *The Soul as Virgin Wife: Mechtild of Magdeburg, Marguerite Porete, and Meister Eckhart*. Notre Dame: University of Notre Dame Press, 1995.

———. "Suffering Transformed: Marguerite Porete, Meister Eckhart, and the Problem of Women's Spirituality." In *Meister Eckhart and the Beguine Mystics*, edited by Bernard McGinn, 87–113. New York: Continuum, 1994.

Howe, John. "The Nobility's Reform of the Medieval Church," *American Historical Review* 93 (1988), 317–339.

Hunt, Tony. "The Emergence of the Knight in France and England, 1000–1200," *Forum for Modern Language Studies* 17 (1981): 93–114.

Jaeger, C. Stephen. *Ennobling Love: In Search of a Lost Sensibility*. Philadelphia: University of Pennsylvania Press, 1999.

———. *The Envy of Angels: Cathedral Schools and Social Ideals in Medieval Europe, 950–1200*. Philadelphia: University of Pennsylvania Press, 1994.

———. *The Origins of Courtliness: Civilizing Trends and the Formation of Courtly Ideals, 939–1210*. Philadelphia: University of Pennsylvania Press, 1985.

Javelet, Robert. "Image et ressemblance." In *Dictionnaire de spiritualité* 7:1341–1353.

———. *Image et ressemblance au douzième siècle: Du Saint Anselme à Alain de Lille*. 2 volumes. Paris: Letouzey et Ané, 1967.

Johnson, Penelope D. *Equal in Monastic Profession: Religious Women in Medieval France*. Chicago: University of Chicago Press, 1991.

Jónsson, Gunnlaugur A. *The Image of God: Genesis 1:26–28 in a Century of Old Testament Research*. Lund: Almquist and Wiksell, 1988.

Kaplowitt, Stephen. *The Ennobling Power of Love in the Medieval German Lyric*. Chapel Hill: University of North Carolina Press, 1986.

Keen, Maurice. *Chivalry*. New Haven: Yale University Press, 1984.

———. *Nobles, Knights, and Men-at-Arms in the Middle Ages*. London: Hambledon, 1996.

Kennedy, Elspeth. "The Quest for Identity and the Importance of Lineage in Thirteenth Century Prose Romance." In *The Ideals and Practice of Medieval Knighthood*, edited by Christopher Harper-Bill and Ruth Harvey, 70–86. Dover, N. H.: Boydell Press, 1986.

Kieckhefer, Richard. *Repression of Heresy in Medieval Germany*. Philadelphia: University of Pennsylvania Press, 1979.

Klibansky, Raymond. *Middle Platonism: The Continuity of the Platonic Tradition during the Middle Ages*. London: Warburg Institute, 1939.

Kloppenborg, John S. "Egalitarianism in the Myth and Rhetoric of Pauline Churches." In *Reimagining Christian Origins*, 247–263. Valley Forge, Pa: Trinity Press, 1996.

Lamau, Marie-Louise. "L'Homme a l'Image de Dieu chez les Théologiens et Spirituels du XIIe siècle," *Melanges de Science Religieuse* 48 (Jan.-June 1991): 203–213.

Lambert, Malcolm. *Medieval Heresy: Popular Movements from the Gregorian Reform to the Reformation*, Second Edition. Cambridge, Mass.: Blackwell, 1992.

Langlois, Charles V. "Marguerite Porete," *Revue Historique* 54 (1894): 295–299.

Leclercq, Jean. *The Love of Learning and the Desire for God: A Study of Monastic Culture*. Translated by Catharine Misrahi. New York: Fordham University Press, 1988.

———. *Monks and Love in Twelfth-Century France: Psycho-Historical Essays*. Oxford: Clarendon, 1979.

Leff, Gordon. *Heresy in the Later Middle Ages: The Relation of Heterodoxy to Dissent, c. 1250-c. 1450*, 2 vols. New York: Barnes and Noble, 1967.

Le Grand, Léon. "Les Béguines de Paris," *Mémoires de la Societé de l'Histoire de Paris et de l'Ile de France* 20: 295–357.

Lerner, Robert E. "An Angel of Philadelphia in the Reign of Phillip the Fair: The Case of Guiard of Cressonessart." In *Order and Innovation in the Middle Ages: Essays in Honor of Joseph R. Strayer*, edited by William C. Jordan, Bruce McNab, and Teofilo F. Ruiz. Princeton: Princeton University Press, 1976.

———. "Beguines and Beghards." In *Dictionary of the Middle Ages* 2:157–163.

———. *The Heresy of the Free Spirit in the Later Middle Ages*. Los Angeles: University of California Press, 1972.

———. "The Image of Mixed Liquids in Late Medieval Thought," *Church History* 40 (1971): 397–411.

Lichtman, Maria. "Marguerite Porete and Meister Eckhart: *The Mirror for Simple Souls* Mirrored." In *Meister Eckhart and the Beguine Mystics*, edited by Bernard McGinn, 65–86. New York: Continuum, 1994.

———. "Marguerite Porete's *Mirror for Simple Souls*: Inverted Reflections of Self, Society, and God," *Studia Mystica* 16, No. 1 (1995): 4–30.

———. "Negative Theology in Marguerite Porete and Jacques Derrida," *Christianity and Literature* 47, No. 2 (Winter 1998): 212–227.

Little, Lester K. *Religious Poverty and the Profit Economy in Medieval Europe*. Ithaca: Cornell University Press, 1983.

Lucas, Robert H. "Ennoblement in Late Medieval France," *Mediaeval Studies* 39 (1977): 239–260.

McDonnell, E. W. *The Beguines and Beghards in Medieval Culture, with Special Emphasis on the Belgian Scene*. New Brunswick, N. J.: Rutgers University Press, 1954.

McGinn, Bernard. "The Abyss of Love." In *The Joy of Learning and the Love of God: Essays in Honor of Jean Leclercq*, edited by E. Rozanne Elder, 95–120. Cistercian Studies Series 160. Kalamazoo: Cistercian Publications, 1995.

———. *The Flowering of Mysticism: Men and Women in the New Mysticism— 1200–1350*. Volume Three of *The Presence of God: A History of Christian Mysticism*. New York: Crossroad, 1998.

————. *The Foundations of Mysticism: Origins to the Fifth Century*. Volume One of *The Presence of God: A History of Christian Mysticism*. New York: Crossroad, 1992.

————. *The Growth of Mysticism: Gregory the Great through the Twelfth Century*. Volume Two of *The Presence of God: A History of Christian Mysticism*. New York: Crossroad, 1994.

————. "The Human Person as Image of God: II. Western Christianity." In *Christian Spirituality: Origins to the Twelfth Century*, edited by Bernard McGinn and John Meyendorff, 290–330. New York: Crossroad, 1985.

————. "Love, Knowledge, and *Unio Mystica* in the Western Christian Tradition." In *Mysticism and Monotheistic Faith: An Ecumenical Dialogue*, edited by Moshe Idel and Bernard McGinn, 59–86. New York: Macmillan Publishing, 1989.

————, ed. *Meister Eckhart and the Beguine Mystics: Hadewijch of Brabant, Mechtild of Magdeburg, and Marguerite Porete*. New York: Continuum, 1994.

————. "Ocean and Desert as Symbols of Mystical Absorption in the Christian Tradition," *Journal of Religion* 74 (1994): 155–181.

McLaughlin, Eleanor. "The Heresy of the Free Spirit and Late Medieval Mysticism," *Medievalia et Humanistica* 4 (1973): 37–54.

McNamara, Joann. "*De Quibusdam Mulieribus*: Reading Women's History from Hostile Sources." In *Medieval Women and the Sources of Medieval History*, edited by Joel Rosenthal, 237–258. Athens, Ga: University of Georgia Press, 1990.

Martindale, Jane. "The French Aristocracy in the Early Middle Ages: A Reappraisal," *Past and Present* 75 (1977): 5–45.

Meeks, Wayne. *The First Urban Christians*. New Haven: Yale University Press, 1983.

Mens, Alcantara. "Beghine, Begardi, Beghinaggi." In *Dizionario degli Instituti di Perfezione* 1:1165–1180.

————. "Les béguines et béghards dans le cadre urban de la culture mediévale," *Le Moyen Age* 64 (1958): 305–315.

Mierlo, J. van. "Béguinages." In *Dictionnaire d'histoire et de géographie ecclesiastique* 7:457–473.

————. "Béguins, béguines, béguinages." In *Dictionnaire de Spiritualite* 1:1341–1352. Paris: Beauchesne, 1937.

Mommaers, Paul. "La Transformation d'Amour Selon Marguerite Porete," *Ons geestelijk erf* 65 (1991): 89–107.

Monfrin, Jacques. "A propos du vocabulaire des structures sociales du haut Moyen Age," *Annales du Midi* LXXXX (968): 611–620.

Monson, Don A. "The Troubadour's Lady Reconsidered Again," *Speculum* 70 (1995): 255–274.

Moore, R. I. *The Formation of a Persecuting Society: Power and Deviance in Western Europe 950–1250*. New York: Blackwell, 1987.

————. *The Origins of European Dissent*. New York: St. Martin's Press, 1977.

Moser, Sabina. "La Mistica di Margherita Porete," *Rivista di Ascetica e Mistica* (1991): 396–414.

Müller, Catherine. *Marguerite Porete et Marguerite d'Oingt de l'autre côté du miroir*. New York: Lang, 1999.

Muraro, Luisa. "La Filosofia mistica di Margherita Porete: Il concetto di ragione," *Rivista di spiritualità e politica* 13 (June 1993): 67–80.

Murk-Jansen, Saskia. "Hadewijch and Eckhart: Amor Intellegere Est." In *Meister Eckhart and the Beguine Mystics*, edited by Bernard McGinn. New York: Continuum, 1997.

———. *The Measure of Mystic Thought: A Study of Hadewijch's 'Mengeldicten'*. Göppingen, 1991.

Neel, Carol. "The Origins of the Beguines," *Signs* 14, No. 2 (1989): 321–341.

Newman, Barbara. *From Virile Woman to WomanChrist: Studies in Medieval Religion and Literature*. Philadelphia: University of Pennsylvania Press, 1995.

———. *Sister of Wisdom: St. Hildegard's Theology of the Feminine*. Berkeley: University of California Press, 1987.

Newman, F. X., ed. *The Meaning of Courtly Love*. Albany: State University of New York Press, 1968.

Nichols, John A., and Lillian Thomas Shank. *Medieval Religious Women*, Volume 1: Distant Echoes. Cistercian Studies Series 71. Kalamazoo: Cistercian Publications, 1984.

Niermeyer, J. F. *Mediae Latinitatis Lexicon Minus*. Leiden: Brill, 1976.

O'Meara, Dominic, ed., *Neoplatonism and Christian Thought*. Albany: State University of New York Press, 1982.

Orcibal, J. "Le 'Miroir des simples ames' et la 'secte' du Libre Esprit," *Revue de l'Histoire des Religions* (July-Sept. 1969): 35–60.

Otto, Stephan. *Die Funktion des Bildesbegriffes in der theologie des 12. Jahrhunderts*. Münster: Aschendorff, 1963.

Pagels, Elaine. *Adam, Eve, and the Serpent*. London: Weidenfeld and Nicholson, 1988.

Parisse, Michael, ed. *Les religieuses en France au XIIIe siècle*. Nancy: Presses Universitaires de Nancy, 1985.

Pearce, Spencer. "Dante: Order, Justice, and the Society of Orders." In *Orders and Hierarchies in Late Medieval and Renaissance Europe*, edited by Jeffrey Denton, 33–55. Toronto: University of Toronto Press, 1999.

Pépin, Jean. "Stilla aquae modica multo infuso vino, ferrum ignitum, luce perfuses aer': L'origin de trois comparaisons familières à la théologie mystique médiévale," *Divinitas* 11 (1967): 331–375.

Pereira, Michela. "Fra Raison e Amour: il Miroir des simples âmes di Margherita Porete." In *Filosofia Donne Filosofia*, edited by M. Forcina et al. Lecce: Milella, 1994.

Philippen, L. J. M. *De Begijnhoven, Oorsprong, geschiedenis, inrichting*. Antwerp: n.p., 1918.

Phillips, Dayton. "The Beguines in Medieval Strassburg: A Study of the Social Aspects of Beguine Life." Stanford University Dissertation, 1941.

Pranger, Burcht. "The Rhetoric of Mystical Unity in the Middle Ages: A Study in Retroactive Reading," *Journal of Literature and Theology* 17, No. 1 (March 1993): 13–49.

Randall, Catherine. "Person, Place, Perception: A Proposal for the Reading of Porete's *Miroir des âmes simples et anéanties*," *Journal of Medieval and Renaissance Studies* 25, No. 2 (Spring 1995): 229–244.

Reiss, Edmund. "Fin'Amors: Its History and Meaning in Medieval Literature," *Medieval and Renaissance Studies* 8 (1979): 74–99.

Reuter, Timothy, ed. and trans. *The Medieval Nobility*. Volume 14 of *Europe in the Middle Ages, Selected Studies*. New York: North-Holland Publishing, 1979.

Rigby, Stephen. "Approaches to Pre-Industrial Social Structure." In *Orders and Hierarchies in Late Medieval and Renaissance Europe*, edited by Jeffrey Denton, 6–25. Toronto: University of Toronto Press, 1999.

Robertson, D. W. Jr. "The Concept of Courtly Love as an Impediment to the Understanding of Medieval Texts." In *The Meaning of Courtly Love*, F. X. Newman, ed. Albany: State University of New York Press, 1968.

Rogozinski, Jan. "Ennoblement by the Crown and Social Stratification in France, 1285-1322: A Prosopographical Survey." In *Order and Innovation in the Middle Ages: Essays in Honor of Joseph R. Strayer*, edited by William C. Jordan et al., 273–291. Princeton: Princeton University Press, 1976.

Roisin, Simone. "L'efflorescence Cistercienne et le Courant Féminin de Piété au XIIIe Siècle," *Revue d'Histoire Ecclésiastique* 39 (1943): 342–378.

Rosenthal, Joel. *Medieval Women and the Sources of Medieval History*. Athens, Ga: University of Georgia Press, 1990.

Rubin, Miri. "Choosing Death? Experiences of Martyrdom in Late Medieval Europe." In *Martyrs and Martyrologies*, edited by Diana Wood, 153–183. Oxford: Blackwell, 1993.

Ruh, Kurt. "Beginenmystik: Hadewijch, Mechtild von Magdeburg, Marguerite Porete," *Zeitschrift für deutsches Altertum und deutsche Literatur* 106 (1977): 265–277.

———. "Gottesliebe bei Hadewijch, Mechtild von Magdeburg und Marguerite Porete." In *Romanische Literaturbeziehungen im 19. und 20. Jahrhundert. Festschrift für Franz Rauhut zum 85. Geburtstag*, edited by A. San Miguel et al. Tübingen, 1985.

———. "Le *Miroir des Simples Ames* de Marguerite Porete," *Verbum et Signum* 2 (1975): 365–387.

Russell, Jeffrey Burton. *Dissent and Order in the Middle Ages: The Search for Legitimate Authority*. New York: Twayne Publishers, 1992.

———. *Dissent and Reform in the Early Middle Ages*. Berkeley: University of California Press, 1965.

Sargent, Michael G. "Le Mirouer des simples âmes and the English Mystical Tradition." In *Abendländische Mystik im Mittelalter*, edited by Kurt Ruh, 443–465. Stuttgart: Metzler, 1986.

Schmitt, Jean-Claude. *Mort d'une hérésie: L'Église et les clercs face aux béguines et aux béghards du Rhin supérieur du xiv.e au xv.e siècle*. Paris: École des Hautes Études en Sciences Sociales, 1978.

Schweitzer, Franz-Josef. "Von Marguerite von Porete (d. 1310) bis Mme Guyon (d. 1717): Frauenmystik im Konflikt mit der Kirche." In *Frauenmystik in Mittelalter*, edited by Peter Dinzelbacher and Dieter R. Bauer, 256–274. Stuttgart: Schwabenverlag, 1985.

Sells, Michael A. *Mystical Languages of Unsaying*. Chicago: University of Chicago Press, 1994.

———. "The Pseudo-Woman and the Meister." In *Meister Eckhart and the Beguine Mystics*, edited by Bernard McGinn, 114–146. New York: Continuum, 1994.

Simons, Walter. "The Beguine Movement in the Southern Low Countries: A Reassessment," *Bulletin de l'Institut Historique Belge de Rome* 59 (1989): 63-105.

Singer, Irving. *The Nature of Love*. Volume 2 (Courtly and Romantic). Chicago: University of Chicago Press, 1984.

Skarup, Povl. "La langue du *Miroir des simples âmes* attribue a Marguerite Porete," *Studia Neophilologica* 60 (1988): 231–236.

Söhngen, G. "Die biblische Lehre von der Gottenbildlichkeit des Menschen," *Münchener Theologische Zeitschrift* II (1951): 52 ff.

Souillac, Geneviève. "Charisme et prophétisme féminins: Marguerite Porete et le *Miroir des simples âmes,*" *Australian Journal of French Studies* 35, No. 3 (December 1998): 261–278.

Southern, R. W. *Western Society and the Church in the Middle Ages*. Baltimore: Penguin Books, 1970.

Spiegel, Gabrielle M. "Genealogy: Form and Function in Medieval Historical Spiegel Narrative," *History and Theory* 22 (1983): 43–53.

———. "History, Historicism, and the Social Logic of the Text in the Middle Ages," *Speculum* 65 (1990): 59–86.

Stein, Frederic. "The Religious Women of Cologne, 1120–1320." Yale University dissertation, 1977.

Strayer, Joseph R. *Feudalism*. Princeton: Princeton University Press, 1965.

Summers, Janet I. " 'The Violent Shall Take It By Force': The First Century of Cistercian Nuns, 1125–1228." University of Chicago dissertation, 1986.

Tabacco, Giovanni. "Su nobilità e cavalleria nel medioevo: Un ritorno a Marc Bloch?" *Rivista storica italiana* 91 (1979), 5–25.

Tarrant, Jacqueline. "The Clementine Decrees on the Beguines: Conciliar and Papal Versions," *Archivum Historiae Pontificiae* 12 (1974): 300–308.

Taylor, A. E. "Regio Dissimilitudinis." In *Archives d'histoire doctrinale et litéraire du moyen âge*. Volume 9 (1934): 305–306.

Tellenbach, Gerd. "Zur Erforschung des hochmittelalterlichen Adels (9.–12. Jahrhundert)." *XIIe Congrès international des sciences historiques*. Vol. 1. Vienna: 1965.

Thunberg, Lars. "The Human Person as Image of God: I. Eastern Christianity." In *Christian Spirituality: Origins to the Twelfth Century*, edited by Bernard McGinn and John Meyendorff, 290–311. New York: Crossroad, 1985.

Torjesen, Karen J. "In Praise of Noble Women: Gender and Honor in Ascetic Texts," *Semeia* 57 (1992): 41–64.

Trinkaus, Charles. *In Our Image and Likeness: Humanity and Divinity in Italian Humanist Thought*. 2 volumes. Chicago: University of Chicago Press, 1970.

Turner, Denys. "The Art of Unknowing: Negative Theology in Late Medieval Thought," *Modern Theology* 14, No. 4 (October 1998): 474–488.

Van Baest, Marieke. *Poetry of Hadewijch*, Studies in Spirituality Series, Supplement 3. Leuven: Peeters, 1998.

Wainwright-deKadt, Elizabeth. "Courtly Literature and Mysticism: Some Aspects of their Interaction," *Acta Germanica* 12 (1980): 41–60.

Watson, Nicholas. "Melting into God the English Way: Deification in the Middle English Version of Marguerite Porete's *Mirouer des simples âmes anienties..*" In *Prophets Abroad: The Reception of Continental Holy Women in Late Medieval England*, edited by Rosalynn Voaden. Dover, N. H.: Boydell and Brewer, 1996.

———. "Misrepresenting the Untranslatable: Marguerite Porete and the Mirouer des simples ames," *New Comparison* 12 (1991): 124–137.

Werner, Karl Ferdinand. "Adel: Fränkisches Reich, Imperium, Frankreich." In *Vom Frankenreich zur Entfaltung Deutschlands und Frankreichs*. Sigmaringen: n.p., 1984.

———. *Naissance de la Noblesse: L'essor des élites politiques en Europe*. Paris: Fayard, 1998.

———. *Vom Frankenreich zur Entfaltung Deutschlands und Frankreichs*. Sigmaringen: n.p., 1984.

Wiethaus, Ulrike, ed. *Maps of Flesh and Light: The Religious Experience of Medieval Women Mystics*. Syracuse: Syracuse University Press, 1993.

———. "Reality as Imitation: The Role of Religious Imagery Among the Beguines of the Low Countries." In *Maps of Flesh and Light: The Religious Experience of Medieval Woman Mystics*, edited by Ulrike Wiethaus, 112–126. Syracuse: Syracuse University Press, 1993.

Ziegler, Joanna E. "Secular Canonesses as Antecedents of the Beguines in the Low Countries: An Introduction to Some Older Views," *Studies in Medieval and Renaissance History* 13 [Old Series Vol. 23] (1992): 117–135.

Zimmerman, Béatrice Acklin. "Mittelalterliche Frauenmystik: 'Feministische Theologie des Mittelalters' als Korrektiv an der herrschenden Theologie?" In *Frauen zwischen Anpassung und Widerstand: Beiträge der 5. Schweizerischen Historikerinnentagung*, edited by Regula Ludi et al., 13–21. Zürich: Chronos, 1990.

Ziolkowski, Jan. "Avatars of Ugliness in Medieval Literature," *Modern Language Review* LXXIX (1984): 1–20.

Zum Brunn, Emilie. "Non Willing in Marguerite Porete's 'Mirror of Annihilated Souls'," *Bulletin de l'Institut Historique Belge de Rome* 58 (1988): 11–22.

———. "Self, Not-Self, and the Ultimate in Marguerite Porete's Mirror of Annihilated Souls." In *God, the Self and Nothingness: Reflections Eastern and Western*, edited by Robert E. Carter, 81–88. New York: Paragon House, 1990.

———, and Georgette Epiney-Burgard, *Women Mystics in Medieval Europe*. Translated by Sheila Hughes. New York: Paragon, 1989.

INDEX